THEY CALL ME CHIEF

WARRIORS ON ICE

THEY CALL ME CHIEF

WARRIORS ON ICE

DON MARKS

J. GORDON SHILLINGFORD
PUBLISHING INC

They Call Me Chief: Warriors on Ice
First published 2008 by
J. Gordon Shillingford Publishing Inc.

Book design by Relish Design Inc.
Printed and bound in Canada on 100% post-consumer recycled paper.

Cover Photos: Hockey Hall of Fame

We acknowledge the financial support of the Manitoba Arts Council, The Canada Council for the Arts and the Government of Canada through the Book Publishing Industry Development Program (BPIDP) for our publishing program.

J. Gordon Shillingford Publishing Inc.
P.O. Box 86, RPO Corydon Avenue
Winnipeg, MB
Canada R3M 3S3

Library and Archives Canada Cataloguing in Publication

Marks, Don, 1953-
    They call me chief : warriors on ice / Don Marks.

Includes index.
Accompanied by a DVD.

ISBN 978-1-897289-34-1

    1. Native hockey players–Canada–Biography. 2. National Hockey League–Biography. 3. Native hockey players–Canada–History. I. Title.

GV848.5.A1M36 2008   796.962'640922   C2008-903067-2

ACKNOWLEDGMENTS

Some very special thanks must be sent out to some very special people who helped immeasurably in the making of this book.

To Kathleen Richardson, who provided me with a spiritual light from a distance. Just to know that such a wonderful and giving person is in your corner is inspiring enough to overcome any obstacles.

To Chris McLeod, Allan McLeod and Sam Anderson and all the folks at the Tribal Councils Investment Group, who got behind this project from the get-go and continue to support my work.

To my publisher, Gord Shillingford, for having the vision and courage to offer me a deal without hesitation, for living up to his end of that deal mostly on time, and for going the extra mile and doing all the work that is required by a publisher and more.

To my agent, Dale Willson, for supporting me through the rough patches and always paying the cell phone bills.

To Bryan Trottier, for becoming a good friend and providing the support and encouragement which reflected on all the Indian and Metis players I became associated with through this project. And to Don Cherry, for his support of the documentary which got everything going.

To the Manitoba Arts Council for providing that Writers B grant.

To Arnold Asham and Gerald Flood for providing writing jobs that paid the rent while I got the book finished.

To Fran and Leo Horoditski and Cindy Gabriel, who provided a shelter where I found myself and I can always return to in my mind when I get lost again.

To dear friends and supporters Dennis Nanowin, Ray Barbour, Curtis Shingoose Jonnie, Clay O'Bray, Marion Ironquil Meadmore, Bob Dubesky, Lisa Lacosse, Meryle Lewis, Jim Bear, Elijah Harper, Charlie Hill, Phil Fontaine, Gary Doer, Greg Selinger, Bobby Jay, Tim Killeen, Hersh Wolch, Gerri Wiebe, Sam Katz, Hippy Nanowin, Scott O'Bray, Larry O'Bray, Calvin Pompana, Eric Robinson, Duke Redbird, Scott Taylor, Allen Aitken, Raven Thundersky, Dan Vandal, Ken Young, Frank "Mawasega",

Ken Young, Gary Zubeck, Val Vint, John "Buddy" Monette, Tom Jackson, Buffy Sainte-Marie, Lisa Hill, Lesley Hughes, Dave and Sharon Cramer, Mogwai, Bizhoons, Clarence Anderson, Eric Hogue, Steve Chyzzy, Ken MacDonald, Barb Prettie, Kahla Prettie, Derek Miller, Ritchie Franzen, Ken Hoover, Aaron Peters, Sharon Stern, Robb Mitchell, Eileen O'Donnell, the Scouts Hockey Club, Evelyn Poitras, Larry Prewada and many more (and please do not get mad at me for forgetting to mention you).

In special memory of Valerie Nanowin (Keewatinomin Binesi Ikwe), Izzy Asper, Lars Sharp, Delann Prewada and George Poitras.

To God, Jesus of Nazareth and the Grandfathers for my Sacred Teachings, Rules for Living, the Sweat Lodge and the Lords Prayer which gets me through every day.

This book is dedicated to a special lady who demands anonymity for her good works. She is the matriarch of my hometown, Winnipeg, and the lives of many human beings and animals have benefited from her generous and sharing nature.

TABLE OF CONTENTS

Foreword   9

Introduction   15

Chapter 1   Chief Running Deer on Skates
             (a.k.a. Chief Thunderstick)   27
Chapter 2   The Chief (and the "up-and-coming" Chief)   51
Chapter 3   The Riverton Rifle   63
Chapter 4   "Little Chief"   87
Chapter 5   They Called Me a Half-breed   105
Chapter 6   The Best Indian Fighter   143
Chapter 7   "They Call Me Coach"   163
Chapter 8   American Chiefs and Other Notable Warriors   189
Chapter 9   Other Notable Chiefs   193
Chapter 10   Heart of a Lion   205
Chapter 11   They Called Me "Boy in a Man's Body"   217
Chapter 12   Future Chiefs   227

Appendix   259
Index   275

FOREWORD

They Call Me Chief tells the fascinating stories of First Nations athletes who overcame tremendous obstacles to achieve success in the greatest hockey league in the world. These stories not only provide inspiration and motivation for all citizens of Canada's First Nations, they provide positive role models for our children and youth to emulate.

Just as important, the stories of these athletes provide readers with a window into the culture, history and lifestyle of Canada's First Nations. Their stories are told in a plainspoken manner, straight from the heart, without lecturing, or blaming, or creating guilt feelings among others. Their lives have been influenced by issues that impact on all First Nations people, and the reader gains a clearer understanding of these issues by witnessing their impact on these prominent individuals who share their experiences in a "user-friendly" way which builds understanding, empathy and unity.

For these reasons, this book is long overdue. It speaks to so many!

But first and foremost, They Call Me Chief is a sports book that tells great sports stories. It is a book about hockey and the stories these First Nations athletes tell are as entertaining and interesting as the many other accounts Canadians have compiled and shared about this country's "national sport"

(First Nations will always argue that lacrosse is really Canada's national sport but we can agree the credit might be shared between these two wonderful national pastimes). We get to join superstars like Reggie Leach and Bryan Trottier, and First Nations warriors such as Ron Delorme and Stan Jonathan, as they give us the inside scoop on things we witnessed from the stands but never really got to experience behind the scenes.

Don Marks relays the stories of these First Nations athletes to the reader in their own words; in their own manner of speaking, with their own style of humour, colour and insight. The stories stand by themselves as fascinating reading, but no account of these players' lives can be considered complete without examining the lifestyle, history and issues that intrude or impact on these accounts of the players' identity as First Nations people. The hockey tales lead us into intimate layers of other interesting and important themes.

And so we learn about the history of Indian residential schools from Fred Sasakamoose's experience with loneliness and abuse as a child, the issues of alcohol abuse as we follow the journey of Reggie Leach to sobriety—a journey that includes workshops to help First Nations youth and children throughout North America to be warned about the dangers of alcohol and drugs (sadly, it is a journey that does not stop in the Hockey Hall of Fame, a regret Reggie attributes to his drinking problem). We meet racism head-on in all its ugliness in South Dakota as Ron Delorme flees irate fans because they were upset that local Sioux tribes objected to being used as mascots by the local university hockey team, which put funding of their new arena in jeopardy. The rights of Treaties are raised when "North American Indian" Stan Jonathan stands up to Boston General Manager Sinden over the rights to do a car commercial in the United States. These themes reflect the obstacles First Nations people face and that these "warriors on ice" overcame.

And on it goes, the lives of these colourful athletes intertwined and inseparable from the issues of the times.

But the book remains, first and foremost, a hockey book. One that should occupy a prominent spot on the lengthy shelf of books that have been written about Canada's national obsession. All of us who have become obsessed with this sport have our own hockey stories, which we share before meetings to "break the ice," in the dressing room before we "take to the ice" with our buddies, and after the game when we socialize (some "with ice," but not Reggie and me, and many, many more like us all the time!). We reminisce about previous victories and defeats, past glories and disappointments, and the funny, crazy things that often happen when groups of guys or gals get together and play games like this. It's just that the stories the First Nations superstars tell in *They Call Me Chief* are better, because they speak of glory at the highest level, defeat that takes place when the stakes are highest, and the zany, fascinating and fun things that take place in heretofore far-off places on the world's greatest stage.

I have known Don for over 25 years, having first met him when he was a community development worker at the Indian and Metis Friendship Centre in Winnipeg. Don was helping my friend Marion Ironquil Meadmore launch some economic development projects to create employment and wealth for First Nations citizens in southern Manitoba. He went on to make films, and often, his news stories and documentaries required a statement from me when I served as Grand Chief of the Assembly of Manitoba Chiefs, or in other leadership capacities in which I have served. I can state from my personal experience that Don has never misquoted me or taken my words out of context. The players Don has written about in this book can enjoy the same comfort and confidence in the book's accuracy. So can readers.

I also met Don on the hockey rink. I have always been a huge hockey fan and, like any other Manitoba boy, I grew up watching and playing hockey every chance I could. In my adult years, I played on various adult recreational or "old-timers" teams, and so did Don. He was involved with a team called the Scouts and I was playing for the Sagkeeng Braves. Notwithstanding the drawbacks that might be associated with these nicknames, both teams were made up of First Nations players and Don's players associated their nickname with scouting for food or enemy tribes (and certainly not for Custer and the 7th Cavalry) while we felt we were honouring warriors or "braves" from our past.

Don had stacked his lineup with some of the youngest and best First Nations players in Winnipeg. Really skillful athletes such as Joe Dumas, Ron Benoit, Dennis Nanowin, Tim Kereluk, Paul McLean, Eli Tachan,

Curtis and Kelsey Lavallee, Clarence Anderson and then some steady older guys like Terry Kadachuk and Jimmy Meadmore. My team had some fairly good players, too, but all well past their prime (like Don and I were!).

Right from the start of the game, we all knew the rout was on. Now, I understand Don would always tell his players to back off when the Scouts were routing white teams in other games. Well, in this one, the Scouts were running up the score and embarrassing my Braves. When the score reached 7-0 by the middle of the second period, I could see Don telling his players to ease off. But, this time, they responded with statements like "Screw you, that's my cousin over there on the Braves and I wanna shut him up for good" or "No damn way! I hang out with those guys at the Savoy and I'm gonna rub this one in good!" and so on.

Well, the final score ended up a massive slaughter and I didn't feel great about it and Don didn't feel so good, either. And, like all old jocks, my primary motivation was to get even.

It just so happened that Don had scheduled a film interview for one of his documentaries with me for 9 A.M. the next morning. I know that Don is a neurotically organized person and that he would have his day scheduled tightly, so he was greeted the next morning by one of my staff who simply said, "The Grand Chief is in a meeting and he will be with you shortly." Which was replaced by "as soon as he can." And on and on for a couple of hours.

After waiting in our reception area for a couple of hours, Don ventured down the hall to my office, where I was sipping a coffee and reading some briefing papers (I had "cleared" the entire morning for Don but, in the end, Don's shooting schedule somehow got "rushed"). Finally, I most politely and graciously welcomed Don into my office and simply said, "That was for the beating your guys laid on my team last night."

Don holds most value in how much he has learned by listening to the people he has worked with or met through various film projects. Important in his background, he often states that the most rewarding experience in his life was making the documentary series *The Everywhere Spirit* which required him to travel throughout Manitoba to interview First Nations Elders to record their story about the history of First Nations contact with Euro-Canadians "from the people who were directly involved or who heard about it directly from their parents or grandparents." Don was blessed to meet and talk with hundreds of Cree, Ojibway, Oji-Cree, Dene, Mechif and Dakota Elders who told him their stories in their own language (using translators). Don has always said that this was an experience which changed his life, and provided him with an education that no school could ever provide.

I have enjoyed a most worthwhile relationship with many of the people Don writes about in *They Call Me Chief.* I have worked beside these most honourable men in meetings and in our communities, and I enjoyed skating with them from time to time whenever we got a chance to lace them up together. I would write more about my association with all of these fine gentlemen, but they are the engaging subjects of this book and their stories are told very well in the following pages.

I found it interesting to note that Don writes mostly about the OCN Blizzard and the Lebret Eagles when he writes about efforts to get more First Nations into elite levels of hockey and that is fine with me (even though Don knows full well that I used to be the owner of the Southeast Blades franchise in the Manitoba Junior Hockey League; perhaps Don thought his objectivity might be sacrificed by his association with me).

Don provided extensive coverage of the Southeast Blades (formerly the "Thunderbirds") through his television production company in any case, even producing a half-hour documentary on the team for his First Nations series on the Global Television Network. I recall how excited Don was when one year, the Blades and the Blizzard squared off in the championship final for the Manitoba Junior Hockey League's Turnbull Cup. For many of us, this was major history! Think about it. Two First Nations-owned teams had become the last two teams standing in this province. This was just about the biggest thrill any of us could ever achieve (besides one of our teams winning the Canadian championship!).

The Blades lost, but just to see one side of the magnificent multiplex on the Sagkeeng First Nation packed full of brown faces who had travelled all the way from OCN/The Pas to bang their noisemakers and fly their flags against the local brown faces jammed together on the other side, was one of the greatest thrills I have ever had in my life.

I couldn't help but notice that Don could barely contain his excitement and pride, as well. Don is always supposed to maintain his objectivity as a journalist, and even though I don't think he cared which of the two teams won the series, I knew that he shared the joy we all felt during that historic, never-seen-before and never-seen-since all-First Nations final. Quite simply, Don has always been supportive of our efforts to develop the sport of hockey in First Nations communities and he certainly has always been there when we wanted or needed coverage of our activities.

I wish to offer my congratulations to Don Marks for his perseverance in getting these stories into print. I hope that *They Call Me Chief* finds the audience it deserves and that this book is able to accomplish the goals of cross-cultural awareness and bridge-building that Don, the link, the messenger, is striving to achieve.

—*National Grand Chief Phil Fontaine – Assembly of First Nations*

INTRODUCTION

They Call Me Chief started out as a television documentary that told the stories of North American "Indians" who played in the National Hockey League. The documentary was a "Top 10" hit with viewing audiences when it was broadcast nationally in Canada on the Global, Prime and APTN television networks; it was highly acclaimed by critics throughout the country and it won awards wherever it was shown.

The producers of this documentary logged over 100 hours of interviews, which had to be condensed into 46 minutes and 50 seconds to suit the needs of commercial network television. There were many stories—people and elements, details and sidebars—that could not be included in the documentary because of time constraints.

This book hopes to overcome that deficiency.

★ ★ ★ ★ ★

A warrior is not simply one who goes to war. A warrior is a provider, a protector and a peacekeeper. The true warrior does not judge his greatness by the goals that he sets for himself but rather by the obstacles that he overcomes. Such tests are to be

welcomed because they provide the challenge a warrior needs to prove himself worthy.
(Traditional)

From a quantitative perspective, the number of Indians who played in the National Hockey League was seriously deficient, considering the fact that Indians may have been responsible for inventing the game.

This popular modern sport is very similar to an ancient Mohawk spiritual practice that was used to prepare Indian warriors in southern Ontario and New York for battle. This spiritual ceremony was called "baggataway," basically a competition wherein the object was to pass a ball between three forwards and two defensemen and score against a goalie by shooting the ball into a net.

Baggataway is now more commonly known as "lacrosse."

Just as in the modern game of hockey, there was plenty of physical contact in the traditional spiritual ceremony of bagattaway. And, whenever a Mohawk warrior got hit especially hard, he exclaimed "haw-gee," which means "it hurts" in the Mohawk language. It's not a big stretch to imagine that the name of the game now known as hockey came from "haw-gee."

Then again, some people think that the name hockey originated in England; after a stick-and-ball game that was played by youth during breaks from selling fruits and vegetables from their "hawk" carts. Nova Scotians claim that a local military man named Colonel Hockey invented the game as a way to keep his troops in shape. But nobody really knows or can prove where the name hockey actually comes from.

In any case, the spiritual practice of baggataway, to prepare Indians for battle, also develops the skills needed to play hockey. Indians have been playing baggataway throughout their long history in North America, and they have played lacrosse and hockey ever since these games became popular with the public. One might think that they are uniquely trained and qualified to excel at the modern sport of hockey, yet the list of Indians who played in the NHL is very short.

★ ★ ★ ★ ★

Qualitatively, however, the history of Indians in the NHL is long and memorable. And the relatively few "warriors on ice" who managed to overcome the large and varied obstacles to make it to "the show" tell some very heartwarming stories of courage, as well as of athleticism.

Until the 1970s, the only players identified as "Indians" in the NHL were Fred Sasakamoose of the Chicago Blackhawks; George Armstrong, the Toronto Maple Leaf who became the longest-serving captain in NHL history; and Jim Neilson, who played mostly with the New York Rangers. They and almost all who followed were called "Chief" by their teammates, their fans and the media.

There were other NHL players of Indian ancestry at the time, but they weren't officially or publicly recognized as Indians. Bill Robinson played goal for the New York Rangers in 1951 but the NHL recognized Sasakamoose, whose debut with the Blackhawks came in 1953, as the first "real" Indian to play in the NHL.

That's because Sasakamoose was a treaty status Indian and Robinson did not have a treaty card, for whatever reason (many Indians, at the time, lost their treaty status to obtain G.I. benefits or "easier access to housing" or any of the many other reasons that led the Canadian government to enact Bill C-31 in 1985 to restore Indian status to thousands of people who had lost that status unfairly). That, or they simply weren't brown enough, or their cheekbones weren't high enough, to be perceived as "real Indians" by the public or the media.

Some players denied their Indian ancestry because of prejudices that existed at the time. It wasn't exactly popular to be known as an Indian during the 20th (and 19th and 18th and 17th and 16th and 15th) centuries. The stereotypes that went with the name Indian were insulting, degrading and generally harmful to one's psyche, career and general well-being.

Other players, for reasons of their own, simply didn't play up their Indian heritage. Names like Ab McDonald and Pierre Pilote are not as readily associated with Indian or Métis as much as Armstrong and the rest of the "Chiefs" were.

★ ★ ★ ★ ★

It wasn't until the 1970s that Indians gained prominence in the NHL again. It started with Reggie Leach, who escaped the stereotypical nickname "Chief" because of his booming, accurate shot. Reggie, who was born and raised in Riverton, Manitoba, became known as the "Riverton Rifle."

Reggie was soon joined in the NHL by Stan Jonathan. This native of Six Nations, Ontario was described as "a six-foot-three man who was placed in a compactor until he came out five-foot-seven." Stanley, therefore, was called "Little Chief."

Just before Jonathan, the best player who ever stemmed from Indian blood came along. Bryan Trottier, who has raised the Stanley Cup over his head seven times, joined a standard of excellence that can only be celebrated by the likes of Bobby Hull, Gordie Howe, Maurice Richard, Wayne Gretzky and Mario Lemieux.

There have been many more "warriors" in the NHL, like Ron Delorme, Ted Nolan, Theoren Fleury, and Gino Odjick. This book will focus on the stories of the warriors on ice whose journey is mostly complete to make sure this book doesn't become dated the day after it goes to print. Therefore, the stories of native stars like Sheldon Souray, Wade Redden, Jonathan Cheechoo or Carey Price are not included, as much of their stories remains to unfold. I hope we will watch the careers of new and upcoming warriors on ice with respect and admiration. Perhaps their stories will be recorded in some future book. But this book is confined to the stories of warriors like Sasakamoose and Leach and Trottier, who "blazed the trail," whose stories are fascinating in and by themselves.

★ ★ ★ ★ ★

As for the book's title, I haven't changed it from the documentary simply because *They Call Me Chief* fits. Almost every Indian who played in the NHL or anywhere else has been called "Chief" at one time or another; therefore, this title seems most appropriate.

And it brings in a lot of interesting background. For instance, some people might consider it racist to call every Indian they meet a "Chief." That's true to some degree, but I believe that most who use the word Chief when they refer to or meet an Indian are not really racist, just ignorant. Ignorance is not a bad thing. Hell, we are all ignorant of many things. It's when people are provided with information that might allow them to know better, but choose to remain ignorant, where problems arise.

I'm reminded of a story that Shingoose, my long-time business partner (and one of Canada's foremost Aboriginal performing and recording artists), once told me about being called "Chief" that might "guide us all to a higher understanding."

"Goose" was riding on a bus one day when a white guy sat down beside him and said, "How's it goin', Chief?" In his younger days, Goose would have been angry and insulted by this kind of greeting. But he had long since learned that you can't catch a fish by trying to whack it over the head with a paddle while it's swimming in the stream it's most familiar with. You have to lure that fish in.

So Goose simply said "Hi" and struck up a conversation with the white guy, who wasn't really a mean person, just kind of ignorant. Goose had learned from his Indian elders that it's no use getting mad at ignorant people (although people who choose to remain ignorant are a different story). By the time the bus reached their stop, the white guy had met a kind of Indian he had never known about.

Goose didn't lecture, or preach or try to lay any kind of guilt trip on the white guy. Goose did as his elders had taught him to do: *We must guide people gently to a higher understanding.*

At the end of their conversation, Goose politely informed the white guy that some Indians might consider being called "Chief" a stereotype, if not rude, racist or just basically offensive. Goose suggested that the white guy might want to look beyond any stereotypes of Indians he might have been told about, or read about, or felt, or thought. The white guy shook Goose's hand as they departed and left with a healthy new attitude toward Indians.

It's the same kind of thing with the white hockey players who call all the Indian hockey players they meet "Chief." Most don't mean any harm; they just don't know any better. And, as we've learned from Goose and the Elders, that's not really a bad thing.

Some activists rant that Indian players were called Chief because the other players didn't get to know their Indian teammates well enough to come up with more creative and meaningful nicknames (like Edouard "Newsy" Lalonde, who had worked his way through junior hockey by hauling newsprint) or even "Red" Storey (because he had red hair).

But this isn't a matter of laziness or carelessness. In the highly competitive world of professional sports, there simply isn't much time to really get close to your teammates. Players come and go (they're cut or traded) and who really wants to get to know people closely who might simply disappear one day? And, don't forget, some of those people might be out to take your job. Nicknames are best kept simple because they can just as easily end up with negative connotations as positive ones. And there are always players who might become your instant enemy, by being traded to the team you will be playing against tomorrow night in another NHL city.

For those reasons, and somewhat because they chose a career in sports over rocket science, hockey players of any background, race or religion have never been very creative when it comes to creating nicknames. So Todd Bertuzzi is "Tuzzi," Jerome Iginla is "Iggy," Mats Naslund is "Matty," Nasty" or "Lundy," and so on down the lineup. A nickname like "Chief" sounds highly creative in comparison.

Some Indians might react to the name of this book by exclaiming "Don't call me Chief!", just as they react to being called Chief in their daily lives. The fact is that most of the Indians written about in this book have been called Chief, and when we understand the reasons, and empower people with information that allows them to overcome their innocence, we are all "guided gently to a higher understanding."

★ ★ ★ ★ ★

As for hockey players being racist at the NHL level, that is doubtful. Oh sure, there are are probably a few ignorant bastards out there but, for the most part, hockey players—indeed all professional athletes—are generally more free of racism than society is in general.

Players rely on their teammates to help them make plays and score, back them up in a fight and win at all costs, and cannot succeed if they let racism disrupt the harmony that a team must have. Children, youth, men and women who play sports learn early on to accept differences, build friendships and play well together.

Oh sure, you still hear about players calling Indian opponents names like "wagon burner" or "prairie nigger." Most of this name-calling is muttered under the breath in a faceoff circle and it's usually just a tactic to throw the Indian off his game. If Shingoose played hockey, he wouldn't have time to guide his opponent gently to a higher understanding but I know he'd try to educate his opponent by winning that faceoff and setting up a goal. The most successful Indian players have handled the racism they've encountered throughout their careers in this way.

Names will never hurt you. Don't get mad, get even. Never lose your cool. All boxers know this, and boxers get punched in the head a lot more than hockey players do. Any boxer who loses his cool because he got called a name is a fool, because when he loses control, gets angry, stops thinking and analyzing, he loses form and is more vulnerable to the devastating shots to the head and body coming at him from the calmer, cooler customer in front of him.

Racism in organized sports is also extremely frowned upon by officials and carefully policed by and on behalf of the players. Therefore racism is rare on the playing field and in the locker room, though some might argue that it does exist in locker rooms. Teasing and taunting about another player's background takes place in this atmosphere all the time (so does teasing about another player's taste in clothes, his mother, his sister, his choice of cars and many other things). But nothing serious is ever intended, and nobody takes it seriously. It's actually a form of bonding that breaks down barriers and brings players together. While it would take a text in psychology to explain all this, perhaps it can be justified by saying that the same sort of bonding took place in the U-boats that stormed Normandy on D-Day. Racism had to be the farthest thing from the minds of those soldiers who taunted each other because of their different backgrounds—they were about to rely on each other for their very lives. A "parting shot"? I think not.

All Indian hockey players know that sometimes they'll be called names when they play a white team. Most simply get used to it. Some return the favour and call the white guys names like "honky" (smelly white man), "mojit" (stinky bum), etc. Good referees, if they hear any of this, eject the offending players; and good leagues, when they get the reports from the referees, suspend the offending players.

Sadly, it's the fans who are responsible for most of the racism in sports. We're the ones who can be the most racist, and we, the fans, are the ones who most get away with it. From the tomahawk chop, to shouting racist slurs from the seats in the stadium, racism rears its ugly head most often in a grandstand.

If a mob of fans, infantilizing a proud and historic culture by wearing cardboard headbands adorned with chicken feathers, are smacking themselves in the mouth with one hand while yelling "Woo! Woo!," and hacking away at the air with an ax in the other hand, well, they could be yelling "I love you" and it would make "Chief" sound racist.

★ ★ ★ ★ ★

Some readers may wonder why, having said all that, I use the name "Indian" when I refer to the people whose stories are told in this book, when words like "Aboriginal" seem to be much more fashionable these days. There are many reasons for this.

First of all, warriors of the First Nations of the Americas have identified themselves as Indians proudly for centuries. Perhaps they were given this name by a white man by mistake—it has long been believed that Christopher Columbus was looking for India when he landed in the Americas and he mistakenly called the Indigenous people he met here "Indians" as in "West Indies." Then again, some historians maintain that Columbus was so taken by the physical and spiritual beauty of the Taino people who welcomed him to what is now known as Puerto Rico that he was moved to exclaim "these people must be made from the body of God." In Christopher's language that translates into *du corpus in Deo* and from *in Deo* comes the name "Indian." God's children.

The latter theory seems more plausible, since the lands Columbus was looking for were not called "India" in 1492 AD.

The Tainos became extinct from new diseases the Europeans brought to them but the name Indian had been given and it stuck—in certain places. To the Indigenous peoples of South America the name Indian is a derogatory term of the lowest order. To be called an Indian in Argentina is to be called a whore. Perhaps that is because Columbus had no right, complimentary or otherwise, to change the historic names of the traditional inhabitants of that land.

The history of North America reveals that the people who lived here first, and were now being called Indians, went on to engage in brave battles against white incursion and negotiated sacred treaties between their nations and the newcomers to America. Many of these same people fought for the United States and Canada with tremendous honour as Indians in the great world wars. They were also Sacred Guardians of our Mother Earth and protectors of the land known as Turtle Island (North America) as much as they were soldiers in the Canadian or American military. The name Indian lives on in the hearts and minds of many of our Elders and veterans and they deserve to be known by whatever name they want to be known by.

And, as stated previously, this book focuses on the warrior athletes whose journey is well-run, if not well-known. These warriors on ice like Fred Sasakamoose have been called, and they've called themselves, Indians all their lives. So why would I call them anything different?

Most Canadians, including many Indians, now use the word "Aboriginal" to describe the people of North America's First Nations. But just because some politicians held a conference and decided to use an Anglo word derived from a dictionary shouldn't mean the name Indian has to become extinct. To call Indians "Aboriginal" or "Native" (without reference to where they are native to) is kind of an insult, I think.

The most proper and correct thing to do is to address the people of the First Nations of Turtle Island by what the people call themselves: Haudanasee, Ojibwe, Kiowa, Inuit and so on. That will take a lot of work because there are hundreds of tribes throughout North and South America. So for now, the name First Nations seems to be most appropriate. But I use the word "Indian" in favour of "Aboriginal" because, at least, there is a proud history associated with the former.

And, to those who associate the name "Indian" with negative connotations, I hope that you have been somewhat "guided gently to a higher understanding."

★ ★ ★ ★ ★

In keeping with all that, this book will focus on feelings rather than facts. One of the major reasons the documentary *They Call Me Chief* was so well received was that it presented the stories of the players through their day-to-day experiences that reached out to the "big-picture" issues of racism, treaty rights, sovereignty, and alcohol and drug abuse without lecturing or preaching. Their personal accounts brought these issues home in a way that no academic, bureaucrat, politician or social activist ever could.

And so, like the documentary, this book will not focus on cold statistics such as how many goals or assists or penalty minutes each player posted during their careers. Anybody can look that up. It's the feelings and thoughts, the motivations and struggles, the pressures and the pain the players experienced, which enhance their stories and enlighten the reader.

The documentary was conceived and sold as a sports production for television but it was quickly recognized as more than that. As readers of this Foreword must realize by now, I am hoping that this book will also be received as more than just a sports book. While I intend to tell good hockey stories first and foremost, I also want to enlighten and inform readers about situations and circumstances that bring history, politics and socio-cultural issues of the times into a balanced perspective. If the book empowers people with information that allows them to make informed choices about social justice and equality, that cannot be bad, can it?

★ ★ ★ ★ ★

I have also at times introduced and incorporated the process I went through to uncover the stories in this book. I did this not only because I hope readers will find it interesting, but because beneath it all I'm a Canadian hockey fan, and we all love to share our unique experiences with the greatest sport in the world with other fans. Researching and writing this book was an incredible experience; I got to travel throughout North America and meet many of the heroes from my childhood. A dream come true for any hockey fan. I hope readers enjoy sharing that journey of discovery, failure, folly and foolishness with me.

We interviewed many more players for the documentary than we could include in the final version of the film. This book is intended to be a much more complete production, and, I hope, a more comprehensive look at this country that we hold dear to our hearts.

When people think of Canada, the sport of hockey always comes to mind. But Canadian culture is much more than just hockey. Yes, culture can be most simply defined as what we do, therefore, hockey is certainly an integral part of Canadian culture. But so are all the other things we do—our politics, our issues, our arts and entertainment, and our different lifestyles—all of which are uniquely Canadian.

The contributions and involvement of Canada's First Nations people in a sport such as hockey, a game they may have invented, has been mostly overlooked. Their experiences have certainly not been well-documented in the specific and personal way this book will try to do. Whenever and wherever it fit, I tried to relate these stories and human experiences to the broader issues of social, economic and political equality and justice.

The history and relationships shared between Canada and First Nations are intertwined in the same way that two opposing teams first used tree branches to pass a "cow cookie" back and forth over a frozen pond in the past. Eventually, rules were formulated and the game of hockey as we know it today evolved.

Conversely, divisive subjects such as treaties, land claims, resource sharing, racism and full and equal partnerships are easier to understand and deal with when they are negotiated in a spirit of friendly competition, fair play and a set of rules that have been agreed to—just like in a hockey game.

It's safe to say that, for the most part, this kind of fair play—using rules that cannot be broken, playing on a level playing surface—has not been accessible throughout much of the history, politics, economic and social development between First Nations and Canada.

We may have dropped the ball in the past, but it's never too late to start again. We might be well served to drop the puck and start that game over.

1

CHIEF RUNNING DEER ON SKATES (A.K.A. CHIEF THUNDERSTICK)

Official NHL records don't tell you much about Fred Sasakamoose. His stats sheet reads "13 games played, 0 goals, 0 assists, 6 minutes in penalties." The record also notes that Sasakamoose was the first Indian to play in the NHL, and that is about it.

Amongst the First Nations in Saskatchewan, however, Fred Sasakamoose is a legend. Not only because he achieved the highest honour of becoming the first Indian to play in the greatest hockey league in the world but because Freddie was one of their own: a real, red pioneer who broke through to the top, but could also be seen playing right next door. Most Indians in Saskatchewan had not only listened to Fred's exploits on the radio through *Hockey Night in Canada* and Canadian Senior Hockey League broadcasts, but they had been able to witness his incredible skill first-hand.

Because he was a star on the national stage, as well as a barnstormer who might be coming to your neighbourhood to play an exhibition game against local boys any day or night, the stories about Fred Sasakamoose began early and spread like wildfire. From the prairies of Saskatchewan to other First Nations communities throughout Canada, these stories grew better and better with each telling.

★ ★ ★ ★ ★

Imagine a cold, prairie winter night in Saskatchewan. An Indian family is gathered around a wood stove in the living room of their log cabin listening to mooshum (grandpa) tell stories. Like the one about Fred Sasakamoose, the first full-blooded Indian to play in the National Hockey League.

One time not too long ago, just out back of this here shack, the one and only Freddie Sasakamoose suited up against a bunch of white boys, who had been having considerable success against teams both white and red in and around these parts and, as a matter of fact, all of northern Saskatchewan.

Well, the game started, and those white boys fired the puck into the Indians' end of the ice and charged after it like a pack of rez dogs after a rabbit. Ha ha! Them poor dumb dogs! Because they didn't know we had a secret weapon! Fred Sasakamoose was visiting relatives in town and we convinced him to suit up with our team and teach those white boys a lesson!

Well, the puck crossed the red line behind our net and ol' Freddie just skated back there quite leisurely and wrapped that ol' bannock biscuit around the blade of his stick, and wound up...first back and forth behind his own net, and then up the ice... Freddie started stickhandling as if by magic through every one of them white boys. He had the entire other team beat by centre ice, so he wheeled back and I'll be damned if he didn't do it all over again. Meanwhile, Fred's teammates went for a smoke.

Now, some people say Freddie did this just for the fun of it, but I knew Freddie personally and he was always worried about giving the people their money's worth. After all, folks on the rez had paid 25 cents apiece to see Freddie play and that outdoor rink was packed. Freddie was just giving the folks a show!

And Freddie was never one to embarrass other players too, too much, so he finally just settled in front of the other team's net...them white boys were nowhere near that net by this time, heh heh, they was sprawled all over the ice looking for their long johns! Just their goalie remained behind, and that poor little white boy, he was shivering and shakin' like a willow in a strong wind.

But instead of firing the puck past that goalie, Freddie just backhanded it high up into the air and skated off the ice to join his teammates for a smoke!

Well, one week later, Freddie led his team back on to that same sheet of ice...just as that puck was coming down from the sky.

Freddie, with a flick of the most powerful wrists that ever fit into any hockey glove, tucked that puck politely into an open net. You see, that goalie, and the rest of his white-boy friends weren't there that one week later, and it's a matter of fact that those white boys never showed up around this part of the prairies again.

This is a true story. I swear on my dogs! And if isn't, then may I be killed by a puck falling out of the sky. Heh heh!

In this way, to the people of Saskatchewan, Fred Sasakamoose was the best and most famous hockey player to ever lace on a pair of skates. He was to prairie Indian kids what Maurice "The Rocket" Richard was to the white kids.

I first heard about Fred Sasakamoose when I started doing work for the Saskatchewan Indian Federated College in Regina. I was contracted to write a play for the World Assembly of First Nations and this work brought me into contact with a lot of Indian Elders (I had to check everything I wrote with the Elders to make sure it was accurate and appropriate).

Most of the Elders were huge sports fans. Athletics have always been a big part of Indian culture, history and lifestyle, and I spent many hours talking hockey with my Indian friends in Saskatchewan (and making bets on my beloved Winnipeg Blue Bombers against their beloved Roughriders of the Canadian Football League).

And almost always, when we talked hockey, the name Fred Sasakamoose would come up. The stories were incredible; many unbelievable. You've heard of urban myths? Freddie was a "reserve myth." The man could do anything on ice, the greatest player ever. I took the stories the Elders told me with a bite of bannock, mostly because I was a huge sports fan as well as a kind of sports historian, and I had never heard of this Indian who supposedly played (and outplayed) NHL stars I knew a lot about, like Gordie Howe and The Rocket. But the Sasakamoose stories were interesting, entertaining and fun to share. I got so caught up in the hype that I started spreading tall tales about Sasakamoose that I heard in Saskatoon to people I met in Regina who had somehow remained oblivious to this legend, just to join in the din.

I didn't have any inclination or major motivation to get any facts straight about Fred Sasakamoose until many years later, when my friend Gary Zubek approached me with the idea of co-producing a documentary about Indians and their history in the sport of hockey. I knew right away that, besides featuring famous Indian players like George Armstrong, Reggie Leach and Bryan Trottier, the documentary would have to include stories about the legendary Fred Sasakamoose. But it would have to separate fact from fiction, so I finally set out to find the truth about Fred Sasakamoose.

There was just one detour, which I had created for myself. The stories I had heard about Freddie were so legendary, iconic and full of idolatry that I quite simply had assumed that they pertained to a "great and late Fred Sasakamoose." Every storyteller's style spoke about Freddie in the past tense, and I confused talking about the past with Freddie's having "passed." My thoughts about his death were as greatly exaggerated as the stories I had heard about his life.

I'll never forget my first research call to Georgie Poitras, a former Chief of the Peepeekisis Reserve, who had such an outstanding junior hockey career himself that he won a Tom Longboat trophy as Best Indian Athlete in Canada, was considered for tryouts with the CFL's Edmonton Eskimos and Saskatchewan Roughriders, and was a killer fastball player. Georgie had filled me with stories about Sasakamoose throughout our long friendship, so I asked him to help me tell Freddie's story by setting up some interviews with people who played with or against Freddie, or who knew Fred as a friend.

"So George, I'm doing this documentary about Indians who played in the NHL and I want to include stories about Freddie Sasakamoose. I was wondering if I could interview you on camera and maybe you could find a few of the old-timers who used to play with or against Freddie and we could cobble together a feature on his life?"

In typical Indian fashion, George's reply was polite. He didn't put me down for my ignorance, but his point was patiently and patently clear. "Uh, Don? Why don't you just talk to Freddie himself? You just have to phone the gas station in Shellbrook and they'll get in touch with Freddie, who's still living in his log cabin in Sandy Lake."

George set up interviews with Fred, his friends and relatives, and some of the guys who played "with 'im or agin him." George's fee for producing this segment of the documentary was two new tires for the back end of his 1971 Oldsmobile.

And, during numerous interviews in and around the Sasakamoose homestead (a log cabin that keeps getting larger) on the Ahtahkakoop First Nation (formerly called the Sandy Lake Indian Reserve), Freddie set me straight. About his life, his career and the times in which it all took place. And it's true what they say: truth is stranger than fiction. And far more fascinating.

★ ★ ★ ★ ★

Fred Sasakamoose is officially recognized as the first "natural born Indian" to play in the National Hockey League, at least according to all the record books and other literature published by the NHL (Bill Robinson, an Indian, but one of many who the Canadian government would not issue a treaty card to at the time, played goal for the New York Rangers during the 1951–52 NHL season). Fred's NHL career only lasted 13 games with the Chicago Blackhawks during the 1952–53 season.

That makes Fred a member of what the people in professional hockey call the "cuppa coffee" gang (the most famous member of this team being former Boston Bruins head coach and hockey broadcaster Don Cherry, who played just one game in the "show"). That wasn't because Freddie couldn't cut it or even that he was cut. It was simply a different time—and Fred Sasakamoose was most definitely different. And it was these differences that cut his career in the show short.

★ ★ ★ ★ ★

The "difference" begins on Christmas Day, 1933, on the Sandy Lake Indian Reserve in northern Saskatchewan (a long hop, skip and a jump from

Grizzly Bear's Head, Lean Man and Mosquito, but a stone's throw from the Shellbrook–Prince Albert area). While many of the other players who rose to prominence in the NHL during the 1950s hailed from small Canadian villages and towns, few to none were raised in an isolated community that could only be accessed by boat, sled or winter road, as Freddie Sasakamoose was.

Fred's early memories are of snaring rabbits and prairie chickens, trapping beaver and muskrats, and fishing rivers and lakes. "We were poor. We had nothing. We lived in a log house that was 20 feet by 20 feet."

Canadian kids who grew up during this era learned to play hockey on ponds and rivers and backyard rinks. Fred skated on a slough near the family cabin, pretty much the same as any other Canuck kid at the time. "It got awful cold out there. That's why you learned to skate fast!"

It was an ideal time, with mommy and daddy standing by, along with kookum and mooshum (grandma and grandpa), other kids, and many aunties and uncles and cousins coming around. Dinner ran wild just outside the front door. Mother Earth, Grandfather Sky and their brother, the river, along with a traditional Indian extended family, provided Freddie with everything he could ever want or need.

Mooshum was the biggest influence in young Freddie's life. "My grandfather gave me the name 'Tootsa,' which means 'solid little guy.' He would take me to this pond on our reserve and he would cut two willow branches. He would carve one of the branches into a fishing pole and the other into a hockey stick. I learned to play hockey on bobskates strapped to my moccasins while Grandpa caught dinner. Then I unstrapped the bobskates from my moccasins and gave them to my brother, because it was his turn to skate, and Kookum cooked dinner."

Fred first heard about the NHL through *Hockey Night in Canada* radio broadcasts, which gathered most every man, woman and child around the radio every winter Saturday night throughout Canada. In this way, Fred and his family were no different from any other Canadian family.

"And it was no different from watching the game on TV, the way that legendary Foster Hewitt called the play-by-play."

★ ★ ★ ★ ★

The major difference between Freddie's upbringing and the raising of most other Canadian children was that Freddie was taken away from his parents at the age of five and placed in an Indian residential school. The intent was to educate Indians in the ways of the white man, but things went horribly wrong.

"The Indian agent kind of ran things on the reserve. They told my mother and father that they would go to jail if they didn't let them take me to residential school. They took me away by...kind of...force?"

Anybody with an ounce of common sense will know that any child who is taken away from his mom and dad at such a tender age is going to feel one emotion. "The main thing I remember was the loneliness. I was always lonely."

While the intentions of the Canadian government and their agents, the churches, may have been "honourable," that is, to educate Indian children in the white man's ways of reading, writing and arithmetic, it has been well documented that the residential schools were also an effort to convert Indians to Christianity at least, and a holocaust of cultural genocide, including physical and sexual abuse, at worst. "We got punished. We got punished pretty hard. I'm not going to complain about it. I learned to behave. But I damn near forgot my language. I couldn't talk my language in that school."

Yet Fred was lucky—in a way.

He didn't become one of the 50,000 children who died in the Indian residential school system in Canada. He wasn't sexually abused. He wasn't slapped across the face for speaking his language. He didn't wear braids in his hair that could be cut off. He wasn't forced to share a bed with another child who had tuberculosis and get the "coughing sickness" himself. He wasn't raped or murdered, like the Indian girls—buried under the floorboards or in the schoolyard—who had been impregnated by perverted priests. Sterilization experiments were not performed on Fred Sasakamoose. And he wasn't forced into full-time slave labour planting crops, milking cows or baling hay like his fellow students at some other Indian residential schools had to do at the expense of the education they were supposed to receive. Mistreatment such as this resulted in the historic apology made by Prime Minister Stephen Harper on behalf of all Canadians to survivors of the Indian Residential School System on June 16, 2008.

The St. Michael's Indian Residential School at Duck Lake wasn't that bad. At least, that's the impression you got from Freddie, because he didn't like to talk about it all that much. "I'm not going to say what kind of abuse I saw there but I will say that I didn't like it. But my time there did lead me to some good opportunities."

Fred, like the rest of his schoolmates, did not receive the education he was supposed to get under the original design of the residential school system. Mornings were taken up by classes. Afternoons were spent tending to the school's substantial farm. Early evenings were eaten up by hockey. "The priests who ran the school were from Montreal and you know how those French men are. They love their hockey. We skated every day. Seven days a week."

Fred didn't mind. He loved hockey more than a child loves ice cream. Literally. "We got one dessert a week. On Sundays. I traded my ice cream with other children for an extra hour of skating."

The priests who coerced Freddie and his mates to play hockey every day coached the hockey team just like they taught school. "The priests never talked twice. The second time, you got the strap. But Father Rousell had a dream. He told me, 'Freddie, I'm going to work you hard, but if you work hard, you're going to be successful.' And, sure enough, 1945–46, we won the Saskatchewan northern midget hockey championship!"

But, by the time Fred was 14, he had enough of being used and abused by the residential school system, and he vowed never to go back again, no matter what. Freddie went home and hid.

★ ★ ★ ★ ★

North American First Nations history is full of legends. It is an oral history, which is valid and full of colour. There are many of tales of bravery and brotherhood and battles with other First Nations. Indians were always on the lookout, mostly to be aware of scouts from enemy tribes.

This Hoop Dance tells the story of a warrior's journey into an enemy's camp. During the day, he would dig holes to hide in when the enemy was about. At night, the warrior would creep closer and closer to the camp. Eventually, the warrior would make his way into the camp and steal some horses, maybe even a wife!

When the warrior returned home, he would tell the story of his journey by way of this Hoop Dance. The number of times he would dance in and out of the hoops let the people know how many holes he had to dig to hide in during the day when the enemy was about. The designs he made with his hoops were the sights of nature he witnessed on his journey…the grass growing…the butterfly in flight…the eagle in its nest.

After returning home at the age of 14, Fred was very wary of "enemy scouts," the Indian agents, or the priests, who would drag him back to residential school. And late one summer afternoon a car pulled up to Fred's house on the Sandy Lake Reserve. And it was indeed a priest who was trying to steer the car through the dirt trails of the rez.

Fred was playing with his brother in the front yard of the Sasakamoose cabin. At first, they were naturally curious about the approaching car, but as soon as they made out the figures of white men behind the wheel, they fled into the bush. It was like they were both wearing the family bobskates at the same time.

But these enemy scouts turned out to be scouts from the Moose Jaw Canucks of the Saskatchewan Junior Hockey League. The bird dogs from "the big city" (Moose Jaw: population 5,000) eventually found Fred, and after a long talk with his mom and dad, and a lot of convincing that it would be in his best interests to join the team in Moose Jaw, Fred left his home and family once again, this time voluntarily.

"Moose Jaw was so much different from Sandy Lake. Street lights, traffic, lots of big stores. Every Saturday afternoon downtown was like a powwow, lots of people crowded around. But one thing was the same as residential school. That was the loneliness."

And now a new element was added to the mix Fred was drinking in so rapidly. Fred had experienced racism in the form of feeling inferior from the nuns and priests at boarding school, who preached that his Indian culture and spirituality were subordinate to the ways of the white man, and sometimes he was called "stupid Indian" or lazy and savage. But they always combined some sort of reason or logic or rationale, however wrong or twisted, with their racist insult or "teaching."

When Fred began travelling through the junior hockey circuit in western Canada, he began to hear racist name-calling so freely, seemingly without rhyme or reason, and so fiercely, he didn't know what to make of it. "Edmonton, Regina, Lethbridge, there was always discrimination. They called you names. I guess I got used to it."

A stranger in a strange land, Fred managed to cope. "I felt at that time I always walked behind everybody else. Played a step behind. After a while, I learned to play their game, then I learned to play their game better than they did."

Fred developed a reputation as a smooth skater with a hard shot. That smoothed over some of the roughest racists in those prairie towns. Then the coach of the Canucks made a clever move that put racism on the rails for Freddie for a while.

Freddie was placed at centre on a line with "Chinaman" Jimmy Chong on one wing and a "black guy from Edmonton" on the other, the three of them skating on sheets of ice as white as snow. What a sight this was! Especially for Indians. Freddie was in the middle of a kind of medicine wheel (which has strong healing powers for Native people and incorporates the four colours of humankind: red, white, yellow and black).

"The fans, they laugh at you, because you are an Indian. When they put the black and yellow guys beside me, I felt a little more comfortable."

As a show of respect, Fred combined red, black, yellow and white skate laces to tie up his skates. His teammates repaid that respect by placing a "C" on Fred Sasakamoose's sweater.

Fred's all-around ease afforded him the opportunity to shine as Captain Canuck, and by the age of 19, Fred Sasakamoose was chosen as the top player in western Canada.

Back when he was 16, Fred had signed a letter committing him to the Chicago Blackhawks (for a cool 100 bucks). And after three long, hard prairie winters, Freddie finally got "the call."

By now, Fred had developed into a compact, brick shithouse of a man, which he remains to this day, but his eyes still well up with tears as he recalls the experience of being called up to the NHL.

"You have a dream. A dream to play in the NHL—couldn't go any higher. The Chicago Blackhawks got a hold of me. They said, 'You report to Toronto on Saturday night.' Being a Native in this world is very hard. I realized my dream: the NHL."

A team official read the telegram from Chicago. He gave Fred a suitcase packed with three suits, shirts and a watch, and Fred caught the next train out of town. Fred claims that Moose Jaw had prepared him for the big city but, stepping out of Union Station in Toronto on February 27, 1952, he was awestruck by the height of the very first building he saw, the Royal York Hotel across the street.

"Coming from the bush, I knew tall trees sure 3-story buildings in Mosse Jaw but this was a different thing, these huge buildings! I thought, 'Where the heck am I?'"

Freddie's first stop was at a radio station, where he was given a box of cigars and a battery-operated transistor radio (payment now more commonly known as "swag") for doing an interview. Fred remembers that the radio interviewers greeted him by saying, "How!", like he was from some Hollywood western B movie.

"I just raised my hand like an old Indian and answered back, 'How! as in Gordie Howe!' They asked me to speak Cree. To speak my language. So I said, in Cree, 'Hello! You'll be able to see me at the hockey game tonight.' I pretended I was talking to all the Indians in the audience. I don't know if there were any Cree out there. I doubt it. And I have no idea what the white people who were listening were thinking!'"

Some listeners in Toronto were no doubt twisting their radio dials back and forth in confusion thinking their reception had gone haywire; maybe some of them harkened back to romantic images of Hiawatha and Running Bear. Who knows? But one can imagine the radio DJs getting a huge kick out of it all, having a "genuine Indian" speaking in a foreign tongue in Toronto (which, by the way, means "meeting place" in the Indian dialect from which the city's name is derived).

Meanwhile, Fred was becoming a nervous wreck, which only got worse at the worst possible time. Just before they dropped the puck to start Freddie's first game in the most hallowed hockey rink in the English world to any man or child who grew up sitting around the hot stove listening to CBC's *Hockey Night in Canada* radio broadcasts every winter Saturday night, Fred was called over to the boards alongside the rink in Maple Leaf Garden.

A man in a suit was waiting there, holding up a telephone. "Number 21? Somebody wants to talk to you."

Fred couldn't possibly imagine who would be calling him, right before the game, way out there in Toronto. Certainly not his family. They didn't have a phone. The Chief of Sandy Lake didn't even have a phone—the community was connected to the rest of Canada by radio. Fred put the receiver to his ear: it was none other than legendary play-by-play man Foster Hewitt.

"He asked me what was my name? Was it 'Saskatoon-moose' or 'Saskatchewan-moose' or what?"

Remember, this was Foster Hewitt himself. The radio voice that boomed through the living room that Freddie grew up in, surrounded by his mom and his dad and his grandma and grandpa and his aunties and his uncles and his brothers and sisters, all of whom listened in awe and reverence to this voice, which was now on a phone talking directly, personally, with Freddie.

But, if you read between the lines, Mr. Hewitt was being kind of condescending.

So Fred simply snorted into that telephone, "Sasakamoose is my name!" and skated away with righteous indignation. Sometimes, somehow, Indian pride just takes over, come hell or high water.

And that was no tall tale from Saskatchewan, but the pure and simple truth (at least the way Freddie remembers it now). And, if it isn't, let us both be struck by a puck falling out of the sky.

★ ★ ★ ★ ★

Chicago Stadium, which always listed its official attendance as 16,066, but regularly jammed 21,000 people into its seats and standing-room-only sections during the 1960s, was even more overwhelming than Maple Leaf Garden.

"I never seen such things as the three balconies there...over 20,000 people! When I skated out onto the ice, the organist started playing 'Indian Love Call'...everybody was yelling, 'Chief, Chief, Chief.' It was insane! I was nervous...I could barely skate!"

But, teammates in Chicago like Gerry Topazzini, swore by Freddie's skating. "It was like his blades never touched the ice—he was that quick!"

That covers Fred's skating. What about his shot? The person who best described that came after Freddie.

Bobby Hull, who started his illustrious career with the Blackhawks the year after Sasakamoose had left the team, says that in the beginning of his career in Chicago he was always being compared to "some Indian guy who had this booming and powerful slapshot." That was Freddie.

Hull's booming and powerful slapshot carried him to the NHL Hall of Fame. Fred Sasakamoose, or "Chief Thunderstick," wasn't around for any of it. With such quick blades and such a powerful shot, why did Fred Sasakamoose only last 13 games with the Blackhawks, registering 0 goals, 0 assists and 6 minutes in penalties? Certainly, Fred, like every other junior who was called up during these times, was "nervous, unsure, certainly not confident," according to fellow rookie Peter Conacher. Despite his obvious skills, Fred's number 21 would be passed onto, and made immortal by the legendary forward Stan Mikita.

The reasons that Fred never achieved similar standing continue to compromise other Indian hockey players to this day. It's much more than the simple fact that, even though Fred's skates never seemed to touch the ice, that at five-foot-nine, his jersey almost touched his knees. Other, even smaller guys, like Camille Henry and Henri Richard, starred in the NHL, while Freddie didn't. There was a problem that simply would not go away, and it wasn't based in the physical or the athletic: "I could never get over that loneliness."

Indian health and success stems from natural, holistic balance. Healing and harmony can only be achieved if all four aspects of the human being—body, mind, emotions and spirit—are in synch. Freddie was a fine physical specimen, but the rest of him was a mess.

From all outward appearances, things looked mighty fine after those first 13 games with the Blackhawks. Fred celebrated the end of his first season in the NHL by stopping in Humboldt, Saskatchewan on his way home, where he bought a brand new Mercury DeSoto for a princely sum, in those days, of $3,900.

"There were no cars on the reserve in them days," says Fred. "Or roads. Just a trail."

Fred recalls bumping along that trail and then stopping in front of the log cabin where he grew up. "My mom looked out and saw a shiny new car with a man in a suit behind the wheel. She started yelling 'Monias! Monias!' (white man! white man!) to the other people inside the cabin. When I stepped out, mom started crying, 'Ni kosis' (my son).

Fred offered to take his parents for a ride anywhere they wanted to go. They settled on a trip to the general store 13 kilometres away, where Fred bought groceries for the family, and a pair of rubber boots for his dad.

Whether Freddie will admit it, or even knew what "culture shock" was at the time, it had to have some impact on his ability to cope and perform when he returned to Chicago the next fall. Notwithstanding the orientation to city life that Fred claims was provided by Moose Jaw, it wasn't Chicago. Fred was an Indian from a remote Saskatchewan reserve who spoke English as a second language, and he was in the home of Al Capone, Elliot Ness, Richard Daley and "Bad Bad Leroy Brown." There's many a sportswriter who has gotten warped by the overdose of acetylcholine that keeps firing across one's synapses every time a new environment requires an adaptation response. It's easy to imagine what was going through Freddie's nervous system—his mind and his heart.

Complicating the situation was the fact that Fred was coping with his loneliness and cultural isolation with alcohol. The last thing management in Chicago wanted was a "firewater" stereotype to be associated with their famous Indian logo (unlike other sports teams, which use a race of people as mascots, the Chicago Blackhawks are named after a World War II fighter plane that honoured the great Indian Chief Blackhawk).

Loneliness, confusion and booze must have been affecting Fred's ability to perform. After all, he had absolutely dominated everybody his age in western Canada but he couldn't keep up with the players who would make up the magic 20 for the final Blackhawks roster.

"They decided to send me down to their farm team in Buffalo, New York. I bounced around from Chicoutimi in the Quebec Hockey League to the Westminster Royals of the Western Hockey League. Finally, I said to the Blackhawks, 'Send me close to home so I can be with my wife!' So I signed a contract with Calgary. It wasn't very much, maybe three thousand dollars a year."

Three thousand dollars a year doesn't sound like much in these days of million-, billion- and gazillion-dollar salaries, but we have to remember the times Freddie was living in. First of all, three grand was good money. For playing a game! For just half a year. And we have to keep in mind the NHL wasn't the dominant force that it is now.

There is a big difference between the present-day NHL and leagues like the American Hockey League, the East Coast Hockey League, the United Hockey League and other minor circuits (trust me, when you watch NHL third-liners like Ron Wilson and Doug Smail of the parent NHL team Winnipeg Jets score seven goals each in a scrimmage against the "meat" provided by the AHL Moncton Jets during a training camp scrimmage, you know the difference, and it is huge!).

But back in the days of Fred Sasakamoose, when there were only six teams in the NHL, there was no room for hundreds of talented players who were just as good as, if not better than the elite "6 times 20" who made it to "the show." Countless talented players slipped under the radar of scouts who were trying to keep up to this talent by train.

The American Hockey League was stocked with great players. Senior hockey leagues with teams like the Saskatoon Quakers and the Winnipeg Maroons thrived before sellout crowds in 10,000-seat arenas. There simply wasn't as big a difference between the NHL and the minor leagues as there is now.

Back in the day of Fred Sasakamoose, playing in a senior league was merely akin to playing bastard son to a slightly more poor uncle. The money in Calgary was almost as good as Chicago. The adoration from the fans, in a hockey-crazy northern outpost like Cowtown, was often better than fan support in that windy city in the American midwest. Most importantly for Fred Sasakamoose, Calgary was closer to home.

"I told the Blackhawks I wanted to go home to get my wife, but they wouldn't buy me a plane ticket. So I took a taxi 700 miles from Calgary to home."

Fred's wife Loretta, who had once refused to move from one side of Sandy Lake to the other because she would get too homesick, now refused to join her husband in Calgary.

"She said, 'I'm not going.' I went back to Calgary and packed my bags. My roommate asked, 'Where you going, Chief?' I said, 'I'm going home.'"

That was the end of Freddie Sasakamoose's NHL career—and the beginning of a legend that would become to the province of Saskatchewan what the Legend of Paul Bunyan is to the state of Minnesota.

★ ★ ★ ★ ★

Back in the days before television came to the Canadian prairies, whenever parents left a living room to fix a between-periods snack for kids curled around a radio for *Hockey Night in Canada*, mooshums were left alone to spin another yarn for wide-eyed children, as all of them huddled around a wood stove in that "little house on the rez." Such stories grew bigger and taller as the children grew big and tall.

And then there was the time they decided to hold this here "fastest and hardest shot" competition over to Balcarres! Well, Freddie Sasakamoose, humble as ever, humble as any man ever was, refused to put his name up for that contest because, as he said, "I only shoot to score and then not too much, if the score gets to be too high."

Besides, Freddie had to use his stick to harvest the grain off his back 40 acres. Fred's threshing machine had broken down and he needed that stick to thresh that wheat. And he also needed that stick to shoot what few pucks he had left to bring down a few deer or rabbits to feed his family for the winter.

Them white boys was laughing and laughing and laughing, as they fired pucks at that empty net, measuring each shot with a stopwatch and jumping up and down, higher and higher, every time the speed of one of their shots got faster! (but not too fast). Well, eventually, the white boys got tired, and it was just no fun just beating up on each other. But just as they were ready to tie up that net and retire to the bar up by Beau Valle for one of their wobbly pops, who else but Fred, Fantastic Fred Sasakamoose, should pull up—in a brand new DeSoto automobile!

Fred didn't take kindly to those white boys prancing around like them fake fancy dancing bureaucrats at one of our powwows, and I swear that Freddie, for the first time in his life, looked, well, just a little upset. Maybe even peeved, you might say. So, with a humble, but proud proclamation, ol' Freddie just said, "Wanna see the fastest slapshot in the entire West?"

Now, to the untrained eye, it might have appeared like Freddie just passed the whole darn competition by, being burdened down as he was by the dead he-wolf on his back and the she-wolf nippin' on his heels, but Freddie proved everybody wrong by looking back just before he crossed through the front door of his home to give his beloved wife, Loretta, the nine-point buck he had wrapped around his waist and said: "You wanna see that shot again?"

★ ★ ★ ★ ★

Fred Sasakamoose followed up his NHL career by barnstorming through Saskatchewan and the rest of western Canada. Every Indian who lived on the prairies wanted to see this Indian who had actually played in the National Hockey League—and for good reason.

As Fred himself has said, "It's hard to be a Native in this world." Success, while still quite attainable within the valid values and traditions of Indian life on the rez, was almost impossible for an Indian in mainstream North American society. Fred Sasakamoose had achieved the ultimate success, albeit for a short while: he'd made it to the top in the white world. That was enough to attract thousands of Indians for a look-see. Caucasians, too.

Children throughout western Canada still had their NHL heroes and followed the NHL by radio the best they could. But on the reserves of Saskatchewan, Indian children had poor access to radio and no access to television. Their heroes were created around the campfire and the wood stove. Grandpas, dads and uncles would regale their Indian children with tales of the great Fred Sasakamoose—the only Indian to play in the National Hockey League. And unlike all the other children at the time who never got to see an actual NHL player in person, these Indian children actually had a chance to watch Freddie fly around the ice against what they always thought were "the best"—good local players, who would end up being completely dominated by the wizardry of "Chief Running Deer on Skates."

For Freddie, barnstorming was almost like being in the NHL. The benefits were similar and there were far fewer hassles. Fred's contract with the Blackhawks had been worth $6,000 per season and that was reduced to $3,000 when he went down to Calgary. For barnstorming, Fred was being paid a couple of hundred dollars plus expenses per game to appear in local rinks, and he was also available as a "ringer" to help teams willing to pay enough for him to help them win a weekend tournament featuring big cash prizes. If Fred played only 40 games a winter at an average take of $300 per game, he was pulling in $12,000. He'd already bought that brand new DeSoto with his Blackhawk money, so he was riding in style with plenty of gas to spare.

Adulation was similar to the NHL in the "barns," if not better. Fred Sasakamoose didn't have to compete with other NHL players for attention; Freddie was the show. The fans adored him everywhere he went. No more travelling into opposition rinks to endure the catcalls of enemy fans who sometimes went too far with their racism. For this time, Freddie could leave that racism behind and this was very important to him.

Indian leaders have often claimed that their people are subject to racism or prejudice or discrimination in employment, housing, the courts and even when they go shopping. It's a point that's difficult to prove and it's often hard to get the impact of racism across. Indian leaders are most effective when they can demonstrate the devastatingly cruel impact that racism can have. And the impact of racism was really brought home by Fred Sasaka-moose's experience with it.

"The fans would call me names but I would just ignore it and skate on. But there was one name that I was called...I will never forget it...They called me 'squaw-humper.' I did skate on, but I will never forget it...it wasn't right because if they're saying that about me, they're really saying that about my wife."

Remember, this was a guy who missed his wife so much that he travelled 700 miles in a taxicab to try and convince her to join him in Calgary. When she refused, Fred Sasakamoose quit the NHL—the most elite league in the world for any hockey player. To imply that having sexual relations with an Indian woman was something degrading is the extreme insult and the most extreme example of racism that can be inflicted, at least verbally.

So you can understand Fred's glee to be free of racism while he barnstormed the Indian rinks of Saskatchewan. Sure, there was the odd white loudmouth or drunk who tried to get under Fred's skin, but they were few and far between, and they were usually hushed up by their kin, who didn't want to offend or incite the hundreds of Indians who were also in the stands.

There was no happy ending for Fred at this time, however. His constant companion, and his main nemesis, remained with him wherever he went. Loneliness. The barnstorming was fun, and he was doing what he did best but, again, hockey was taking him away from his wife, and his now growing family. There didn't seem to be any answer. Hockey was the only way he knew how to provide for his family, but it was also hockey that kept Freddie away from them. All of this created a bigger problem; the biggest challenge Fred would ever face in his life.

It soon became common knowledge to organizers of the exhibition games and tournaments who were counting on appearances by Fred Sasakamoose that the biggest problem the organizers had, and Fred had, wasn't showing up, but sobering up.

According to the owner of the gas station in Shellbrook, SK, "Freddie could still dominate games and win tournaments for teams single hand-edly...that is, if you could keep him sober long enough to play."

Fred would often show up for the first game completely sober and put on a dazzling display. But any beer league player will tell you that nothing goes down like a "barley sandwich" after a game. That's why they call them "beer leagues," and not milk or Kool-Aid leagues. And why you see so many beer ads during hockey telecasts.

Some guys can have a beer or two and then get ready for the next game. Other guys go home. And then there are the guys who down two too many between games. Fred was often part of the latter group, and the booze that went with the barnstorming began taking its toll.

Back in Ahtahkakoop First Nation, Loretta was left alone far too often to raise a rapidly growing family. Fred was great with Loretta and the kids when he was around, but there were too many moments and memories that were being missed. As is usually the case, it was the children who were most seriously affected.

Some people mistakenly believe that being the offspring/beneficiary of a star professional athlete provides sufficient compensation for all the travel and turmoil involved. That is often not the case. Unique circumstances arise that cannot be anticipated but must be dealt with. Such as what is revealed in the following response to what I thought was a rather simple question I posed to one of Fred's children.

★ ★ ★ ★ ★

Transcript of Interview: Tyler Sasakamoose (son)

Q: What was it like to be the son of the legendary Fred Sasakamoose?

A: It was horrible, just awful. I can remember the first time I played hockey. I was just a little shaver and I didn't know anything about the game. They dressed me up and put me on the ice and all of a sudden, I heard this loud roar and I looked up and the whole arena was full of people. They had all come out to watch the son of the legendary Fred Sasakamoose and I couldn't even skate! I remember the referee kept picking me up and putting me on the other side of the blue line because I didn't know what offside was. Then, when I was about 12 years old, they picked me for the provincial team ahead of a lot of other players who were better than me…again, just because I was the son of Sasakamoose. The parents of those other players all got mad at me. So I got mad at my dad. I quit hockey and it wasn't until years later that things got patched up between me and my dad and I started to love the sport of hockey like a Canadian prairie boy should.

The interview with Tyler raised issues that the media and public are most likely not aware of, or cannot see, or realize. Even though professional athletes supposedly live in a fish bowl, the uniqueness of their situation goes far beyond what happens to most people. Couple all that with all the booze and separation from his father and you can realize why Tyler was so upset.

It would be a long way to healing, and ironically, the first step towards the healing of the Sasakamoose family came from that very distance, that geographical separation that took place every weekend between Fred and his family as he headed off to tournaments throughout western Canada. The loneliness—and all that goes with it—eventually provided a clean sheet of ice.

The Creator moves in mysterious ways. Separation and loneliness were always the major problem, yet Fred found the foundation for solving his problems in faroff Kamloops, BC when the Kamloops Chiefs (the name providing even more irony), a senior hockey team located far from home in the British Columbia interior, offered Fred a permanent position on their team. And as luck, or fate, would have it, Loretta just happened to have relatives in Kamloops. For the first time, Loretta was willing to leave Sandy Lake to join her husband on the road. Step one.

Everything was perfect, except for the fact that Fred was still drinking. It wasn't that Fred was a mean drunk. As a matter of fact, Fred was fun to drink with; he made a good drinking buddy. But in the end, only drunks really appreciate other drunks, and the irresponsible behaviour of an alcoholic always takes its toll on the teetotallers.

Freddie was being paid good money to play for the Chiefs. When someone keeps missing work or screwing up on the job, something has to be done. It's the old "I can't tell you where to take a leak, but when you are pissing off the company dock…"

Maybe it was the ceremony the Kamloops Indians held for him where they honoured Fred with his Indian name "Chief Thunderstick." Perhaps it was Loretta's patience and understanding. Maybe it was the way Fred's children looked at him at certain times. Whatever it was, Fred woke up one day in 1982, far away from home in Kamloops, and swore that he had to find another way. He threw away the bottle, and Fred Sasakamoose hasn't had a drink of alcohol since.

Fred threw his hockey career away along with that bottle, at least that part of hockey that made it the primary focus of his life, and his primary source of income. Fred traded centre stage on the ice for a political stage, by deciding to run for Chief of Sandy Lake in 1982.

There was no doubt Fred has the leadership qualities that most elite athletes have. They lead their teams to victory by bringing people together to work towards a common goal. The greater the challenge, the more it is relished, because if they can beat a supposedly superior team, then that makes the victory even greater. Leaders overcome the bumps that appear along the road, the hardships and obstacles to success.

Fred was elected Chief of the Ahtahkakoop First Nation in 1982. That created other obstacles, because politics is a completely different game; a much dirtier game than hockey. There were backstabbers amongst his own people, as well as a huge white bureaucracy/political system to overcome. But Fred had already won the biggest fight of his life against that demon alcohol, so you didn't hear any whining from this warrior.

"The greatest thing that ever happened to me was when I entered political life and became a Chief. I quit drinking at that time and I've never looked back since."

★ ★ ★ ★ ★

Fred was one of the Chiefs who made the decision by the Federation of Saskatchewan Indian Nations to stage the World Assembly of First Nations in Regina. That was the group who hired me to write the play *in Deo*, which was presented at the Saskatchewan Centre for the Arts in 1982. One of my favourite memories from that time was the reaction of three good friends of mine to the play. George Poitras, Felix Musqua and Dutch Lerat were three big Indian guys, jocks really, who had all played junior hockey and were now well-respected leaders in their communities.

The play *in Deo* tells the history of First Nations in North America through music and dance (traditional Indian, rock, blues, opera, ballet, modern dance and jazz). At the end of Act One, Indian children sit at their desks in a residential school, dressed in white shirts and black pants, studying their textbooks. A young traditional dancer, representing the spirit and traditions of a proud Indian past, dances proudly in and around the desks. But the harder he dances, the more the other children bury their heads in their textbooks. Finally, the little traditional dancer dances to the corner of the room and bows his head in despair.

Then BOOM! The curtain rises and the house lights come up.

I knew the scene would have an impact, but I didn't know that it would almost cost me a good licking! You see, Georgie, Felix and Dutch, macho men that they all were, did not enjoy being caught in the full light of a theatre intermission with tears streaming down their faces. They had all been victimized by residential school. I had caught them at a vulnerable moment, and exposing their weakness was very embarrassing to them. In the end, they realized that opening wounds is a first step towards healing, and cooler heads prevailed. We all had a good laugh later.

Fred Sasakamoose was in the audience that night, because all of the Chiefs in Saskatchewan were there. Fred may have even cried at the end of Act One like his jock brethren did, but I'll never know. It's good enough for me that Fred is laughing now.

Fred Sasakamoose is retired and lives in that log cabin on the Ahtakekoop First Nation. He works a farm by that slough where he first put on those bobskates, and operates a water truck at times. But mostly, Fred and his wife Loretta spend their days keeping track of their 8 grown children, 16-

plus grandchildren and 57-plus great-grandchildren. Fred coaches hockey (imagine how many team rosters a family tree like Freddie's can fill), and he fills water bottles, opens the gate for the players, laces up skates, and tapes sticks. He is also in demand as a speaker at banquets, for celebrity golf tournament appearances, memorabilia signings, and to conduct anti-alcohol and anti-drug workshops for youth and children, which he does wherever and whenever he's asked to go.

He's even invited to play exhibition games on the road and sometimes he goes. But he never takes his problems with him anymore—he left loneliness and the bottle behind him on another road a long time ago. That time when he became a warrior.

Chief Running Deer on Skates doesn't run away from anything anymore. He is running towards goals that are more important than turning on a red light behind a hockey net. The lights Fred wants to turn on are the ones that appear over a young child's head when ambition, motivation and inspiration come together as one.

2

THE CHIEF (AND THE "UP-AND-COMING" CHIEF)

Although almost all Indians who play hockey at any level get called "Chief" at one time or another, the man who was, and will always be, the most well-known "Chief" was George Armstrong. You can call any Indian anywhere "Chief," but George Armstrong was "*The* Chief."

George Armstrong is the longest-serving captain in NHL history. The Chief led the Toronto Maple Leafs to four Stanley Cup championships. He was elected to the Hockey Hall of Fame in 1975. Details of Armstrong's career are readily available in any library or on the Internet.

Jim Neilson followed Armstrong into the NHL a couple of years later. When he entered the league, Neilson was called the "up-and-coming" Chief. Neilson proved worthy by starring for the New York Rangers for well over a decade, even finishing second to the legendary Bobby Orr in votes for the NHL's top defenceman one year. Neilson's exploits are also well-covered in libraries and on the Internet.

The fact that Armstrong is the Indian who is most readily associated with the term "Chief," and that Neilson was quickly slapped with the same moniker, makes for some incredible irony. Because neither man was raised in the Indian way, and both were quite unfamiliar with most things Indian.

At the same time, when these two played, there was a fascination, a kind of mystique, with all things Indian. Romantic notions of the forgotten American, the noble savage—stoic, patient, with high cheekbones; one who can run through a forest without snapping a twig. These images were perpetuated in some Hollywood westerns and Buffalo Bill's Wild West Show. The entire image of Indians was cast in the past: buckskin and beads, head-dresses and bows and arrows. Meanwhile, Indians were being bombarded by modern technology, automobiles, televisions, electric stoves, suits and ties. The United States supposedly had a policy to assimilate Indians, and Canada had a multicultural society that recognized the sovereignty of First Nations, but both bounced back and forth depending on the time and the tribe. It can safely be said that Indians were the least well-known and most misunderstood minority group in North America. Perhaps the best way to make this point is on a personal level. And what could be more personal than someone's name?

When the white man first came to North America, he met Native people with very strange-sounding names (at least in the European language). One of the most well-known Indians in North American history has been called by a misnomer because of misunderstanding, poor translation or simply laziness on the part of the whites who first met him.

When this great Elder and medicine man first met white people, they asked him what his name was. He replied: "As a child, it was foretold that I would one day become the head of a herd (of buffalo or tonka) who would lead his followers to a safe valley, then I would go up to a high vantage point to rest on my haunches to watch for predators. My name is 'Resting Monarch on the Plains.' To the white man, this Indian leader became known as 'Sitting Bull.'"

Similarly, "Even His Horses Are Afraid of Him" became known as "Man Afraid of His Horses" and "Face like a Storm" was called "Rain the Face."

Such simple, but personal and important misunderstandings aside, it can also be safely said that Indians remained so mysterious and unknown because, of all ethnic groups or nations, they were least subject to assim-ilation. This is partly because Indians were the only societies who were completely segregated from the main by geographic isolation on reserves (in Canada) or reservations (in the United States), and partly because Indian people are sovereign First Nations who did not come to North America to seek a new life like all other ethnic groups. Indians have always struggled to preserve their culture and lifestyle in their own lands, which they love most sacredly, with a spirituality that is infinitely connected with this land. And—bottom line—Indians are, like most others, very proud of who they are, their identity, and will simply never give up being who they really are.

In the 1950s and early '60s, the only Indians most people saw were in those Hollywood B films; westerns, or so-called "cowboy and Indian" movies. It was a rare experience to encounter a real Indian in real life unless you happened to live near a reserve or reservation. Indians who somehow managed to gain a high profile in white society were often treated with fascination and attracted a lot of attention.

Think about it. How many Indians were well-known or famous in the 1950s? Perhaps Jay Silverheels, who played Tonto in the Lone Ranger series. Will Rogers was Native American but few people knew that. The only "Indians" we saw or read about were "Wop-ahos" —olive-skinned, Italian actors like Sal Mineo, who portrayed Indians in movies (then again, blond and blue-eyed actor Chuck Connors played Geronimo in a movie; that's why Indians who parachute out of planes yell "Chuck Connors" on their way down!). Historical figures like Resting Monarch on the Plains (Sitting Bull), Crazy Horse, Peguis and perhaps Ira Hayes (Iwo Jima, Flags of our Fathers) were somewhat known to the mainstream. The most famous Indian athlete was Jim Thorpe, who was chosen Top Athlete of the First Half-Century by *Time* magazine. And that was about it.

This was the social scene that George Armstrong and Jim Neilson entered when they started playing professional hockey. Indians were so unseen and unheard that they had just won the right to vote in Canada. As Armstrong began to star in the NHL, with English Canada's favourite hockey team in Canada's favourite sport, he began to attract a lot of attention. Having Indian blood in him, and being strikingly Indian in appearance, George quickly became all that most people knew about Indians. The task of representing the Indian people of Canada, and the rest of North America, fell on George's shoulders. And then Jim Neilson's shoulders.

This wasn't fair because neither grew up going to powwows, praying in sweat lodges or voting for Chiefs and Councils to fight for self-government, land claims and socio-economic development programs. Armstrong was raised in Falconbridge, Ontario and learned to play hockey on local rinks while his Caucasian father worked in the nickel mines and his Indian mom ran the home. Neilson grew up in an orphanage, where he was the only Indian; child, woman or man.

It is quite ironic that when you google "George Armstrong" on the Internet, material about America's most famous "Indian fighter," George Armstrong Custer, pops up. Custer was the American US General who commanded the 7th Cavalry during the so-called Indian wars of the 1870s. As historian Dee Brown documented in her book, *Bury My Heart at Wounded Knee,* Custer slaughtered the innocents (almost 300 men, women and children) and innocence of Chief Black Kettle (who believed that his people would be safe as long as the American flag flew above his teepee) at the Washita River in the winter of 1872 ("battles" such as Washita, Sand Creek and Wounded Knee are depicted in movies such as *Soldier Blue* and *Little Big Man*). Custer was ultimately vanquished by the vision of Resting Monarch on the Plains (Elder) and War Chiefs Crazy Horse and Gall and their warriors, at the Little Big Horn in 1876.

There is much less material on the Internet about the most famous Indian who ever played hockey. Obviously Indian (and proud of that fact), George Armstrong would have to deal with stereotypes, imagery and role models that he was not intimately familiar with and this would create problems, because George was not the kind of man who would exploit or misrepresent the culture and lifestyle of a race of people whose blood flowed through his veins.

Throughout Armstrong's NHL career, he was besieged by requests for interviews by all types of media outlets and he was obligated to try and cooperate. A born leader, he represented the Maple Leafs well in all things hockey, but when it came to answering questions about current events, history, politics or the culture of Canada's First Nations, it was unfair to expect George to represent all that.

George lent his name and image to various role-model programs sponsored by Indian and Northern Affairs Canada and non-governmental Indian groups to encourage children and youth to excel, but his public appearances started to become more and more rare. Eventually, George Armstrong stopped doing interviews about any subject, and he hasn't given an interview to the media or made a public appearance since the early 1980s. This author completely respects George Armstrong's position in this regard, although it left a big hole in the documentary and in this book, as we can only recap the highlights of this great player.

I made numerous attempts to interview George, but I was rebuffed every time by the Leafs public relations guy, who simply said, "George does not do interviews with anybody for any reason." When they spotted me hanging around a Leafs practice like a hungry dog, I gather somebody finally asked George to contact me personally and let me down easy. George did just that, and I vividly remember receiving a call on my cell phone while having lunch at a Toronto restaurant. George was infinitely polite and nice, and despite my desperate attempts to persuade him of the merits of doing an interview for the documentary, he was unwavering. He was able to make me feel better because his sincerity was so real when he said he appreciated what I was trying to do and that he believed in my project, but he had made a decision that had become a rule and he couldn't break it for one person over another. And that was that. Except for the fact that I got to talk to The Chief, George Armstrong. Even for just a little while, it was good.

★ ★ ★ ★ ★

George Armstrong was born on July 6, 1930 in Skead, Ontario, which sits on the shores of Lake Wanapitei, about 25 kilometres northeast of Sudbury. He spent most of his childhood in Falconbridge, where he learned to play hockey while his father worked in the nickel mines. George was big for his age, and by the time he was 16, he was starring for the Copper Cliff Redmen of the Northern Ontario Hockey Association, along with future Maple Leaf teammate Tim Horton. They were both put on Toronto's negotiation list and George moved south to Stratford, where he starred for the junior Kroehlers. The Leafs wasted no time moving George up to the Toronto Marlboros system, where he dominated the OHL, and it was more of the same with Pittsburgh in the American Hockey League.

Then it was on to an NHL career characterized by two words; leadership and longevity, and best described by Toronto's assistant manager, King Clancy, in a 1952 prophecy: "This kid's got everything. He has size, speed, and he can shoot 'em into the net better than any hockey player I've known in a long time. I'll be surprised if he doesn't become a superstar."

Clancy wasn't surprised. Armstrong wasn't a consistent superstar; he was a superstar because of his consistency. You could count on Armstrong for 15 to 20 goals a year which, during the 1950s and '60s, was the equivalent of a .300 hitter in baseball. He was not only the longest-serving captain in NHL history, he was, as Leafs owner and manager Conn Smythe said, "the best captain, as a captain, the Leafs ever had."

Armstrong and the Leafs spent the '50s in futility, but the '60s brought success. The Chicago Blackhawks, led by young sensation Bobby Hull, were expected to stretch a string of Stanley Cups through the 1960s and they started in 1961, but the Leafs, led by Armstrong, snatched the Cup away in 1962 and then swept it three straight. By 1967, Leaf stars like Armstrong, Tim Horton, Allan Stanley, Bobby Baun, Frank Mahovlich and even Dave Keon were getting long in the tooth, but the Chief led them to one more—the final of his career (and the beginning of the use of an adjective that would stick with Leaf fans for at least four decades: "long-suffering").

Armstrong hung on for about five more years, through a couple of retirements (final stats: 296 G, 417 A, 713 P), and then served as a scout for the Leafs. At one point he was reluctantly hauled in to coach the team on an interim basis, to replace the highly volatile John Brophy, but The Chief proved to be a better leader on the ice than behind the bench.

During the 1997–98 season, George Armstrong was awarded the highest honour a player can receive from his team, when the Leafs retired his Number 10 jersey. And then, George Armstrong was bestowed the highest honour of the NHL and hockey worldwide, as he was inducted into the Hockey Hall of Fame.

★ ★ ★ ★ ★

During the early stages of his career, Armstrong made numerous public statements and appearances which tied in with his Native background. But there were reports of an incident where George had been embarrassed by the appearance of his Indian grandmother at a public gathering (one insensitive reporter, spotting the old-fashioned long dress, wool sweater and kerchief that George's grandmother was wearing, called her "shabby"). Speculation, inaccurate guessing really, went that George began to play down his Indian heritage after that. Other reports claim that George was so ashamed that he had been embarrassed by his grandmother that he stepped up appearances that tied in with his mother's Indian bloodline. Only George knows what really happened, and he isn't talking.

★ ★ ★ ★ ★

"I remember one time, the PR guy from the Rangers wanted me to wear a hair dress, I mean, a headdress. But I wouldn't do it."

Jim Neilson, like George Armstrong, is strikingly Indian in appearance. And Neilson, like Armstrong, did not grow up in a Native environment. "I grew up in an orphanage. All the rest of the kids were white so I didn't know anything about it [being Indian]."

And, like Armstrong, Neilson has spent his adult years catching up on the culture he was denied as a child. Unlike Armstrong, Neilson is willing to talk about Indian stuff, within the limits of what he knows. Just like any good defenceman, Neilson plays within his game. He has even had some fun with it.

"Red Fisher is a reporter from the *Montreal Gazette* and he coveted this painting, a Native painting, that Glen Sather [then general manager of the Edmonton Oilers] had at his cottage. We used to gather at Glen's cottage sometimes and Glen set Red up by saying that he was going to give him an

'Indian painting.' Well, Glen and I got the media out and photographers and we all gathered at Glen's cottage for a kind of gala ceremony where Red would be presented with this Indian painting. The thing that Red didn't know was that, for the first time, I put on a headdress and they gave me a can of paint and a brush and when Red got there, I started painting the side of the cottage. Red got an Indian painting. It was a picture of me painting a house!"

★ ★ ★ ★ ★

"I only saw my father once a year. He was always off mink ranching. I was placed in St. Patrick's Orphanage at the age of six and I was there for 12 years so it is the only home that I knew. St. Patrick's was a good experience for me because that is where I was introduced to hockey. I don't know where I would be if not for that orphanage.

"My hockey career took off very fast. I still had a year of junior left when I went to the Ranger camp in New York. It wasn't like some dream I had since I was 10 years old. It just happened so fast! I was lucky because the Rangers weren't a very good team at the time; well, we had good players but it was the six-team NHL and there were some outstanding teams which kept us and the Bruins out of the four-team playoffs. I was just good enough at that early age to stick with the starting roster but I also picked up a lot of those 'little sticks' in my butt, slivers from sitting on the bench. But that gave me a chance to watch and observe…guys like Doug Harvey and Harry Howell. I picked up a lot while picking up slivers.

"I had a good year my last year in junior in Kitchener [Ontario] so the Rangers, well, they were kinda desperate, too, so I guess they were willing to take a chance. But a good year with the Kitchener-Waterloo Beavers doesn't even come close to your experience with the New York Rangers. All of a sudden, you're playing defence against the Howes and the Beliveaus! They can make you look small so you have to really get to know yourself. Know what your capabilities are. Whereas you have to realize that you are progressing at the same time, you still have to have confidence. You don't let your mistakes beat you. You learn from your mistakes.

"I truly believe that it was also a good thing that I was married. I only spent one year in New York as a single man. I was married in 1963. Yeah, that took care of a lot of things I may have fallen into. Some of those traps that are big-time in New York."

Neilson avoided those traps so well he enjoyed a long, long (12-year) career with the only team in New York at that time. "Things were way different back then. There was nowhere near as many players moving around and changing teams. And you didn't get too buddy-buddy with players from other teams. They were the enemy."

That philosophy prevented Neilson from developing anywhere near the kind of Indian camaraderie with George Armstrong that, say, Ron Delorme would develop with Gino Odjick. But that doesn't mean that Neilson wasn't intimately familiar with Armstrong.

"I remember Armstrong was a rangy fellow. Getting around him was like getting around an octopus. An Eric Nesterenko kind of reach. That's when I decided not go up the ice that much. Just throw it up to the forwards and that's their job." And that became one of the strengths in Neilson's game. He became a master at "head manning" the puck.

The nicknames that were given to Armstrong and Neilson were rather apt. "Armstrong was The Chief, and I was the 'up-and-coming' Chief. I've been called Chief all my life, everywhere else I go. In hockey, you know that your teammates were calling you Chief in a friendly, natural sort of way. But then you would play guys from other teams and you knew it wasn't so friendly. Most of it was just during the heat of the battle and they were trying to throw you off your game and you just ignore it."

Despite the patience and understanding Jim seems to be able to muster up to deal with ridicule and racism, there have been times when the "red line" was crossed. "Yeah, it's that 'FBI' (f'in big Indian) type of thing that just gets you shaking your head. Hockey is a tough game and professional hockey is so competitive…it's a fight to the death to keep your job…the pressure…But to sink to that level of insulting somebody because of their race…you are insulting the children, the innocent children, the women, the good people of that race."

Racist barbs got thrown Jim's way from the stands as well, but one incident of racism that came from the newsstands really stands out in Jim's mind.

Norm Mclean wrote the following in a publication called *Hockey World*; what this ignorant author thought was a tribute piece to Jim Neilson: "Like most Indians, Jim Neilson is swarthy of skin and dark of hair. Unlike most Indians, Neilson keeps himself in good physical shape and does not over-imbibe in the kickapoo joy juice."

Jim's response to McLean's piece wasn't shock. It was almost child-like in its innocence. "Kickapoo joy juice? Well, a lot of things got written and there were stereotypes. Little or no homework was done. How can they get away with it? I mean, don't they have editors? Man! Can you imagine if they ever tried that with the coloured people? Wow! There would be a little bit of an explosion or something... Anyways, they can't do that kind of stuff anymore."

Neilson's reaction to McLean's article kind of sums up the man that Jim is. Not only a thoroughbred like, say, the great filly Ruffian who is trained to run 'til you drop, Jim put on a set of blinders that, while they didn't prevent him from seeing his goals, filtered out the side shows. This was a perfect mindset for a player in New York. Take in the sights on the side but don't allow them to become real distractions. According to Jim, this is why he was able to walk away from the game when his playing days were over.

"I guess I regret not putting more back into the game. How come I never got into coaching? I was never that smart. All I knew about hockey was a tap on the shoulder, go out, and do your job. I never studied what I didn't need to know other than my job."

Neilson did his job well enough to finish second to the legendary Bobby Orr in votes for the Norris Trophy (given to the NHL's top defenceman in 1967–68) and was named to the NHL's second All-Star team. And, just as Doug Harvey and Harry Howell had helped Neilson develop, Jim played an instrumental role in the development of a young Brad Park when those two were paired up 1968–69. After 12 years with the Rangers, Neilson wound down his career on the West Coast and also played one year with the WHA's Edmonton Oilers and a young Wayne Gretzky.

After he retired, Jim considered an investment in a golfing business and then worked for the federal government in Canada for a few years. Nothing much stuck and he developed a drinking problem, which was serious to the people around him, but not to Jim himself.

"I like beer and I am well aware of what people think about my drinking. And, yes, I lost my family, but we are all still good friends."

Jim has not asked for and he says he does not want any help with his drinking problem. He doesn't want any counselling or interventions and he does not want to go to meetings of Alcoholics Anonymous. "I like my beer and I like getting drunk and that is my choice."

During the production of the documentary and as I wrote this book, many of the other Native players, knowing that I live in Winnipeg, would ask caringly, "How's Jimmy doing?" Their faces revealed a concern but also a knowing resignation. They care, but they know there is nothing they can do. And that's how Jim Neilson wants it.

At the time this book was written, Jim was living in a tidy one-bedroom apartment in a nice block in downtown Winnipeg. He is comfortable, with income from pensions, including the NHL. He gets out to play old-timers recreational hockey when he can and he is an avid student of First Nations current events, culture and history.

Jim Neilson had a long and successful career in the NHL. He is now retired and living the way he chooses to live.

3

THE RIVERTON RIFLE

" I was sitting by this white guy on an airplane one time, and he knew who I was, and he asks me what I've been doing lately. And I told him about the anti-alcohol and anti-drug workshops I was doing with the Native kids. And this guy says to me, 'Isn't that a waste of time?'"

Former NHL superstar Reggie Leach rolls his eyes when he tells that story.

"Trying to help one, two, or 100 or 200 young people to stay off drugs and alcohol is never a waste of time. If I can help just one kid, then I've done my job."

★ ★ ★ ★ ★

Reggie Leach had a spectacular career in the NHL. "The Riverton Rifle" scored 381 goals and was an integral part of the "Broad Street Bullies" who won NHL championships wearing Philadelphia Flyers uniforms during the mid-1970s. Leach even gained the rare honour of winning the Conn Smythe trophy as the Most Valuable Player in the Stanley Cup playoffs while a member of the losing team in the championship final.

"But I never reached my goal, and that was to make it into the Hockey Hall of Fame," says Leach. "And that was because of overdoing it in my drinking."

★ ★ ★ ★ ★

Reggie Leach has been called "Chief" hundreds of times; starting in Riverton, Manitoba, where he was born on April 23, 1950. And then at school, in playgrounds, and on hockey rinks. But Leach is better known as the Riverton Rifle, partly because of his hard shot, partly because of his birthplace, but mostly because sportswriters, including this one, love alliterations. We use them far too often, thinking that stringing together words that simply begin with the same first letter somehow passes for creativity, but we are addicted (adamantly, aggressively and always).

Reggie was raised by his paternal grandparents, who adopted him at the age of two. He called grandma and grandpa "mom and dad" because they were the only parents he knew (Reggie's biological dad was a miner who never spent much time with his son; his biological mom was from Ontario and didn't come around much until Reg was in his late teens).

Grandma hailed from Berens River First Nation, but Reggie never lived in this community from where he derives his status as a treaty Indian. "I grew up with a bunch of Icelanders and Ukrainians in Riverton. It was a fishing village and a farming community."

Reggie also grew up "dirt poor," with six brothers and six sisters, and he didn't start playing hockey until he was 10 years old, simply because he couldn't afford a pair of skates. "At the age of 10, I was old enough to be trusted enough for someone to borrow me a pair of skates, but I had to play by myself a lot, outside. My grandparents didn't have the money to pay for ice time at the local indoor arena. It was 25 cents an hour or $2.50 for the season. So I skated around on the outdoor rink. It was cold, and sometimes lonely, but a 10-year-old kid is never really alone because, in your imagination, you're playing on some NHL team against another NHL team for the Stanley Cup."

"I remember that first pair of skates that I borrowed. They were size 11. My feet are size 7 now, so you can imagine how big those skates were on my 10-year-old feet! I stuffed newspapers in the boot so those skates wouldn't fall off. And that's how I started to skate."

Finally, at the age of 14, Reggie got his own pair of brand new skates. He will only say that "the town of Riverton" bought those skates for him. Most important, they fit like a glove (okay, a shoe) and those blades were like wings. Reg was a natural hockey artisan, and he was soon in demand all over. As a matter of fact, at one point, Reggie was young enough (or old enough, but mostly good enough) to play bantam A, midget, juvenile and senior all at the same time, juggling the schedule of four different teams, which involved vastly different calibres of competition, against wildly differing age groups.

But the environment young Reggie was growing up in wasn't all fun and games. Or maybe there was too much time for "fun and games." Drinking alcohol was not only accepted in Riverton, it was expected by people of all ages. "I picked it up at the age of 12. It was considered normal."

★ ★ ★ ★ ★

"When you're young, you can get drunk and you have a pretty rapid recovery time. You're not quite as up to snuff as you could be the day after, but if you only get drunk maybe twice a week, you don't really notice the negative impact alcohol has, except, of course, when you're actually drunk."

Reggie didn't play hockey when he was drunk, but sometimes he played hungover. He fought through the headaches and dehydration and, because he was a cut above the rest, he still dominated whatever players he faced and whatever games he played. And on those occasions when Reggie said "beddy-byes" at 8:30 p.m. after some "warm milk and cookies," he was simply spectacular.

Reggie wasn't too keen on school, even though he was rather a bright child. Reggie dropped out after grade 8, which left him with two options.

Pursue a career in hockey, or join a regular Riverton crowd, who worked at whatever job they could find during the day, and "drank it up" at night.

That's not to say there weren't plenty of solid working-class and business people in Riverton. Reggie's background and upbringing simply didn't fit the rural Manitoba norm. For him, it was going to be either a spectacular crash or landing.

This was most clearly laid out for Reggie one day by his coach, Sigg John, who sat the kid down and gave him a good talking to. Sigg knew that Reggie had been drinking a fair bit, so he met him in a restaurant across from a local bar, where they sipped coffee and watched a couple of local guys, who had become the town drunks, as they came staggering out of the bar. Sigg pointed out that the two drunks used to be pretty good hockey players, not unlike Reggie, but they chose booze, and "there they are." This cold, hard, tough-love talk had an enormous impact on Reggie, and he straightened out his act, at least somewhat, for the time being.

And it steered Reggie up to Flin Flon, where he met up with Bobby Clarke. This pair would star for the Flin Flon Bombers of the Western Canadian Junior Hockey League, before starring for fans across North America and all over the world.

"I knew about Clarke from midget hockey and we had a lot of respect for each other," Leach says. "Flin Flon was the totally overwhelming experience. There were 18,000 people living there and, to me, that was a big city! Clarkie and I handled it all together. We even bought our first car together. It was a clunker we got for $80. We used to fill up with oil and check the gas!"

Leach and Clarke weren't paired together on the ice immediately. Reggie came up to Flin Flon as a defenceman, but GM/Coach Pat Ginnell quickly realized that Leach was too quick to play back. Leach was soon moved up to a line with Clarke and they clicked, to say the least. "I scored about 65 goals my first year in junior, and Bobby set up a lot of them. The fans started making up nicknames for us. I remember one of the first things they called us was 'Tonto and the Lone Ranger.'"

Reggie was rather unique in avoiding being called Chief. Even later in his hockey career when he played for a brief while in Boston, they would call Reggie "Little Beaver" because Johnny Bucyk, a Ukrainian from Edmonton who wasn't even an Indian but had an Indian appearance, had already been bestowed with the nickname Chief. Nicknames like Tonto, Kemo Sabe and even "the masked stranger" hinted at the kind of atmosphere that existed in the northern mining town of Flin Flon at the time.

"There were a lot of white people and a lot of Indians and Metis. On Friday nights, people would go downtown to socialize (or, in more simple language, drink and get drunk). There was a white bar on one side of the main street and an Indian bar on the other side. At midnight, people would spill out of the bars into the street and it was like *Twelve O'clock High*. Lots of fights. Lots of racial tension in the afternoons, too."

That conflict didn't spill over into the hockey arena, however. Leach was clearly an Indian in his appearance, and Clarke appeared to have been raised where mushrooms thrive, but all the fans in Flin Flon, red or white, loved Leach and Clarke.

According to Reggie, "Hockey was the way we could bring people together and get them pulling for the same thing. And the fans in Flin Flon were the greatest in the world."

Or the worst. The arena in Flin Flon, the Whitney Forum, more commonly called "the smelter," was one of the most feared and dreaded places in the world for visiting teams. Young junior players had to deal with some of the most obnoxious behaviour that has ever been displayed, anywhere.

"It was very intimidating and we would often see players from teams from the south come down with what became known as the "Flin Flon Flu"—they would stay home pretending to be sick rather than get on that bus heading up north."

Leach and Clarke dazzled junior hockey fans throughout western Canada. Reggie led the Western Canadian Junior Hockey League in goal-scoring twice, lighting the lamp 188 times in three seasons with the Bombers, including an incredible 87 snipes in 1967–68. Leach always made the WCJHL First All-Star team.

"But I wasn't strictly known as a goal scorer or a play-maker, because Clarkie was 155 pounds soaking wet and I had to protect him. I was considered big at that time, 185 pounds, and Bobby was always in there whacking people with his stick and I'd be in there trying to help him. I wasn't one of the fighters on the team, we had guys for that, but I still racked up about 300 minutes in penalties."

Clarke was drafted by the Philadelphia Flyers in 1969, a year earlier than Leach, who was picked by the Boston Bruins third overall in the 1970 draft.

"That was the year the Bruins won the Stanley Cup for the first time in a long time. I was in awe, this Indian kid dressing next to Bobby Orr, Phil Esposito, Wayne Cashman and all these guys who had just won the Cup! I had watched them the year before on TV and then there I was sitting in the same dressing room as them!

"But I wasn't going to get a chance to play. Teams don't change much right after they win the Stanley Cup. I signed a contract which was very good, and then I sat around for three or four weeks until they sent me down to Oklahoma City, which I wanted, because there I could play. I played 40 games down there, and then Johnny McKenzie got hurt, and I was called up, and I never went back down."

But instead of staying in Boston, Leach ended up heading west, to California, as part of a package trade that brought defenceman Carol Vadnais to the Bruins. The Oakland Golden Seals were a terrible team, over-matched almost every night, but that gave Reggie a chance to play, and he recorded consecutive 20-goal seasons. By his second year in California, Reggie was anchoring the team's top line.

Meanwhile, in Philadelphia, the Flyers were just starting to fully embrace the leadership of their new captain, Bobby Clarke. They won the 1973–74 Stanley Cup, and then they took the biggest step they needed to repeat, by stealing Leach away from Oakland so he could join his old pal Clarke in the City of Brotherly Love. Leach was put on a line with Clarke and Bill Barber, and it became one of the top units in the NHL. Reggie scored 45 goals during the 1974–75 regular season, and then helped the Flyers repeat as Stanley Cup champions by chipping in with eight goals in 17 post-season games.

Yet it would be in failure where Leach shone the brightest. As the Flyers strived for their third straight championship the next year, Leach led the team during the regular season with 61 goals. And he would save his best for the playoffs.

The Flyers found themselves over-matched by the Montreal Canadiens in the 1975–76 Cup final, but Leach's 19-goal effort throughout the playoffs earned him the Conn Smythe Trophy, given to the Most Valuable Player in the post-season. It's extremely rare for this honour to be awarded to a player who is not a member of the winning team. It has only happened twice before, both times it was a goalie who won the Smythe while on the losing team (Roger Crozier and Bernie Parent). This most unlikely accolade capped off the best season of Reggie's career, one of the finest seasons by a goal scorer ever, as his combined 80 goals (regular season and playoffs) broke Phil Esposito's NHL record, which was set in 1970–71.

Leach's goal totals went up and down the next three years as he battled with off-ice problems, but in 1979–80, the 50 goals he scored played a major role in helping the Flyers set an NHL record by going undefeated in 35 consecutive games. Leach added 16 points in the playoffs, but the Flyers fell to the New York Islanders in six games in the Stanley Cup final.

The fleet winger added 60 goals during his last two seasons in Philadelphia before moving on to the Detroit Red Wings as a free agent. Reggie scored his final 15 goals for Detroit in 1983–84 before closing out his professional career with the Montana Magic of the Central Hockey League.

Leach finished with 381 goals in 934 regular season games and will always be remembered as one of the top snipers of his era. One would expect that any player who had a career filled with the kind of lofty statistics that Reggie compiled would have few regrets. But Reggie Leach had many.

His biggest regret? "Drinking. I never reached my goal and that was to make it into the Hockey Hall of Fame. And that was because of overdoing it in my drinking."

★ ★ ★ ★ ★

"I think I could have probably played another 4 to 5 years, but I cut myself short. The people in the NHL didn't want to take a chance on me. I had a great career. But my personal life was a mess. Alcohol was always a big part of my life.

"I lost one brother that froze to death in Riverton, I had another brother that wrapped himself around a telephone pole and I had a sister that, I don't even know what it was from…froze to death in a car…fell asleep…and then I had another brother that strangled himself to death. So it runs in the family, and you know it's tough, and it's like anything else, you can say it's never going to happen to you, but it's a disease that creeps up on you until it's too late, then you've gotta straighten yourself out."

Being involved in sports made it especially difficult for Reggie to deal with his drinking problem, because alcohol is so closely associated with the game. Witness all the beer commercials during hockey (or most other sports) broadcasts. An ice cold beer "goes down great" right after a game. And, of course, there is a lot of pressure in performing before thousands of people in the most highly skilled, competitive hockey league in the world. Alcohol provides an escape from the stress, at least for a little while.

"Alcohol was available all the time in the NHL. It was in the dressing room, on the bus, on airplane flights. I played many games hungover. I would quit, but then I would start right back up again. Some years, I couldn't tell if my lower scoring totals were the result of stress trying to sober up, or because I was still drinking. There was no relationship between the number of goals I scored or I didn't, and whether I was drinking or I wasn't."

But there was a relationship between drinking and whether or not Reggie was going to live… or die.

★ ★ ★ ★ ★

"I had a real bad stomach, heat waves and cold sweats and all of that stuff. So I went to the hospital and Dr. Corbino had all these tubes in me and I still felt like hell, so Corbino gave me a shot of something and I spent the night. The next morning, he says, 'Reg, you're a mess,' and I starts laughing because he's a good friend and I used to drink with him!"

But then, once again, a tough-love talk turned Reggie around.

"He said, 'Reg, you have two choices. Either quit drinking, or you're going to die, because your liver is not up to par right now.' I knew I should quit and I tried, but I was always doing it for somebody else. My teammates, my wife, my kids. You have to do it for yourself."

Reggie Leach finally realized that fact, and quit drinking for good in 1984, the same year his marriage ended in divorce. There was a lot of change going on in Reggie's life, but it simply had to be done. A completely new beginning.

"I went into rehab, and one of the first things I learned is that you not only have to make changes in yourself, you have to change your place and other things. People that you hung around with. I ended up becoming a sort of hermit for four or five years. It wasn't easy. I still remember going in there the first day [to a rehabilitation clinic] kind of sick or hungover or whatever…and they give you this sheet of paper to fill out…all these questions on being an alcoholic.

"Being a con artist, as all alcoholics are, I'm lookin' at this paper and sayin', 'What do they want to hear?' So I'm trying to figure this all out. Rehab lasts a month. That couple of days before you get out, they give you that same sheet of paper. But now your mind is all straightened out and you compare your answers…and you think: who is the idiot who filled out that sheet of paper a month ago?

"You have to change your habits. That became easier when I stopped going to the bar. My friends were people that hung around in the bar. Nothing against them but they were never my friends. They were people I drank with, got drunk with. I hope they ended up quittin' drinkin', too. But they never came around when I started staying home. It wasn't that we had anything against each other. We just had nothing in common except drinking. And I wasn't drinking anymore.

"What turned out to be really ironic was that my biggest and best support group turned out to be the one that I had been drinking with most of my life! It was the Philadelphia Flyers Alumni.

"Every addict who is trying to kick the habit needs support, like a sponsor, something you can turn to when you get tempted or need advice or reinforcement or even just someone to talk to. Those guys turned out to be my support. They understood what I was going through, and even if they didn't understand, they knew that I wanted to quit—that I needed to quit—and they backed me up 100 percent.

"We would have all these golf tournaments, and banquets, and other social functions that we had to go to…and alcohol is always associated with those kind of events. Any time I had to go out in public, the guys would pick me up, and make sure that I went straight home afterwards.

"The biggest thing was people who didn't know what I was going through, or trying to do, what they would always say to me was, 'Come on, Reg! Have one drink! It'll never hurt you.' There was guys like Bob Dailey and Orest Kindrachuk and they would actually get quite mad at these people and they would say, quite sternly, 'Reggie does not drink…and don't offer him anymore, and that's it!'

"I still get together with all those guys…and the stories come out…and we have a good time. But I don't drink, and that's the only difference."

Reggie managed to keep his family of Flyers, but he lost his own family. "It's hard to believe that my wife put up with it for 14 years. And it hurts your kids. They were teenagers (daughter Brandy was 11, son Jamie 14) when the divorce happened, so they could realize and feel it all. And, of course, I missed out on the best part of them growing up. Then again, I wasn't around for the teenage years when I hear kids are the most trouble.

"But then I remarried and became stepfather to a teenage child. As they say, 'God always gets you back.'"

★ ★ ★ ★ ★

Regrets? Reggie's had a few. But regrets are useless unless you learn from those situations and choices and mistakes that caused you to have regrets in the first place. Reggie knows this, and he also knows that if you truly regret the bad things you've done in your life, you've got to do more than just say "I'm sorry," and move on. Somehow, you've got to make up for your mistakes. Make good, even up the score.

"My generation made a lot of mistakes in the 1950s, '60s and '70s. Now it's time for us to make up for those mistakes by giving back to those kids that are here today which is going to be our future. We put them in this bind and I think it's our responsibility to help them get out of it."

Reggie Leach is making up for his mistakes by crisscrossing the country conducting anti-alcohol and anti-drug workshops in First Nations communities wherever and whenever he can.

The following is a compilation and condensed version of the videotape we shot of an anti-alcohol and drug workshop that Reggie hosted on the Roseau River Anicinabe First Nation, approximately 60 miles southeast of Winnipeg, Manitoba. (Note: some of the dialogue has been approximated and/or drawn from other workshops Leach has held in other communities throughout North America.)

REG LEACH ANTI-ALCOHOL AND DRUG WORKSHOP
(ROSEAU RIVER ANICINABE FIRST NATION)

TRANSCRIPT OF VIDEO

INTERIOR—ESTABLISHING SHOT—WIDE (a school gymnasium full of elementary and junior high school age children. Former NHL player Reg Leach is conducting an anti-alcohol workshop)

CUT TO: TIGHT SHOT—REG LEACH (Leach speaks to the children through a handheld microphone. He is intense, passionate and animated. He moves around a lot, pacing back and forth in front of the children)

LEACH: "Thank you for inviting me to your community. I played in the NHL for 14 years and I scored 382 goals. I won a lot of awards, I still hold the record for most goals in the playoffs, I hold the record for most consecutive games with a goal in the playoffs. I was the first player ever to score 80 goals in the league counting playoffs. I won the Conn Smythe trophy, the only forward to win that who played on the losing team…a couple of goalies have done that, too.

Yet I'm from the same kind of small community as you live in here. I grew up poor like many of you. My mom and dad were on welfare. I had to stuff paper in my first pair of skates so they wouldn't fall off because they were size 11 and I had size 7 feet. You might be wondering why I'm telling you that but it's really what I'm here to say today: It's not the skates that make you a hockey player. It's what you have in your heart!"

DISSOLVE TO: BG (background shots of children, some sitting on the floor, some in chairs, all listening attentively) CAMERA PANS from audience to Leach, who starts moving in and around the students with positive messages. CAMERA FOLLOWS ACTION.

Reggie says "I came from a small town like this and I did it!" "What grade are you kids in?" "You can't make anything out of yourself if you don't get an education." "It's good to come back to a First Nations community where our culture is still alive!" "When do you hold your powwow here in Roseau River?" "Do you dance?"

Reggie ends up back in front of the audience.

TIGHT SHOT: LEACH

"How many of you drink in here? How many of you drink?" (beat) "Yeah, I can see some hands going up, but most of you older kids, 13, 14, you don't want to admit it. But I know you might be drinking. I picked it up at the age of 12. Back home where I lived in Riverton, it was natural. Everybody drank. It was accepted. As a matter of fact, people thought you were weird if you didn't drink!

"But I found out the decision I made to drink was a bad choice. I remember the first time I drank. This other kid…he was 14. Big kid. I didn't know it at the time, but he was what you would call a bully, I guess. I thought he was a leader. Anyways, I had earned some money cutting grass and he convinced me to spend it on some white rum. Two mickeys. One for him and one for me. Well, I drank mine and I got real drunk. Later, I never got so sick in all my life! One might think that if you drink something that makes you sick, you would know better not to take the stuff again, but I had been introduced to alcohol and, as I said, everybody else was doing it so I continued to drink. And it ruined my life. I lost my career. My family. And my health.

"I'm an alcoholic. I played in the NHL but I was lucky enough that I had the talent to get where I wanted. You know, as youngsters, we all have goals and dreams."

CAMERA FOLLOWS ACTION: Reggie starts walking around in the audience again, asking questions. He approaches a Native youth.

LEACH: "What's your name?"

CAMERA PULLS INTO A TWO-SHOT as the youth answers.

NATIVE YOUTH #1: (shy, kind of moves away from Reg) "Frankie."

LEACH: "And do you have any plans or dreams about what you are going to do when you finish school and you're all grown up?"

NATIVE YOUTH #1: "I don't know…I guess…well…I was thinking… well, maybe a teacher… because the teachers here at school seem to enjoy their job and they drive pretty nice cars so they must make a good living."

LEACH: "A teacher? That's a good job. Do you play hockey or other sports?"

NATIVE YOUTH #1: "Yeah, I play on a team in Letellier… Bantam. Double-A."

LEACH: "Well, you must be pretty good, then. Have you thought about maybe someday making it to the NHL?"

NATIVE YOUTH #1: "Well, yeah, but…I don't know…"

LEACH: "Well, I hope you have the talent, because all it takes is hard work and commitment…And, of course, staying away from drugs and alcohol!"

Leach moves on to a 15-year-old girl who is holding up her hand. CFA/ 2-SHOT, etc.

LEACH: "Yes! You have a question?"

NATIVE YOUTH #2: "Yeah. I was wondering…did you pass out when you got drunk?"

LEACH: "You mean did I black out?"

The girl nods her head.

LEACH: "Yeah, many times. I would black out…or pass out…or I would wake up in the morning and couldn't remember what happened…how I got to where I was. I didn't even know where I was at the time."

Some children giggle. Leach reacts.

LEACH: (to audience in general) "Hey! I know that sounds funny…or maybe it even sounds like fun…but I'm here today to tell you that it really isn't fun. It's no fun when you can't remember what you did the night before. Because you might have made a total fool out of yourself. Or maybe even got angry and hurt someone. You might have hurt somebody's feelings by saying something stupid! You might even have gotten violent and hit someone. You're not yourself on alcohol. And, too many times, you'll regret what you do on booze. I'm here to talk from experience. I'm not proud of what I did. Sometimes I'm ashamed. But I have to live up to those things I did and make up for it. The best place to start is to never do those kinds of things again. And that starts by not overdoing it with the alcohol and drugs!"

V/O: (a Native youth yells from across the gymnasium) "Are you saying we can drink but don't drink too much?"

LEACH: "That's really up to you. I can't tell you never to drink because a lot of you are going to at least try alcohol if you haven't already. I'm just trying to let you know what I've been through and I hope you'll believe me when I say that alcohol and drugs can ruin your life if you let them take over. I had the greatest career in the world! I played in the world's greatest hockey league... I travelled all over North America and the rest of the world. I made lots of money...but I would give all of that up to be alcohol-free! I mean, I am now alcohol-free, but if I could have lived my life...like from the time I was a teenager until I was 40, without alcohol, I would rather have that than the NHL career that I had. Alcohol took away everything...and it ruined everything I could have enjoyed...I would rather have just lived a normal life...maybe work construction or be a fisherman...and raised my kids...and had a good family life. I would rather have that than the glorious career that I had in the NHL because during all that career, I was drinking and, overall, when I look back, I didn't enjoy it all that much...certainly not as much as being able to enjoy each day sober and enjoy the love of my family and my friends...and do stuff like go hunting and fishing...and not be so out of my mind that I don't know what I'm doing and I don't really enjoy each day and I don't remember any of it."

10-YEAR-OLD GIRL: "Do you smoke?"

LEACH: (laughs) "Okay...I will admit that I smoke...that is an addiction that I picked up but it's not like I'm proud of that or anything. I quit but then I started up again. It's stupid, but that is what addictions usually are. I hope that none of you start smoking, if you haven't started already. I'll bet there's a lot of you who do smoke. Try to stop. It's not that much fun and it harms your health."

Reggie starts to laugh.

LEACH: "Let me put it this way. When you smoke, you're basically picking up some leaves, rolling them up, then putting those leaves in your mouth... and setting them on fire! That sounds pretty stupid, right?"

ANOTHER CHILD: "What about drugs?"

LEACH: "No! It was strictly alcoholic beverages with me. I believe today, with all the drug abuse going on and all the trouble that professional athletes have been getting into with drugs, that if I ever did get involved with drugs, I wouldn't be here today. Besides, I was goofy enough on alcohol."

ANOTHER CHILD: "How many times have you been hit by a puck?"

Reggie laughs wholeheartedly.

LEACH: "Can't you tell? I've been hit by a puck way too many times! (laughs) I even got knocked out a couple of times because, when we played, we didn't wear any helmets."

CAMERA pans the audience where almost every child is holding up a hand.

LEACH: "Let's go to this little guy right over here."

CHILD: "Do you got a mom?"

LEACH: "Yes, she passed away five years ago."

ANOTHER CHILD: "Some of my friends take alcohol. Why shouldn't I?"

LEACH: (shrugs his shoulders) "It's really up to you. You have a choice." (turns very serious) "If you want to be a follower...make mistakes...you know. Let me put it this way...the way you probably heard it from your parents or the teachers here at school. If your friends jumped off a bridge... (laughs). Hey! Sometimes it's fun to jump off a bridge, so long as there's a safe landing. But if you're jumping off a highway overpass into heavy traffic, it's stupid. That's suicide. And that's what alcohol is. You're just throwing your life away. It's like jumping in front of a semi-trailer. I know that sometimes your friends drink and, if you don't, you feel left out. But there are other ways to have fun. Really. Just look at some of the kids who are dancing powwow or playing on hockey teams or going hunting and fishing."

ANOTHER CHILD: "But my mom and dad go hunting and fishing. And they play baseball together, too. But they always get drunk when they do that."

LEACH: "That's a difficult situation, for sure. For you. Now, I don't want to show any disrespect for your parents. I'm sure that they love you and want to do what is best for you. But you have to make your own choices sometimes. All I'm saying is that I have had a terrible experience with alcohol and my advice to you and everybody else is not to drink. Then it comes down to what choice you make. Whether to drink or not, that's your decision."

ANOTHER CHILD: "Did you ever meet Wayne Gretzky?"

LEACH: "Yes, I have. Many times. He's a really nice man. And he achieved many great things. That's why they call him 'The Great One.' And he didn't have the problems I had with alcohol. Maybe I could have been a 'great one.' Or, at least a greater one than I was."

ANOTHER CHILD: "How about Mario Lemiuex?"

LEACH: "No, I retired the year before Mario Lemieux began playing in the NHL. But my son, Jamie, played with Mario in Pittsburgh and they won two Stanley Cups together. Mario is another great person who never compromised his career because of alcohol and drugs. But, you know, it's interesting. Mario had to overcome some tremendous obstacles in his life. Mario had a serious back injury, and he also had cancer. When Mario had cancer, people knew that he was sick and that he needed a cure. Or, to heal. Now, it might not make sense to you right now, but when I was drinking, I was sick, too. Just like Mario, but you might think that there's a difference, because when you drink, people say well, you brought that on yourself. But people have to understand that alcoholism is a disease, like cancer, or pneumonia. You don't use that as an excuse, but people who don't have the disease of alcoholism have to understand that their friends, who are addicted to alcohol or drugs, are sick and they need help. If your friend had cancer, you would help them. It's the same with alcohol. We must help our friends who are sick with this illness."

ANOTHER CHILD: "Who helped you?"

LEACH: "Some very good friends. They were former teammates of mine with the Flyers. Once they knew I was sick, they would come around my house and visit and keep me company and just basically be my friend. And they would be by my side when we had to go out to events that involved drinking and they would watch me and support me and remind me not to drink and how bad it would be if I did and, if needed, they kept me in line. And they told other people who might offer me a drink to back off and leave me alone in that regard."

ANOTHER CHILD: "Did you ever win a Stanley Cup?"

LEACH: "You haven't been paying attention. Or maybe I didn't mention that I was part of the Philadelphia Flyers team that won the Stanley Cup in 1975. Oh, that's right…I just mentioned the Conn Smythe Trophy when we lost. Well, anyways, I guess I should have flashed my ring at the beginning, but I can certainly show it to you now."

Reggie holds up his hand and the CAMERA ZOOMS IN TO A TIGHT SHOT on the ring.

CUT TO: Shots of admiring glances from the audience.

AUDIO OVER: (oohs and aahs from the audience)

LEACH: (joking) "Aww! I really just found this thing in a crackerjack popcorn box!"

The audience laughs. A child, who had been patiently holding up his hand, interrupts the scene.

ANOTHER CHILD: "Have you ever been involved with a street gang?"

LEACH: "Whew! Now there's a big switch in subjects! But okay! (chuckles) No! We didn't have street gangs in Riverton, where I grew up. You guys see a lot of street gangs out there today and maybe they even ask you to join. I never joined a street gang, but I can tell you, they are just another way for kids like you to get together and hang around together. It's just that street gangs do a lot of bad things, like stealing and violence and a lot of them end up spending time in jail. A lot of what they do is wrong and they hurt their own people. But you can look at it like, well, a street gang is kind of the same as a hockey team, or a powwow group, or a rock band. Except street gangs do bad things. If you want to join something, join something that is positive. A sports team. A powwow dance group. A drum. A rock and roll band, uh, rock band…a rap group! Maybe try and get closer to your own family."

Reggie notices a young girl whose hand is halfway up. She wants to ask a question but she is kind of shy.

LEACH: "Hey, little one! I think you have a question. Don't be shy! We're all friends here. You can ask anything…"

The girl remains hesitant, but then stammers out.

GIRL: "Have you ever been sexually abused?"

LEACH: "No, that has never happened to me. I know that it has happened to a lot of our children. And my heart goes to anybody in this room who has gone through that. And I would say that to anyone who has been, or is being sexually abused, whether that be in your home, or at one of your relatives'…or in school…or at the arena…the most important thing you can do is find somebody that you can trust and tell them what is happening to you. (Reggie deliberately looks away from the girl and starts talking to the audience in general) I know it's hard not to be scared and you might feel like you're going to get into trouble or you might get hurt, but nothing can hurt you as much as what's happening to you now…and you can get help and also help to get out of that situation."

AUDIO/VIDEO FADE OUT (as Reggie addresses the audience sincerely and passionately)

VERY SLOW DISSOLVE TO: interview with Reggie after the workshop

LEACH: "I thought the kids were great today. Once we got going, they really responded and I think we opened up a lot of things and we really got the message across. It's too bad the parents and the leaders in the community, like the Chief and Council, weren't able to be there, because that's where the real action has to take place. You know, we're getting better facilities all the time and kids can, at least, get a pair of skates that, even though they might be secondhand, they are probably going to be the right size. Now, some kids are crazy, like I was, and I played hockey no matter what I had to go through because I simply loved the game, but there are lots of other kids who might simply need some encouragement and support and that might just mean going to the rink with them or shooting some pucks back and forth.

"But the kids gotta come through, too. They have to get off their asses and not accept being spoiled and show some appreciation for what they are being offered or given. They shouldn't take everything or anything for granted. At the same time, they have to believe in themselves. Don't let anybody tell you what you can or cannot accomplish."

★ ★ ★ ★ ★

Reggie Leach has been clean and sober since 1984. He continues to live in the Philadelphia area, where he owns a landscaping business in Delaware. He still plays hockey, but only at a recreational level, suiting up for various teams at Native tournaments. He also plays for the Philadelphia Flyers alumni/old-timers team.

Reggie has made the positive development of youth a priority in his life. Towards that end, he has developed a hockey school, but not one located in a permanent, central location. Along with his son Jamie, he travels to Native communities where they pass on their shooting, skating and stickhandling skills to Native youth at hockey camps held right in the First Nations communities; an idea which they developed for the winter of 2007–08.

Leach continues to devote a lot of his time to anti-alcohol and anti-drug workshops, traveling throughout North America to meet children and youth and pass on his experiences and his positive message, just like he did in the Roseau River Anicinabe First Nation. And that should be enough to pay for the mistakes of "the 1950s, '60s and '70s. Now it's time for us to make up for those mistakes by giving back to those kids that are here today which is going to be our future. We put them in this bind and I think it's our responsibility to help them get out of it."

★ ★ ★ ★ ★

Fast-forward to 2008, and there was Reggie, planning to kick back and spend some time between gigs relaxing with his girlfriend, Dawn Madabee, on the Sucker Creek First Nation on beautiful Manitoulin Island in Ontario, when a call came.

Depending how you look at it, Reggie was in the wrong/right place at the wrong/right time when the owners of the Manitoulin Islanders Junior Hockey team phoned looking for a coach. Reggie, who has had so much trouble in his life because he couldn't quit, now found himself unable to quit saying, "Yes!"

The Islanders were in poor shape on the ice when their new coach Reggie Leach took over the team. Their record was 2 and 42 and they were 56 points out of fifth place in a six-team league. "We were losing games 9-1. Most recently, we lost 7-3."

★ ★ ★ ★ ★

On Friday, January 25, 2008, Reggie and his son, Jamie, brought the Stanley Cup to Reggie's hometown of Riverton, Manitoba, to be showcased during the Reggie Leach Classic Hockey Tournament, an event Reggie stages every year to raise money to support hockey programs for children and youth in his hometown. Reggie had to hound the holders of hockey's Holy Grail for two years to make this happen.

Over 500 people came out to touch the Cup. And what was most important to Reggie? Riverton won the Atom Division of the tourney. The

Peewee Division went to Arborg, and Stony Mountain took the Bantam Division. And all of the players were wearing skates that fit.

★ ★ ★ ★ ★

I cannot end this chapter without passing along the details of an exchange that took place between Reggie and me and provides some insight to one of the themes this book is pursuing, to define the characteristics that make a "warrior."

Between breaks at Reggie's workshops and our filming, Reggie and I had a lot of time to talk, about hockey, and things like resolving the Middle East crisis, the cure for cancer, how to find Osama bin Laden, and so on (for sure, I jest). At one point, we talked about the infamous 1972 Summit Series between Canada and the USSR—a historical confrontation in which Leach and teammate Bobby Clarke played an integral role.

I have always maintained that Canada's victory in that battle for global hockey supremacy will always be tainted by Clarke's two-handed slash that broke Russian superstar Valeri Kharlamov's ankle and removed an opponent who was fairly and squarely killing Canada.

Reggie's reaction when I mentioned this was as violent (verbally) as Clarke's action towards Kharlamov had been physically. "You have no idea what you are talking about! It was war out there, man! Anything goes! We wanted to win. They wanted to win. They did everything they had to do, and we did everything we had to do. And that was that. And we won. So that's that."

Some people will have some difficulty accepting Reggie's argument. I did. But then I recalled the video CBC colour commentator Howie Meeker showed us after four games of the series that isolated the dirty tricks the Russians were pulling in the corners and behind the play. Kneeing Canadian players in the groin. Slew-footing behind the play. Spearing. Elbowing.

Okay. Reggie might be right. It was indeed, a "war," symbolic, but all-out. But most important, I, the fan, or the sportswriter, wasn't there, on the ice, like Reggie and the boys were. We can venture our opinions and believe whatever we want, but, in the end, I have to concede that we simply were not there, all suited up and skating and hitting and fighting and trading shots with the Russians. We simply have to respect that fact.

So maybe Reggie was right, after all. Because he was really there. And like it or not, taking an opponent out by "any means necessary" is another characteristic of warrior, if we want that definition to be complete.

★ ★ ★ ★ ★

Reggie provided a much more important element of that definition, off the ice, anyway. This man overcame the horrible and difficult challenge of addiction. I have always admired those people who can muster up the courage and resolve to beat the demon rum, who can resist the mental temptation and the physical pull of alcohol and drugs. It takes great strength and moral fibre to do this.

Some sportswriters seem to like to pass judgment on players who screw up because of alcohol and drugs. Holier-than-thou hypocrite scribes maintain that these players don't deserve a second chance, let alone a third or a fourth. All I can say to that is remember the story of one member of the New England Patriots of the National Football League.

The Patriots were playing in the Super Bowl and this player had arranged for tickets for his family, including his parents and grandparents, to watch him play in the big game. This was to be the greatest day of his life.

But the night before the Super Bowl, this player passed by a washroom where some people were snorting cocaine. They invited him to join them. I imagine he thought that maybe he could have a few toots and then go to bed, but cocaine is a most addictive drug, and this player ended up going on a binge that caused him to miss the big game.

Think about that. Here was this human being, not that much different from you or me, except that he made his living playing football, about as good at that as we are at what we do for a living, on the eve of the most important day of his life—and somehow, for some reason, he threw it all away. This doesn't make any sense, and nobody in this world can be that stupid or careless or lazy.

This human being wasn't weak, nor was he selfish. He was sick with a disease and he deserves our empathy and support. And if and when he beats the beast, he deserves our respect. As does Reggie Leach. For overcoming his addiction, just as much as we respect him for his accomplishments in the NHL.

The true warrior does not judge his greatness by the goals that he sets for himself, but rather by the obstacles that he overcomes.

4

"LITTLE CHIEF"

Stan Jonathan has been described as a six-foot-four man who was placed inside a compactor until he came out five-foot-seven. A full-blooded Mohawk/Tuscarora Indian from the Six Nations Reserve in Southern Ontario, Stan's nickname was "Little Chief" (another indication of the amount of thought and creativity that went into hockey nicknames).

"They called me Little Chief and I didn't mind that. It was when they called me 'wahoo' or 'F#$%'n little Indian' that I didn't like. I'm full-blooded Mohawk on my mother's side. I have some Tuscarora from my grandpa's side, but full-blooded Mohawk. I'm Turtle Clan, like you see on my front door."

Stan's pride in his family and his Native heritage is matched by the pride he will always carry as a Bruin. Stan's home on Third Line Road in Oswegan, Ontario has a stained-glassed turtle on its front door, which leads to a hexagon-shaped living room full of family pictures, Indian art and other treasures. In the centre of the room hangs a chandelier in the shape of an arena score clock adorned with a Boston Bruins logo.

But Stan Jonathan will always best be known as an "Indian fighter." Not to be confused with other well-known Indian fighters like Davey Crockett and Daniel Boone and John Wayne in Hollywood B-movie westerns. Stan was the first Indian fighter to become well-known in hockey circles, and some of his fights were legendary. Stan was often referred to as "pound for pound the toughest man in the National Hockey League."

To understand Stan's toughness—which was accompanied by an incomparable work ethic—you have to look at his childhood. Stan was the sixth child in a family of 14 (nine sisters and four brothers). "I'm right in the middle. I think I'm seventh."

Stan didn't grow up in abject poverty, because his father made a good living "working the high-steel" (Indians from the Six Nations Reserve were legendary for not having a normal, human fear of heights and many found jobs high up on the girders of the many skyscrapers under construction in nearby cities like Detroit, Buffalo, Toronto and New York). But when you are a middle child in a large family, you learn to fight for everything you got.

"At the dinner table, you learned how to grab with both hands or you didn't eat. And if you didn't get into the back of the family pickup truck right quick, you got left behind!" That ability to fight for food with both hands would come in handy later in Stan's hockey career.

None of the children in the Jonathan family were spoiled, because even a good living doesn't go very far when it has to be split 14 ways. Everybody chipped in so there was enough to go around. That meant chores around the house and after-school jobs at an early age. Stan had to compete for work with older boys, and that meant working twice as hard. He cut grass. He worked the tobacco farms. He played semi-pro lacrosse at the age of 15 ($25 for a win and $15 for a loss). Most importantly, Stan developed a strong and steadfast work ethic which he transferred to hockey.

"I didn't play organized hockey until I was 11. I can't remember when I started skating. All I remember is that there was a pond in back of the house; you got out, scraped the ice and enjoyed yourself in the ice cold weather."

Stan's childhood hockey idol was the most sportsmanlike Toronto Maple Leaf, Dave Keon, but by his teens, Stan admired the skills of the Buffalo

Sabres' smooth-skating centre Gilbert Perrault. Strange tastes for a kid who played his hockey like a bowling ball.

Stan played well enough on local teams to advance to the roster of the Peterborough Petes of the Ontario Junior A Hockey League. And, like Keon and Perrault, Stan was quite a playmaker and goal-scorer in his junior years. He was focused on hockey, and his Indian heritage was simply something he accepted and carried within himself. Creating a positive image for Indians or trying to be a role model for his people wasn't a consideration at this young age.

"I remember meeting George Armstrong when I played Junior A and that was a big thrill. I didn't know much about him because we didn't have a TV when I was a kid. I knew Reggie Leach was a player in the NHL, but…"

Besides, Stan had much more important things on his mind at this time. "While I was in Junior A, Cathy (who would eventually become Stan's wife) got pregnant. We weren't married at the time, and if word about that got out, it would have killed my hockey career. That's just the way people thought at that time. These kinds of things are accepted nowadays but things were so competitive in my day and there were so few spots open, any 'character flaw' could compromise your standing. And it's not as if I was the next 'Bobby' [Hull or Orr].

"Cathy had to care for that child mostly by herself. I would slip away to be with her whenever I could. Of course, as soon as I got my NHL contract and got settled, Cathy and I got married and it's been a heavenly union. But it was really tough on Cathy, and I take my hat off to any woman who has to go through childbirth and parenthood mostly alone."

That story came out quite innocently after we had finished videotaping Stan's interview for the documentary *They Call Me Chief.* Our crew had been carrying around a hockey stick that we wanted all the Indians who played in the NHL and whom we had interviewed, to autograph, so we could auction it off for a charity in Winnipeg that provided housing, education and nurturing know-how to single teenage moms. When we asked Stan to autograph that stick, his reaction was, at first, somewhat strange. Stan stood up, turned on his heel and headed straight for his basement, before calling over his shoulder: "Wait! I've got something else for you!"

Stan returned with another hockey stick, this one autographed by players from an NHL Legends All-Stars Gathering Stan had played in. There were names like Dickie Duff, Bob Nevin and other valuable autographs. "Here! Use this to raise money for those kids, too!" Stan said. And then he autographed our stick.

Stan carried Cathy in his heart throughout his junior career. And, because junior hockey doesn't pay anything near an NHL king's-ransom kind of salary, and Stan wanted to give everything he had to support Cathy, he followed his dad in working the high steel.

"I worked as a rigger, building apartment and office towers in the US and Canada from the time I was 16. I was scared the first couple of times I went up. But soon I learned it wasn't all that dangerous if you followed the safety precautions. I think I only went up maybe 125 to 150 feet without any safety rigging, but it's the same as hockey. If you get careless, you get hurt. The difference is that if you make a mistake in hockey, you get a second chance. If you make a mistake working the high steel, well, you don't get a second chance!"

Stan was a good enough hockey player that his coaches soon showed their disapproval of his high-climbing days. While that was bad news for his summer income, it was good news for his hockey psyche—because Stan was starting to stand out as a junior with the Petes. Between 1972 and '75, he showed a lot of scoring potential, amassing 176 points (69 goals and 107 assists) in 204 games. Stan was the beneficiary of coaching from Roger "way ahead of his time" Neilson (a.k.a. Captain Video) in Peterborough.

Stan even got the chance to play in the unofficial World Junior championship in 1973–74. His team did well to finish third in the competition, since it was a club team up against the top juniors from anywhere in the USSR, Sweden, Czechoslovakia, Finland and the United States.

But Stan really wasn't the kind of player who stood out or would attract the attention of most NHL bird dogs. "In Peterborough, we played an aggressive style, take the body and forecheck like hell! It was small arenas and you jumped on top of their defence as quickly as possible and you never let them get turned around. And you always took the body!"

Fortunately, Stan got a lucky break late in 1975, when the correct combination of player and personality happened to come together. Don "Grapes" Cherry, then the Head Coach of the Boston Bruins, was scouting a game in Oshawa with Bruins General Manager Harry Sinden. These two Bruin bosses were actually there to check out Boston's number-one draft pick, Doug Halward, but their chosen one got injured in the game they went to see. Instead, as the game progressed, Cherry noticed a feisty little player named Stan Jonathan.

"I couldn't help but notice this rugged little Indian. He didn't play an exceptional game, but there was something about him that made me take notice. I didn't say much about Jonathan to Harry, but I filed his name in the back of my mind for future reference and, at draft time, I called Harry aside and said, 'Do you think you could get me just one hockey player?'

"Harry was not as impressed as I was, and bypassed Jonathan on the first, second and third picks. We finally got him the fourth time (in the fifth round, 86th overall) around and sent him to the Dayton Gems of the IHL. A year later, he made our team. Of all my discoveries, Jonathan is the one in which I take the most pride."

In Dayton (1975–76), Stan played for an $8,000 salary and he did that very, very well. He led all playoff scorers with 13 goals and 6 assists for 21 points in 15 games. Stan cracked the Bruins lineup the next year and immediately became a fan favourite in Boston, which has a reputation for its hard-working, tough, labour class Irish who know how to settle arguments quickly.

Stan Jonathan had his own way of describing things. "The kind of game I played, you had to be in the corners digging the puck out and you stuck your nose in there and you took the body and well, you're going to get into scraps here and there. Well, in my case, a few more than most people.

"I was just happy to be there. Being small, and being a Native, you had to get in there and show them that you weren't going to be pushed around. I always had more penalty minutes than I should have, but I was always there for the other players, too."

As Don Cherry would say on numerous occasions, "I think Stanley is being modest here!"

In Stan's first NHL fight, he completely destroyed Chicago Blackhawks' tough-guy defenceman Keith Magnuson (who would later die in a car crash coming home from a funeral in Ontario in a car driven by Rob Ramage, who would receive a sentence of four years in jail for this tragic incident). Some other early victims of Stan's ferocity and fisticuffs included two of the biggest and baddest Broad Street Bullies, Dave "The Hammer" Shultz and Andre "Moose" Dupont of the Philadelphia Flyers. It was small wonder Boston's NHL team began being called the "big, bad Bruins," with even their smallest player as tough as anyone in the League.

Stan's pugnacity and overall toughness would label him, and he had no problem with that. But deep down in his heart and mind, Stan always possessed a deep admiration for the sport and the skill that can be displayed when hockey is played by the pure artisan.

For example, late in Stan's rookie season, he was placed on left wing with centre Jean Ratelle—a future Hall of Famer, a playmaker who could feather passes over to his wingers à la Wayne Gretzky.

"Who wouldn't want to play for a centreman like Jean Ratelle?" Stan exclaimed as a rookie. "Ratelle just had some fantastic moves. There's one Jean makes coming in on the defence. Really, it puzzles the defensemen. If they move at him one way, he dumps a pass to me on the right side. If the defence plays wide for the pass, well, then Jean just keeps going in on the goaltender. Incredible!"

Stan managed 17 goals and 13 assists in his rookie year and then, after spending a couple of seasons bouncing between Boston and Dayton and Rochester of the American Hockey League, he made the show for sure. His best scoring season was 1977–78 when he tallied 27 goals while adding 25 assists. Notwithstanding that scoring prowess, Number 27 of the Boston Bruins will always be most famous for his infamous fight with Number 3 of the Montreal Canadiens, defenceman Pierre Bouchard, in an epic Stanley Cup playoff battle.

The date was May 21, 1978. The Bruins, led by superstars Bobby Orr and Phil Esposito, were evenly matched for firepower against Canadiens

Guy Lafleur and Steve Shutt. Right from the start, Montreal coach Scotty Bowman had wanted to send out a "no-nonsense" message to the "big bad Bruins" of John Wensink and Terry O'Reilly et al. He got his chance in Game 4.

Late in the game, Bowman sent out Bouchard (six-foot-two, 205 lbs.), Gilles Lupien (six-foot-two, 210 lbs.) and Rick Chartraw (six-foot-two, 210 lbs.). Boston coach Cherry countered with Wensink, O'Reilly and… Stan Jonathan.

"Peter McNab, who was a helluva finesse player, was supposed to go out there, but Don decided to send me out there. I'll tell ya, the atmosphere was so tense and thick that Peter was just happy to get the hell offa the ice…but I was, I think, already over the boards before Don called my name. Before all this crap happened, earlier in the game during a whistle, I was along the boards by the Canadiens bench, and Lupien and Bouchard were hollering at me, 'You @#$%^& Indian' and all that. I said, 'You tell that cement-head, the guy with the metal plate in his head behind you, that if they ever let you out to play real hockey, then you can come out and play with us real players!' And I think that really pissed them off, as you might put it, because at that time I was standing right in front of their bench and they couldn't do anything about it."

When they finally got all the protagonists in this play—which was rapidly resembling a cross between Shakespearean drama and professional wrestling—all on one stage, it was obvious that World War III was in the making. All it needed was a spark, and Jonathan held the match. And he struck it when, for some reason, Bouchard, a defenceman, and Jonathan, a forward, were lined up side by side in the faceoff circle. At that fatal faceoff, Stan gave Pierre a light shove or maybe a slight shot, just enough to stir up a scrap, which even the popcorn vendor in the concourse knew was coming. Jonathan and Bouchard quickly dropped their gloves and started swinging, like pistons in a 283-cubic-inch V8 engine from a '57 Chevy.

At first it looked like the much bigger Bouchard was going to win because, though they were trading blows one-for-one, there's an old saying that goes, "A good bigger man will always beat a good smaller man." Cherry said from behind the Boston bench, "Fellas, I think Stanley's bitten off a little more than he can chew this time!"

"At first, I was just trying to keep my head on," Jonathan recalled. "I think he weighed 220 at least. I was five-foot-seven...well, five-foot-eight when you wore those high shoes that were in style at the time, but anyways, he had me by the shoulders and he was shaking me...and we were trading shots."

The best way to describe what happened next is to transcribe the exact script as originally presented in the documentary *They Call Me Chief.*

JONATHAN: I switched hands...

CHERRY: And he caught Bouchard with a left.

JONATHAN: I switched hands on him and...

CHERRY: Not many people know that Stan can throw as good with his left, as good as he can with his right! (Cherry demonstrates with his hands of many-ringed fingers.)

JONATHAN: I come from a family of 14...you learn to grab and throw with both hands at the supper table.

Jonathan caught Bouchard with a left that broke the huge defenceman's nose and cheekbone and drove his orbital bone up to his eye. Bouchard dropped like a tall tree cut down by a lumberjack's ax, his face a bloody mess that stained the ice and linesman John D'Amico equally.

JONATHAN: It was a desperation move, really. He got me in close and he was a lot stronger than I was and I just had to do something. I switched hands and I caught him in the right spot.

TV INTERVIEWER: Didn't all that blood freak you out?

JONATHAN: No.

TV INTERVIEWER: Why not?

JONATHAN: Because it wasn't mine!

Stan's junior coach, Roger Neilson, was in the stands that night. "Jonathan is a little like boxer Joe Frazier. He'll take two punches to get in one of his own, and that one punch is usually a dandy!"

Bouchard's reputation and career were never the same after the fight. Bouchard showed a lot of class, however, when he joked with Cherry later by stating, "I think I'll take up the organ. It's a lot safer up there in the balcony."

That's not to say Jonathan escaped the "most famous fight in NHL playoff history" unscathed. "I was sore. I never got cut, but the side of my head and my face hurt like hell. And I looked like a balloon for, the next couple of days." (Stan's eyes looked like two buttons on a big throw cushion.)

And to think it all goes back to that "training" Stan received at the Jonathan family supper table, where three squares a day were served to 14 hungry mouths; the hands with equal dexterity winning more than losing. That certainly came in handy during that bout with Bouchard, and during the many other scraps Stan was involved in during his NHL career. The problem was that Stan Jonathan, all-around hockey player that he was, was never appreciated by hockey "purists," despite some flattering testimonials from universally acknowledged hockey gurus.

Roger Neilson once said, "I've known Stanley and his folks for years. Stan will fight, yes, but he doesn't look for trouble. He won't back away when it comes, either. He's just a good, tough hockey player, but he'll score his share of goals, too." Such testimony from a respected hockey mind like "Captain Video" turned a few heads towards considering Stan Jonathan as more than just a "goon."

And it was all backed up by the father of "Rock 'em Sock 'em Hockey," Cherry himself. "When people think of Stan Jonathan, they always think of his fights, and he was probably the best I ever saw. But that year, 1977–78, when Stan scored those 27 goals, people don't know his scoring accuracy was something like 26.7 per cent, which was right up there with Mario Lemieux!"

Cherry was and remains fiercely loyal to Stan Jonathan. Stan deeply appreciated that, and repaid Cherry by giving everything he had every time he stepped on the ice for Grapes. But that camaraderie doesn't prevent Stan from being critical of Cherry in his description of events that led to the Bruins' downfall in that most memorable 1978 playoff series with the Canadiens.

"We had the Canadiens down and out, we were leading 3-2, in the third period, right in their own palace, the Forum, but we blew a line change late in the game," Jonathan recalls. "Our strategy all game had been to put Don Marcotte on Guy Lafleur. Lafleur headed to the Montreal bench and it was our line's turn to go on. Wayne Cashman and I looked over for a signal but Grapes wasn't even watching the game! He was arguing with some fans who were harassing him from behind the bench. So we jumped on the ice.

"Anyways, when Cherry turned back to face the play, he sent Rick Middleton out and the game went on. I ended up down in the corner, fighting Claude Lemieux, I think, for the puck. That's how far the play had gone on...the linesmen let it go that far...hopefully somebody would get off the ice...but I never really knew what was happening, until the whistle blew and they called us for too many men on the ice.

"Guy Lafleur scored on the power play and forced overtime. Then Lafleur won the game for the Canadiens with a sudden death goal. I really believe we would have won it all that year if we could have hung on to win that game in Montreal. I never really got another good shot at the Stanley Cup."

Jonathan proved to be prophetic because, the following season, the Canadiens had an even more powerful lineup, and swept the Bruins in the playoffs four games straight.

Meanwhile, Cherry was fired and the Bruins adopted a new system. It was a system that didn't fit players like Stan Jonathan, who were often planted squarely on the bench until they were "needed." The new management in Boston, perhaps frustrated by the lack of success that can only be truly measured in sips from Stanley Cups, did not understand the value of a player like Stan the Man. Certainly not like the fans in other cities, like Montreal.

"I remember, after the Bouchard fight, the boos were pouring down so loud, I couldn't hear myself think. But then I remembered, 'Hey Stan! You're on the road. They're booing you so you must be doing something right!' The more I got booed on the road, the harder I played.

"Unfortunately, after Don [Cherry] left, all the Bruins management wanted me to be, more or less, was a fighter. It's frustrating. You want to be out there to play, but you are a fourth-line player, and only when there's a tough team coming in, you get to play regular. And some of the young kids coming in, I didn't think they beat me out of my job, and I wasn't going to protect them if they weren't going to protect me. I asked one guy, 'If something happened to me, if I dropped my gloves, would you be in there,' because I had a bad shoulder and I had a sling on it, and he more or less said, 'No.' So I said, 'I'm not jumping in for you either then.'"

Cherry summed up Stan's situation best: "You can't keep these talented players on the bench like chained dogs! You have to let them play!"

But Cherry was long gone, and Stan had to deal with an entirely different environment in Boston. "The team had changed quite a bit. We had younger players that were given a job who didn't work as hard as I did, to be a Boston Bruin, and I wasn't going to be there to protect them if they weren't going to be there to protect me.

"It was a very difficult situation because nobody ever asks to leave the Boston Bruins. The city is great and the fans treat you so well. And if I quit, that would just mean that Harry Sinden would win, and I don't like losing to anybody. I had two years left on a three-year contract and I went to Pittsburgh for the remainder of one year because they gave up some conditional draft picks [5th and 8th rounds] but the deal was to return to Boston if I didn't fit in with the Penguins.

"Well, Pittsburgh had the type of team where everybody liked to carry the puck. I was used to having that puck dumped into the corner and then going into that corner, biting off some kneecaps or necks if I had to, and coming out with that puck. Or I would take up position in front of the net and whack and push back and forth and fight for position, tying up the defense no matter what. It was weird because I would hit the blue line full-steam and then just stop because somebody was dipsy-doodling around in the centre ice area. So I ended up back in Boston but they only wanted to play me the way I didn't want to be played.

"I talked to some of the guys I really trusted, like Cash [Wayne Cashman] and Don Marcotte and they reminded me that if I quit, Harry would win, and that's the last thing I wanted. So I went down to Baltimore [AHL] for a while and then I accepted a payout, which made me hang around Boston for a couple of years so I could collect on that contract. I checked out a few businesses and the kids were in school but it was still pretty hard to hang around this city I loved without giving something back on the ice. As soon as my contract was up, I left."

And so "Little Chief" retired from professional hockey. He was only 28 years old. But the career of Stan Jonathan will always be remembered for his work ethic, his tenacity, and his pugnacity. Stan was a true Indian fighter, but not only for his fistfights with the likes of Bouchard and Schultz and Dupont.

It isn't well-known, but Stan Jonathan also fought for the legal and political rights of all Indians in North America while he was in Boston, by standing up for some very hard-earned sacred treaty rights.

★ ★ ★ ★ ★

The territories of North American First Nations often straddle the border between the United States and Canada. It has been well established legally and politically that the forty-ninth parallel defines a border between lands to which First Nations have not ceded their sovereignty. Therefore, under what is commonly known as the Jay Treaty, Indians are supposed to be allowed unfettered passage between Canada and the US. Indians are also allowed to work on both sides of the border without paying taxes to either country, because most treaties recognize that Indians paid their taxes "in advance" by agreeing to share land and resources rather than going to war.

As strange and unfamiliar as all this may have been to Boston GM Sinden, it was those treaties that were really behind numerous battles that took place between Little Chief and the General (Manager).

"I remember doing a car commercial down in Boston and Harry said to me, 'You can't do that, because players from Canada are just down here to play hockey and that's all the work they are allowed to do.' But I said to Harry, 'I'm a North American Indian and I can work both sides of the border and I can do things like car commercials and I'm going to do them and that's that.'" Advantage Jonathan.

But NHL general managers are always looking for an angle or an edge. So, after Sinden realized that the Bruins, or Stan, didn't require a green card or visa for this Indian to work in the United States, Harry figured that he could keep an extra Canadian on his roster because roster limits on US-based NHL teams were dictated by a certain number of visas per team.

But Little Chief would have none of that, either. "I told Harry that I'm not going to allow him to bring in another guy and create an extra space on our roster, because that guy might take my job! I told Harry, 'I'll make you get me a green card or a visa if I have to!'" Sinden retreated, and Little Chief had won another battle.

Stan Jonathan is by no means a politician, and he didn't make a big show of standing up for his rights, but by refusing to back down against an NHL mogul like Harry Sinden, Little Chief was defending and fighting for treaty rights that not only protect Stan's individual right to make a living under treaty, but the social, cultural, political and economic rights of First Nations people throughout the Americas by making the powers that be live up to, and enforce those sacred treaties. Stan's victory might seem individual and small, but ask any lawyer or constitutional expert: it is the victories won by individuals that set precedents that are vitally important in re-establishing the legitimacy and authority of the broad-based laws and agreements.

Sometimes white people forget the significance of these treaties, which were signed by our forebears and remain in effect "as long as the sun shines, the grass grows and the river flows."

"Those treaties were signed a long time ago and I had nothing to do with them," is a common refrain. I'm afraid that isn't so. How can we negotiate pacts like NAFTA and softwood lumber agreements if our track record says that we didn't live up to similar treaties in our past? Some people might even be surprised at how much white people have benefited from the treaties with North America's First Nations.

We are all treaty people. Even the immigrants arriving today who become citizens of Canada and the US benefit from the treaties (as well as assume their share of responsibilities). We are all in this together. Treaties 1 to11, which were an agreement between nations to share the land and resources of the western Canadian plains, provide billions of dollars in wealth through agriculture, forestry, mining, hydroelectric power and other bounty to the people of Canada, albeit disproportionately to white people. The share of these resources that were guaranteed under treaty to help Indians develop economically and socially have never been adequate, and this has created Third World conditions for many First Nations throughout North America.

At the most basic, and perhaps most important level, most treaties were signed to prevent further bloodshed like what happened at Sand Creek, the Washita River, Ulm, Wounded Knee and Little Big Horn. Somehow we forget that the people who died through those conflicts were not able to perform the most basic function of any species of animal or plant. To reproduce: to bear children. There are spaces among us that belong to the great-great-great-grandchildren who were never born because their great-great-great-grandparents were killed in wars of the past. Treaties spared all of us this loss.

And therefore, it is egregiously incorrect to say that the white settlers, with superior firepower, defeated the Indians and to the winners go the spoils. Treaties were signed to avoid this very kind of conflict. And finally, to those who cling to the notion of manifest destiny, or "might makes right," they would be well advised to heed world-renowned biologist W. P. Keeton, who proves mathematically that the odds we are the only form of intelligent life in this universe are absolutely zero. Which allows us all to "walk a mile in an Indian's moccasins."

Imagine if an alien life force came to Earth and conquered the human race. What would you say to that alien life force if it told us to speak its language, give up our culture and follow its religion? "Hell no!" is what most of us would be likely to say. Even if we had to go underground to teach our children our culture, our lifestyle, our beliefs and our history, we would fight to keep our way of life alive. Just like the Indian Elders did, by moving their powwows further back into the bush when the Indian agents came around to enforce laws banning powwows in Canada and the United States.

Most likely, we would sign treaties with the new arrivals to protect our rights and our share of the resources of this Mother Earth. Treaties that we would expect to hold up for as long as our race or even "species" survives.

We are all "treaty people," equal and sharing. Stan Jonathan's fight with Harry Sinden may seem like some minor business squabble but when you consider Stan's stand in terms of re-establishing the legitimacy of treaties that shaped and still govern modern North America, Stan and Harry were scrapping over much, much more than a 30-second car commercial.

★ ★ ★ ★ ★

Stan was stubborn enough to hang around until his contract with Boston expired, and then he and Cathy and their growing brood returned to Oswegen, Ontario, which was truly home for both of them. As much as Stan loved Boston and the welcome he received there, the friends he made there, and even the potential for business opportunities that remained in Beantown, it wasn't very difficult to return to the rez.

Stan recalls one of the reasons why. "I remember a time while I was playing in Boston, my brother called me on the phone and said, 'You're out of bullets.' I didn't know what he meant but then he explained that he had 'borrowed' this special rifle I'd bought for when I retire, He said that he had gotten lucky and bagged three more moose that year. 'Send me some money because I ran out of bullets!' he said. Of course, he was just teasing me, but it sure made me wish I could be home during the fall hunting with my friends and family—but I couldn't because I was always in training camp. Your relatives back home always zing you with kidding around like that and you sure wish you could be home deer hunting or moose hunting or fishing."

The first thing Stan and Cathy did when they got back to Six Nations was design their dream home. But they had no place to build it. "The greatest love and honour would come from my grandfather, who was 95 or 96 years old. He always wanted to stay on his land, but when he heard I was moving back, he moved out of his cabin and he let me build my home for my family on his spot.

"I worked construction as a teenager, so it was easy to learn carpentry. And, with all the brothers and sisters and aunts and uncles and cousins I have, the house went up pretty quickly. And what a huge relief it was to have a house that was all bought and paid for. I admit that we made pretty good money playing in the NHL in my day, but it wasn't anywhere near the money they make today. I'll just say that it was a huge relief to Cathy and me not to have a huge mortgage hanging over our heads, because we were pretty much like any other Canadian family. And that house is located right on my grandfather's spot!"

Back at home and free from the discipline, demands and travel of professional hockey, Stan could spend more time with his family. But that didn't mean he was through with the game. "Senior hockey is a pretty good calibre of hockey and I found a challenge there. I played with the Motts Clamatos Senior A team and we went to the Allan Cup [Canadian Senior Hockey Championship] finals."

And then there were the Indian hockey tournaments. There are a lot of really great Indian players who didn't end up on the path that led to the mainstream professional leagues. But across Canada, there are tournaments in First Nations communities that feature top-notch competition and some serious prize money.

"They would pay my travel and food and hotel and give me a few hundred bucks just to play the game that I love for a weekend. It wasn't NHL money by any means, but I think I enjoyed it more because you got to play with your friends and you got to prove that you can still play. And you return home with a trophy after meeting a lot of good players from across the country and making a lot of new friends.

"Just as important, those tournaments brought me into First Nations communities where I could meet young people and try to offer a role model example of hard work and other positive values. I was surprised at how many of these young people knew who I was, but I guess their parents had talked about me and I really started to get into the pride we should have as Native people, and I tried to pass that on.

"You know, my grandfather made it to 100 and when he died, I learned that he had made a sort of potion that would bring us good fortune against Montreal in that playoff. I remember he used to pick things off the ground and off the trees in the forest and make medicines for us kids. I remember that they worked, too, because we always felt better after we got treated by grandpa.

"And his potion worked for me despite what happened against the Canadiens. Just knowing that my grandfather and grandmother were always there for me is the greatest blessing. His medicine was most powerful because it protected me and took care of the big picture, the most important things in our long-term future."

Stan looks around the walls of his living room. Every conceivable space had long been covered with family photos, Native art, memorabilia and other personal treasures, shining under the light of that Boston Bruins arena scoreboard clock lamp in the centre of the six-sided room. "Just look where I ended up!"

5

THEY CALLED ME A HALF-BREED

The life stories of sports heroes are often made into movies. The stories of the Indian hockey players in this book would make for some great movies-of-the-week, with all the ingredients needed for a good film— strong plot, conflicts and resolutions, a wide variety of interesting elements and fascinating character arcs.

But, it would require much more than a movie to tell the story of Bryan Trottier's life. Or should I say nine lives?

So many huge and different things have happened to Bryan, his life could fill a television mini-series. We'll have to settle for a long chapter in this book. Certainly one of the most interesting—and moving. Like, back and forth between Canada and the United States and between white and Indian.

★ ★ ★ ★ ★

Bryan's father was a Cree/Metis man who married an Irish woman. Bryan was the second youngest of five children. "My first recollections of child-hood are in the United States. I can remember Dad working construction down in the Dakotas and in Colorado. We moved to Montana, then Wyoming. I have a brother who was born in Buffalo, Wyoming. We moved back to Canada from Fort Collins, Colorado, when I was six years old."

The Trottiers finally settled into the humble surroundings provided by a family ranch in Val Marie, Saskatchewan. "My grandfather had home-steaded this piece of land. It was early December, and everybody 'up there' was playing this game called hockey."

Young Bryan loved sports, and hockey was *the* sport in Saskatchewan. Bryan learned how to skate on the river near his family's ranch (which was always "a buck above or below break-even"). "There was a river flowing about 100 feet back of the house and that's where I learned to skate. You know, to 'get the stride!'"

★ ★ ★ ★ ★

"When I started school, I would get into fist fights all the time," says Bryan. "They called me a half-breed. I didn't even know what a half-breed was!

"In a way, it was a form of recognizing. And I got past it.

"We had a dog named Rowdie, a border collie. A real sheep- and cattle-herder. The cows would come into the yard, or the horses or even the chickens, and we'd say, 'Sic 'em, Rowdie!' and boy, did those things head right out of the yard! Rowdie became very good at fetching rocks. And hockey pucks.

"My little brother Rocky started it all [Rocky Trottier also played in the NHL for a short spell]. He had a little stick and a rubber ball and he would try to shoot the ball out of the door of the house and Rowdie would catch it in his mouth.

"I came home from school one day and I said, 'Okay, just how good is this dog?' So we took Rowdie out to the barn and I just starting firing balls at the barn door and this dog was a heck of a goalie—there wasn't too much that you could get by him! If he wasn't catching that ball with his mouth, he was blocking it with his body just like a good 'butterfly' goalie.

"Rowdie passed away at the age of 12. He had not one tooth left in his head when he died, and he probably passed away just because he couldn't chew food anymore. Rowdie is in dog heaven. He was a good companion, not only to me, but to the whole family. Everybody loved Rowdie. It was a sad, sad passing for the whole family."

★ ★ ★ ★ ★

Bryan was a natural athlete and was soon starring for the Prince Albert Raiders, then the Swift Current Broncos of the Western Junior Hockey League. His parents dearly wanted to see him play, but they could rarely afford the cost of transportation and lodging. And a player's allotment of tickets would certainly have to be stretched in the Trottier family's case.

These problems were solved by a rather endearing family trait. Most prairie "half-bloods" whiled away long winters playing some sort of musical instrument, and every member of Bryan's family played something.

"The ranch was supposed to support us, but it didn't pay all the bills and in order to, what Dad would say, 'put food on the table,' he would play music on the weekends. And he got us all involved in music at a relatively young age.

"Everybody had a song. My older sister had a song, I had a song, my younger sister had a song. Then, all of a sudden, it was like, 'start playing this bass guitar' and Dad taught me all the changes and I said, 'This isn't so hard! I can stand in the background and just play the bass guitar.' Then my little sister took over the bass and I started playing rhythm guitar. Dad played every instrument under the sun. He played the accordion, he played the fiddle, he played lead guitar, and we had a family band."

The Trottier family became a musical act that could be booked into the beverage room of the local hotels in Saskatchewan wherever Bryan was playing. In this way, they earned enough money to pay for food, accommodations and tickets for Bryan's games. The family was able to watch entire games that were played in the afternoons, and the first or second period of evening games. Then, while Bryan's teammates gathered at a local pizza joint, java joint, smoked a joint, or downed a beer to celebrate a victory or mourn a loss, Bryan hustled off to the hotel to play bass or rhythm in the Trottier family band.

"Native people have an inherent love of music and art. And a natural talent for both. So many of our young people show this today. It was like this in my family and my father encouraged our love of music and art in all his children."

This aptitude for music would also help Bryan to overcome the same problems that plagued Fred Sasakamoose. "I had to deal with the loneliness of being away from my family, travelling and playing junior hockey.

"Our father used to tell us that there's nothing more important than family and that is because of our Native blood. And the music and the family band helped us to bond together and stay together and enjoy each other and be there for each other, especially for me, because it cut down on the time I spent alone playing hockey. That's why I refer to myself as a 'half-white.'"

★ ★ ★ ★ ★

After a standout junior career, Bryan was drafted in 1975 by teams in both of hockey's professional leagues, which were competing for players at the time (the NHL and its rival World Hockey Association). Bryan favoured the more established NHL.

Negotiations got a little complicated. The New York Islanders had selected Bryan in the second round of the NHL entry draft. A typical signing bonus for such high draft picks was a car. Any car of the kid's choice!

Other top draft picks picked a Ferrari. Or a Mercedes. Bryan's pick? A four-door Chrysler for his dad.

"The short story of the signing bonus was that I was chosen by the Cincinnati Stingers of the World Hockey Association and the New York Islanders of the NHL. When the Islanders offered you your contract, they said 'Look, we'll give you the standard bonus of an annuity to cover you for the rest of your life...you'll have money coming in for the rest of your life...and a car of your choice! So what would that be?' And I started thinkin', 'Oh, man! I want a big car! I want a Chrysler New Yorker!'

"And they said, 'A Chrysler New Yorker? Are you sure you don't want a Mercedes? Denis Potvin took a Mercedes. Billy Harris took a Cadillac Eldorado. Are you sure you want a Chrysler New Yorker?' I said, 'Absolutely! I want a Chrysler New Yorker for my dad.'"

Some people might think that Bryan made a poor choice, but really, he had done "the right thing."

"When I pulled up in front of the ranch driving that Chrysler, I saw the smile on my dad's face, and I knew I had made the right choice. The Chrysler became the family car. It was big and we could all fit in it. And we could get all of our musical instruments in the trunk." And when you stop to think about it, a Mercedes on the prairies of Saskabush would have stuck out like a Harley-Davidson at a rally of rice rockets.

"Then when I said, 'I'm going to New York now and I can make my own way out there so you guys keep the New Yorker here on the ranch for the family,' I saw another big smile on my dad's face, and my mom's face, and I knew again that I'd made the right choice."

★ ★ ★ ★ ★

As much as Bryan loved his dad, and though there were a lot of good times in the Trottier household, life and happiness were compromised by a familiar foe.

"The family on our dad's side had alcohol abuse and a lot of alcoholism. It caused the death of some of my aunties. And, because of that, you get depression, lots of arguments, and that wasn't much fun.

"But you learn at an early age that alcohol is not something that I'm going to make a big part of my life. Number one, I didn't like the taste, thank goodness! Number two, I didn't like what it did to change the personality of people, especially my dad. He was not a happy man when he drank. I think a lot of that had to do with the fact that we didn't have much money and there was pressure paying bills. And he got somewhat abusive at times, and I used to say to myself, 'I'm going to make darn sure I'm not going to be like that!'

"Thank goodness he got help; he was involved with Alcoholics Anonymous for 15 years prior to his death. Both he and I were very proud of that and he was a changed man because of it. And I saw a more loving man. I saw the man I wanted to be.

"It's like Reggie Leach says in his workshops. Alcoholism is a disease. A sickness. It's not your fault. You can get help. We should help our friends and relatives with this sickness."

This attitude towards alcohol turned out to be a great gift. When Bryan headed off to the glamour and glory of the "show" which is the National Hockey League, there were times and situations that were difficult, perhaps unfair, but full of stress for sure. Stuff happened that might have turned many other men to drink.

But Bryan wouldn't turn to alcohol—some very basic lessons had been handed down from his late father that he would put to good use.

"I believe that Dad is looking down smiling, happy that his family, his kids, are staying away from alcohol. We've learned the lessons that were very important to him. A handshake is very important. Look someone in the eye. Your word is better than any contract. And love your Mom!"

★ ★ ★ ★

Bryan's rise in the NHL was nothing less than meteoric. He led all first-year players in scoring and won the Calder Trophy as the NHL's Rookie of the Year. Trottier became the face of the Islanders franchise, the image behind a dynasty that would win four straight Stanley Cups (1979–83). Bryan was a top scorer and an all-star on an annual basis. He went on to win two more Cups as a player with the Pittsburgh Penguins, and another as an assistant coach with the Colorado Avalanche. He served a half-year as Head Coach of the New York Rangers and at last word, Bryan had returned to the Isles as executive vice-president for Player Development.

That's the official line on Bryan. On the surface, it all looks so smooth, like a Hollywood movie with a trailer that reads "Young boy, growing up on the prairies, strikes it rich in the world of professional hockey…"

But if we retrace all the steps in detail, Bryan's career wasn't a tiptoe through the tulips. It was full of more bumps and bruises than a Stanley Cup winner's face. Words like bankruptcy, boycott and bigotry do not fit in with a smooth, sweet life. But that was what Bryan would face in his life.

★ ★ ★ ★ ★

From the fisticuffs at five, through numerous punch-ups defending himself or his teammates in junior hockey, Bryan's approach to sports never seemed to match the kind of huge, finesse-type numbers he was posting on the scoreboard. Too small to be a true power forward, Bryan was a banger nonetheless, and he never needed an enforcer to stand up for him or to protect him. Yet he always finished in the top 10 in scoring in his prime. This was also Bryan's approach to life, and he got as good as he gave.

Bryan's feisty attitude, in particular his willingness to stand up for his rights, along with his prolific profile, got Bryan elected president of the National Hockey League Players' Association. One might question his credentials for that post if you recall the naivety he displayed in that car deal, but Trottier was long removed from the hay wagon he might have ridden in on his way to the Big Apple. He knew what the players were worth and he proved to be as feisty a negotiator in the boardroom as he was on the ice. It was during Bryan's tenure that the NHL and the NHLPA started down the road to the historic impasse that could only be settled by a lockout of the players by the owners.

Despite being raised in the home province of the Co-operative Commonwealth Federation (which evolved into the socialist-leaning New Democratic Party), things like unions and collective bargaining between labour and management were about as important to Bryan as backchecking is to NHL rookies—in the beginning.

"The Players' Association was going through a nice growth. Salaries were growing and there were collective bargaining agreements going on. I was in a profession where I was making good money and I was like, 'Let's just keep it going and growing!'"

But Bryan was captain of the successful Islanders, a leading scorer, a champion, and a high-profile guy and…"The Players' Association asked me to get involved and I said 'Absolutely!' After three or four years, NHLPA President Tony Esposito retired and bingo bango, I'm next in line for the job."

Bryan had learned a lot as a front-line player in the NHLPA, but he soon found out he had to juggle and balance seemingly diametrically opposed roles of player/captain and referee during his tenure as President of the Players' Association. The organization was constantly negotiating with management and the owners over various issues. At the same time, the NHLPA was going through a highly charged internal power struggle.

"I served eight years as president, the first seven with Alan Eagleson as executive director, and one year with Bob Goodenow. I was part of the selection committee that got Goodenow."

The sordid chapter of the NHLPA's history that ended with Eagleson in jail is well-known. The founder and long-time executive director of the players' union was deemed to be "too tight" with the NHL owners, and the players decided this conflict of interest had been compromising their interests at the bargaining table. Obviously, this was exacerbated when Eagleson feathered his own nest through outright fraud.

"I am real proud of those years because we went through some good growth, and some turmoil that was very good. We had a union uprising, so to speak, where the players said they wanted a change in executive directors. I am very proud of the work the search committee of Mike Liut, Mike Gartner and I did. God, we had a good crew there! And Goodenow proved to be a knowledgeable and tough representative who gained a lot for the players.

"I maintained right from the very beginning that I was not an Alan Eagleson stooge, or someone that he could control. Bobby Smith [Minnesota North Stars] was definitely not an Eagleson trooper. And we became the ones that said, 'Hey! This is becoming too much!' And when you have 500 players saying 'We don't want this anymore!,' that is a big message to the Executive Committee. We had to start making decisions.

"Yeah, there were some conflicts and Eagleson did some bad things, but he paid for that and he is still paying for that. I still consider him a good friend. And players like Bobby Clarke and Phil Esposito were doing the best they could with the information they had. The benefits were growing, salaries were going up, the pension was growing, medical benefits, everything was growing. But we had to go through a change and the process was a real learning experience. You can go to school and get an education but when you are going through that historical transformation that took place in the NHLPA, this is a greater education because it's going to help in later life."

But how in the world did a shy kid from Val Marie, Saskatchewan become a hardline union negotiator? Again, Bryan claims it all goes back to family, and that red blood flowing through his veins.

"You know, that shy kid, and the Native side of things keeping quiet, kind of slowly disappeared over the years. I felt more comfortable, and again, I give my family great credit because they pushed me. They said, 'Look! You're going to come on stage and you are going to sing songs. You are going to go out there and play sports and you are going to represent your high school.' And so on for everything.

"You are going to do all these things that are very important, and once you get out there and get exposed to it, you're going to get less and less nervous. At first, I felt very uncomfortable, you know, something new, but, after a while, you can look the owners in the eye, and you can look the presidents of the various teams in the eye, and the negotiators, and say, 'Hey look! This isn't fair. And this is fair.' You do your homework, and you speak from the heart, with the truth, and they respect you for that.

"I had some great conversations, some good discussions and some strong arguments across that table with ownership. I respect them because they are successful and they are our bosses, but I know the respect became mutual."

The end result—long after Bryan had moved on—was a historic over-reach by Goodenow that resulted in a lockout of the players by the owners. A balance was eventually achieved that is being put to the test as this book is being written. Goodenow was gone and lackey Ted Saskin proclaimed himself the new executive director of the NHLPA. That lasted about as long as an Al McInnis slapshot.

The players are now absolutely in control of the NHLPA.

★ ★ ★ ★ ★

Bryan's role with the NHLPA had him bouncing back and forth from battles between the players and their own management, to battles between the players and NHL management. At times, it was hard to tell who was the enemy.

If that wasn't confusing enough, or big enough, Bryan's next great challenge can truly be described as a war, because it would pit two entire countries against each other. Friends became enemies, and enemies became friends. And, once again, Bryan felt himself being batted back and forth like a proverbial puck.

It all started when Bryan, recognizing that he could "play" both sides of the border—like Stan Jonathan had, because of their special status as Indians—decided to play for the United States in the 1984 Canada Cup, after he had suited up for Canada in two previous such competitions. "It wasn't a very popular decision. But I felt very strongly that I wanted to give something back to the country I was making my living in [New York/USA]. Plus, there was also a little stubborn side that, when the Committee said you can't do this, I said, 'I'm a North American Indian and Yes! I can!'

"They said I couldn't get a passport quick enough. By God! They got my dander up! But because of my Native background, it was easy. And I made sure that was the prime reason…my Native background…I could play for both countries, and I could go back and play for Canada if I wanted to.

"And it's something I'm very proud of, and my kids are very proud of. I took a bit of flack from the media up in Canada."

And a lot of flack from hockey fans throughout the north country, who vividly recalled Bryan's exploits in a red Maple Leaf jersey during the first two Canada Cup competitions. Now, their hero was suiting up with the red, white and blue enemy.

"Traitor. Ingrate. I got called all sorts of names!

"I didn't feel I was Canadian. I didn't feel I was American. I knew I was North American Indian because my dad handed me my Indian card and he said, 'You can go anywhere you want in the North American continent.' I thought this was awesome, no one can stop you at the border.

"I've had a couple of problems with certain customs agents at various times but, eventually, their supervisors would come out and ring them out and say, 'Don't ever give this young man a hard time again.' It became the same thing with customs agents no matter whether they were Canadian or American. Both sides were saying, 'Come on home, young man!' And that helped to sustain me through this battle. I wanted to repay the country I was making my living in and honour my American wife and I did just that."

★ ★ ★ ★ ★

Bryan Trottier has always respected his unique citizenship status as a North American Indian. He also recognized that this special status is a right, but also a privilege which is never to be abused.

There are advantages to this status, which was earned centuries ago by First Nations leaders who signed treaties that govern all citizens of Canada and the United States. Bryan used those advantages to play for the country of his choosing in the Canada Cup competitions, and he was willing to avail himself of opportunities to work without a visa, just like Stan Jonathan. As is his right. It has been long agreed that there is no forty-ninth parallel crossing through the First Nations, whose traditional territories stretch across both sides of the borderline developed by the newcomers to North America (or what Indians call Turtle Island).

The treaties guaranteed many other rights to Indians, among them, that in exchange for agreeing to share the resources of this land and move to smaller areas (reserves or reservations), the Indian people have paid their taxes "in advance" (besides, it made no sense for First Nations to pay taxes to an outside or "foreign" government). Therefore, the citizens of First

Nations living on First Nations land do not have to pay taxes—income, property, inheritance or otherwise.

This has rarely created any problems because, for most of modern North American history, Indians have been so poor they don't make enough money to pay any kind of taxes. But recently, with the development of Indian casinos, some Indian tribes and the citizens who live on the reserves where casinos are located make so much money that some other people are demanding they share that wealth by paying taxes.

The original idea for granting gaming licences to Indian tribes was to use the wealth that was created to eradicate the widespread poverty that existed on Indian reserves. Gaming was to be the "white buffalo" to create employment and wealth for First Nations, and this has been accomplished on a kind of hit-and-miss, helter-skelter basis throughout the United States.

But there are certain situations where Indian tribes have created so much employment they have simply "run out of Indians" and are importing white labour; and so much wealth that their cups runneth over. How is the tax question affected by this?

One answer can be found in Ledyard, Connecticut, the home of Mystic Pizza (the setting for a minor film success), and where the Pequot Indians own the Foxwoods Casino. Foxwoods is the only casino located in this area, which is one hour north of New York City and one hour south of Boston—a huge hinterland. The Foxwoods Casino Resort Hotel dwarfs anything in Las Vegas. It's the largest in North America—with a 15,000-seat convention centre, three hotels, a theme park and the $100-million Museum of the American Indian.

This gaming-rich Indian tribe is willing to share its wealth, but not by paying taxes, because this would set a precedent that violates the treaties. Therefore, the Pequots agreed to provide "grants" in lieu of taxes.

For example, the Pequots provided $500 million to the City of Hartford for inner-city renewal one year, as a way to avoid paying taxes. The Pequots were not trying to save money—they're willing to pay the exact equivalent of what their income tax bill would be. But they cannot pay taxes, because that would set a precedent that violates the sacred treaties.

Still, problems arise, because treaties and law and economics and legislation are inherently complex. For example, the Pequots, with so much excess in disposable wealth, began to invest in long-term, stable investments such as land. The problem is that every time the Pequots buy up a piece of prime Connecticut real estate it becomes Indian territory, which is not subject to the tax rolls of this great state, and is removed from the Connecticut tax rolls, forever. How should this conflict be handled? There always seems to be another angle or complication when it comes to taxes.

Similarly, treaties were not simple documents signed by Indians with an "X" and stating, "Sign this, move over there, Mr. Indian!" There are also ways to work around the treaties, sometimes by unscrupulous people who might try to take advantage of certain favourable provisions. Such as taking advantage of the provision that states that "Indians have paid their taxes in advance" to avoid paying taxes they rightfully and dutifully owe.

Bryan Trottier was offered an opportunity to take advantage of his Indian status to do just that. "I was invited to the Shinnicock Reservation in New York by the Chief, I believe his name was Soaring Eagle. I learned that I had to have residence on a reserve in order to not have to pay taxes. The Shinnicock people invited me to live in their territory but I said to myself, 'I am not of Shinnicock blood. I will do whatever I am asked to help these brothers and sisters, but I couldn't live on the reservation and avoid paying taxes! That kind of tax break simply isn't right.'"

As things things turned out, Bryan could have used some kind of break.

★ ★ ★ ★ ★

Bryan's success at increasing the financial standing of his fellow players through the NHLPA did not transfer over to his own personal financial success. During the early 1990s, Bryan faced crippling debt.

"In 1990, I was bought out of my contract with the Islanders, and that started a whole series of problems, because now the banks came down on some loans I had taken out to invest in real estate. The banks started saying 'How are you going to repay these loans if you have no contract?' I tried to tell them that it was real strong real estate and it should pay for itself, but the banks started calling in their loans and then the media got hold of it."

Some media estimates had Bryan $9 million into debt. Other accounts had Bryan on the verge of suicide. Both were highly exaggerated.

"The media in New York exaggerate everything to the nth degree. I might have said at one time or another that there were days when I wanted to run into a brick wall and just finish it all, but I never did get to the point where I contemplated 'pedal to the metal,' and just let it go.

"I felt great grief over the whole thing and fell into a depression. Because of that, I recognized what depression really is, it's a form of anger toward yourself, and I just said to myself, 'I don't want to be in this spot anymore.' So, I went and I found some help for that and because of that, I think I am a stronger person today.

"The thing that brought me back was, 'Who is going to take care of my kids?' I want to spend a lot of time with my kids, and they need their dad to help them and I want to be there for them. You find out who your friends are, you find out how strong your family is. I have three great kids and I just kind of had to start my whole life over. It took me three or four years to come out of it and know that Bryan Trottier's a healthy individual.

"I think all of these things happened for a reason. I never turned to alcohol. I never turned to drugs. I got the help that I needed, I relied a lot on the strength of my family, and my character, and I am a better man for it."

And we are all better off for the fact that the word suicide does not play a large role in Bryan's biography. I wish it were the same for our Native youth throughout North America, where the rate of suicide is so disproportionately high compared to any other segment of our young people.

★ ★ ★ ★ ★

Our documentary was a better film for including Bryan Trottier, but that almost didn't happen. My line producer, Clay O'Bray, had become increasingly frustrated in his efforts to set up an interview with Trottier by a PR director who had moved to the Colorado Avalanche from the Quebec Nordiques when that WHA/NHL franchise moved west (or, more accurately, from a small, hockey-crazed Canadian market to a large, hockey-happy American city).

This PR guy kept stifling our requests for interviews with Bryan, and it all reached a head in Montreal, when and where Clay had arranged interviews with Sheldon Souray and Aaron Asham (two indigenous players on the Canadiens roster). We bagged those interviews during an afternoon practice session, but Clay had an ulterior motive.

There was an evening game between the Avalanche and the Habs taking place in the Molson Centre, and Clay believed that our media credentials would get us into the Avalanche dressing room following the game, where we could snag that interview with Bryan.

But as Clay, our camera operator and I tried to enter the visitors' (Colorado) dressing room, that prick PR guy blocked us and threw us out. I was so pissed off that I simply decided to drop Bryan Trottier's story (obviously, we had enough material for a 26-part series, let alone a one-hour "one-off" documentary). We faxed Bryan a note outlining all the hassles we had been going through and we thought that was that.

We wrapped shooting on the doc a few weeks later, and we were in the process of viewing and time-coding our videotape (basically, transcribing what was said over 100 hours of videotape), when we got a phone call from Bryan himself.

By sheer coincidence or fate, Bryan happened to be walking through the Avalanche front office one day, and he emptied his mail slot. Our "final" note was incorrectly stuffed into the box above Bryan's.

Maybe it's because hockey players are used to "seeing all the ice," but Bryan happened to notice that his name was on our fax, and he pocketed it. And realizing our frustration, which was clearly, and quite angrily, outlined, he took it upon himself to act.

"Don, ignore that PR guy. From now on, deal directly with me. Take this down, now. It's my home phone number. I will be home tonight at 8:00 PM Colorado time. Call me then."

Long story short, we were on our way to Parker, Colorado to spend a couple of days getting to know Bryan, and recording the substance of what appeared in the doc and in this book.

Now, let me digress, for the benefit of all struggling (i.e., financially challenged) filmmakers, to pass on some travel tips that will save you plenty of coin. Clay had been informed that it would cost $2,300 for each of us to fly to Denver return from Winnipeg. Brilliant line producer that he is, Clay knew the price was way over our budget, but he didn't know of any other way to hook us up with Denver.

Fortunately, I am as big a fan of Las Vegas as I am of sports in general, and I know full well that you can grab a charter flight to Vegas from Winnipeg (or whatever city, town or village the casino owners can draw VLT or blackjack money in from) for next to nothing, and they have flights all over the American Southwest in and out of Sin City for next to nothing. So we booked a charter out of Winnipeg for $189 return and grabbed a Southwest Airlines flight from Vegas to Denver for about $50. And that is some practical advice to filmmakers who are trying to live within a budget.

It did cost us some coin to spend a couple of extra days at the Excalibur in Vegas while we awaited our charter home. Between driving down the strip in a fully loaded convertible playing powwow songs at 10 and a half, we earned our money going over time-code notes by the pool. Yes, we had to deal with a hot desert sun and being force-fed beverages by bar beauties, but oh well, it had to be done.

The original estimate for airfare alone for this trip was $4,600. We spent about two grand all-inclusive, and bagged it all.

Enough digression. We also got a great interview with Bryan, who was willing to talk openly and honestly about anything.

★ ★ ★ ★ ★

We hired a local film crew and arrived at Bryan's modest (by superstar athlete standards) home in Parker, Colorado. We were met by Jennifer, Bryan's wife by a second marriage, a stunningly beautiful young blonde.

Jennifer is a very accomplished human being in her own right. Having earned a Master of Business Administration, she has a number of her own things on the go, but she is also most supportive of her hockey husband's career. Her relationship with Bryan reminded me of the pairing between Colleen and Gordie Howe, and the successful partnership in romance, life and business that legendary couple forged together in their lifetime.

Bryan had met Jennifer during a meet-and-greet with fans of the Pittsburgh Penguins when he was playing for that NHL franchise. Jennifer was not especially a hockey fan, but her mother was a true fanatic, who dragged her daughter along to a gathering of Penguins at the Igloo (which is what the hockey arena in Pittsburgh was called because it looked like an ice house and housed a team of black-and-white-clad birds from the South Pole).

Bryan and Jen fell in love, got married, and they have one child, Christian, who is following in his father's footsteps by being involved in hockey and roller hockey.

Jen's love and support for Bryan was obvious. First of all, she had spent a busy afternoon moving most of their family rec room to the living room, simply because I had dropped the smallest hint that we might require some space and light. She had redecorated pretty much the entire first floor of their home!

And then there was this guitar sitting on a stand in the middle of all the memorabilia.

★ ★ ★ ★ ★

Bryan noticed the guitar first as he walked in the door, and we both gave it a curious glance, but we had an interview to do. And following the on-camera chat (which is what all of my interviews with these Indian NHL greats became, just two guys shooting the breeze in a relaxed, informal atmosphere, but somehow bringing big issues home out of what appeared to be simple small talk), Bryan and I retired to his living room while the crew struck the set.

It was during this informal conversation that I learned about the cultural side that this NHL Hall of Famer is dying to cultivate. I happened to be packing some DVDs of an Indian television variety show called *Indian Time* which featured First Nations performing artists like Buffy Sainte-Marie and Tom Jackson and Shingoose—and which I had been honoured to produce and direct—and some CDs of the kind of music entertainers like C-Weed and Aaron Peters had recorded. Bryan didn't accommodate my request to put them on out of politeness, he was an absolute sponge for whatever First Nations content he could get his hands on.

And when Bryan learned about our project to raise money for unwed mothers, he signed our stick, and more. Like Stan Jonathan, Bryan had a treasure in his rec room (which Jennifer had somehow managed to over-look), and he dug down to give it to me on behalf of our charity for unwed teenage mothers.

It was a 500-goal stick, a hockey stick signed by every player who has scored 500 goals in the NHL to that point in time, including the auto-graph of Maurice "Rocket" Richard, just before that legend passed on the Great Forum in the sky. There will be many more 500 goal sticks, but the ones with the Rocket's signature will be exceedingly rare. Bryan gave it up without a second thought.

That stick was donated to the charity, the documentary was made and broadcast, and I didn't really expect to hear much from Bryan again unless we somehow happened to cross paths at some rubber-chicken dinner or something.

But I will always remember the final act which took place during this very special evening with Bryan Trottier and the love of his life, wife Jen. You see, that guitar had been laid out by Jennifer for a very special reason.

Bryan, for reasons that are best kept between Jennifer, Bryan and a very special family member who had preceded Christian, had written a song; a very special tribute to…their cat, "Butch."

It seems that whenever Jen and Bryan's feline got upset, he would, like all instinctive animals, expand his appearance to make himself more large and fearful to whatever enemies cats encounter in the real world, or their imagination. He did this quite often, and Bryan had taken to calling him "bushy cat." Jen thought this was endearing, and, Bryan, in a fit or relapse of romanticism that might appear ludicrous to outsiders, spent one night penning a song called "Bushy Cat."

Perhaps it isn't that often that a retired NHL superstar has a professional film crew, complete with audio and lights, in his living room, or perhaps Jen was just sharp enough to seize the opportunity, but we ended up complying with her request to record Bryan singing "Bushy Cat" to his…cat. I couldn't help but wonder if Rowdie had been taught to "roll over," but I imagined he was rolling over in his grave over this act! As we struck our set, I found myself hoping the Trottier family band had at least allowed Rowdie to howl along when they rehearsed songs at home on the ranch.

These were certainly not the thoughts I expected to depart with after meeting one of my NHL heroes, to interview Bryan Trottier for a network television documentary, also to be able to socialize with Bryan, to spin some tunes with him, to watch some videotapes with him—only to end with the production of a music video, featuring Bryan Trottier on guitar and vocals, singing to his wife and their cat, which Jen was stroking gently as the animal purred contently before our cameras. The experience was rewarding, in the end, welcomed and appreciated, but also rather bizarre.

Anyway, Bryan, if you ever poke fun at my skating, or giggle at my shot, I've got you on videotape singing to a housecat!

★ ★ ★ ★ ★

I had not heard from Bryan for a few years, when he called one morning to inform me that he was in Winnipeg to play in a fundraising hockey game, and he wanted me to join him for breakfast at the local Radisson Hotel (which, by the way, is owned by the Tribal Councils Investment Group, an incredibly sharp and successful group of Indians who have created significant employment and wealth for their people through this hotel and other enterprises).

Bryan was having breakfast with Richard Brodeur ("King Richard," the goalie who led the Vancouver Canucks to the Stanley Cup final once).

Bryan's invitation to join him for breakfast was a courtesy call, but it turned into much more.

About a year before, I had been contacted by John Chabot, another Aboriginal hockey player who had made the NHL, who also carried his heritage and a deep concern for the future of his people wherever he played or went.

Chabot had the idea of an NHL Aboriginal Alumni Role Model Hockey team, and I had been working kind of loosely with John to organize an exhibition game between Indian stars of the NHL against some local Winnipeg team to raise money for charity.

Bryan took over that very morning and the result was "Legends and Legacies," an exhibition hockey game between local Aboriginal players led by Bryan and Stan Jonathan, against a Winnipeg Jets Alumni team headed up by Dale Hawerchuk, Morris Lukowich and Thomas Steen.

The show itself was a huge smash. I'd been fortunate enough to play with the best Aboriginal players in Manitoba at one time or another, and they were more than excited and willing to suit up for this showcase. Of course, all their business associates, family and friends wanted to come out and watch. We featured Native performing arts talent between periods, entertainers such as Aaron Peters, Sierra Noble, the Asham Stompers Square Dance Group, C-Weed, Rhonda Head (who sang the national anthem before the game in Cree as well as English), Metis jigger Ryan Richard and powwow dancers. We sold over 7,000 tickets, half of which were sold to junior and senior high schools in First Nations communities throughout Manitoba. The show was entertaining, provided a positive showcase of Aboriginal talent, athletic and artistic, and provided inspiration and hope to our audience by featuring role models they could aspire to.

Financially, it was a "push." Proceeds were to be donated to help the White Buffalo Spiritual Society to create employment within a framework of instilling knowledge and pride about First Nations history and culture. But the costs of staging such an event are high, and admission costs had to be kept down so that citizens of all incomes could afford to attend, so we barely broke even. This despite the fact that the entire event was organized and staged by volunteers—and we are forever in the debt of about 100 Winnipeggers, especially Wayne Mezzo, Glenice Smith and Dale Willson.

The feedback we received about this event was overwhelmingly positive. Everybody agrees that we should do it again. But six months of eighteen-hour days seven days a week, burned everybody out. We're happy that we accomplished what we did, and we have all moved on. If anybody else wants to pick up this ball and run with it, I have a box full of files that contain a game plan and precedents for everything that you need to do to stage such an event (posters, fundraising letters, etc.) in the future.

★ ★ ★ ★ ★

Bryan stays in touch with Winnipeg by playing in an NHL Legends Game against the Winnipeg Police Service to raise money for charity every year. He has also developed a hockey school in Winnipeg with former Winnipeg Jets superstar Thomas Steen and Shaun Chornley of the Winnipeg Police Service, where Bryan passes on tips to local prospects. And, of course, it is all much more than stickhandling tips, and tape-to-tape passing tips.

"My teams are going to be competitive. My teams are going to kind of reflect Bryan Trottier. Do I expect them to play like Bryan Trottier? No. But I expect them to play with passion and the same intensity that Bryan Trottier played with. Because, you know, I can have a system and I can have a group of individuals that play. It doesn't mean that I need 20 superstars. I just need a group of guys that are committed to each other and committed to winning."

And that—with all the rest that you have read here—says it all about Bryan Trottier's philosophy towards hockey. Towards Life?

"There is more good in life than bad," Bryan summed up. "I am not 'anti-anything.' I come 'right down the middle.'" Spoken like a true centre man.

GEORGE ARMSTRONG

was a tremendous athlete who led the Toronto Maple Leafs to four Stanley Cup championships. The longest serving captain in NHL history is a member of the Hockey Hall of Fame. George is immensely proud of his First Nations heritage and was often asked to represent Canada's indigenous people. It was difficult for this sportsman to reconcile racial stereotypes, Indian history and culture and issues like Treaty Rights, land claims and self-government with his background growing up in southern Ontario.

O-Pee-Chee/Hockey Hall of Fame

Imperial Oil-Turofsky/HHOF

BLAIR ATCHEYNUM

spent most of his professional hockey career in the minor leagues but Blair learned the values of "giving back to his community" from his father (also a career minor leaguer). The Atcheynums, father and son, recognized that hockey allowed their family to escape the poverty of life on an Indian Reserve and Blair was one of the first to volunteer at the Aboriginal Role Model Hockey School in Saskatoon.

HENRY BOUCHA

was well-known for wearing an Indian headband in the (then) helmet-less NHL.

JOHN CHABOT

spent most of his professional hockey career playing in Europe, but also spent time with the Montreal Canadiens, the Detroit Red Wings and an NHL Aboriginal Alumni team which is available to play exhibition games and conduct skills clinics and role model workshops for young people.

RON DELORME

ended up playing for the Colorado Rockies and their Head Coach Don Cherry. While player and coach would develop a solid friendship and working relationship based on mutual respect in Denver, the relationship between Delorme and Grapes got off to a sour start in Boston when then Canuck Delorme taunted then Bruins Coach Cherry by pretending to shoot an arrow into the Boston bench. Cherry was held back physically from fighting Delorme, so this feisty Indian ended up battling (period by period) Boston tough guys Terry O'Reilly, John Wensink and Stan Jonathan.

THEOREN FLEURY

The diminutive Theoren Fleury (seen here dwarfed by a couple of American players) overcame his small size to set almost every scoring record established by the Calgary Flames. Fleury may be just as well-known for sticking up for Native-Canadian teammate Everett Sanipass against the Russian Bear in what would turn into a bench-clearing brawl squaring off the world's top two junior teams called the "Punch-up in Piestany."

Paul Bereswill/HHOF

STAN "LITTLE CHIEF" JONATHAN

is commonly referred to as a "six-foot-three man who was put in a compactor until he came out five-foot-seven" and "pound for pound the toughest man in the NHL." Here Stan is pictured in a more unfamiliar role as a "peacekeeper."

REGGIE LEACH

"The Riverton Rifle" winds up for a rush from behind his own net in this game against the Toronto Maple Leafs. More often than not, such a rush would cullminate in a "rifle blast" at the other end of the ice.

LEBRET EAGLES

Surnames like "Bird" and "Keewatin" and "Cardinal" and "Bull" dot the lineup of the 1996 Lebret Eagles, whereas previously, the rosters of teams in the Saskatchewan Junior Hockey League rarely included any players from First Nations backgrounds.

Noel Starblanket

JIM NIELSON

rose from an orphanage to finishing second to the legendary Bobby Orr in balloting for the Norris Trophy—which is given annually to the top defenseman in the NHL.

TED NOLAN

achieved his greatest success as a Head Coach, leading his teams to Memorial Cup Canadian Junior Hockey Championship tournaments four times. Ted is pictured here with the Jack Adams Trophy which honoured him as Top Coach in the NHL—a trophy that Ted would throw down the stairs to his basement after he was blacklisted—an exile that would last ten years, reasons for which will remain unclear forever. Unfortunately, the very day this book was going to press, Nolan was relieved of his duties as Head Coach of the New York Islanders because of "philosophical differences" with Isles General Manager Garth Snow.

OCN BLIZZARD

The OCN Blizzard won the Manitoba Junior Hockey League championship five years in a row. Ho Hum. Here's another trophy for the most successful Junior A franchise in Canadian history.

EVERETT SANIPASS

shown here in his Windsor Spitfires Ontario Junior Hockey League uniform, is best known for being the "first man in" for the "Punch-up in Piestany"—the bench-clearing, lights out brawl between Canada and the Soviet Union which got both teams kicked out of the World Junior Hockey Championships in Czechoslovakia.

GARY SARGENT

was "all-American"—who excelled in baseball (Sargent turned down offers from the Minnesota Twins) and football (he turned down 15 college football scholarships). Sargent made his mark in professional sports in the sport most associated with Canada—hockey.

FRED SASAKAMOOSE

was the first Indian to play in the National Hockey League "I got very lonely but the Blackhawks wouldn't buy me a plane ticket. I ended up taking a taxi 700 miles to home. My wife, Loretta, said 'I'm not going.' I stayed home."

HHOF

BRYAN TROTTIER

was truly a leader on and off the ice. Leading the New York Islanders to four Stanley Cups as their captain, adding two more NHL titles as a sage veteran leader in Pittsburgh, then another as an Assistant Coach in Colorado. Bryan served as President of the National Hockey League Players Association and here, Bryan leads the fans in Nassau Coliseum in a celebratory cheer.

Paul Bereswill/HHOF

Mecca/HHOF

6

THE BEST INDIAN FIGHTER

If anybody knows who was the absolutely best Indian fighter, the toughest "Injun hombre" in the NHL, it would be Don Cherry. Not only did this legendary AHL and NHL player and coach skate alongside and stand behind the bench with some of the top scrappers—white, red, yellow or black—Cherry coached Stan Jonathan, who is regarded as the best Indian fighter most people ever saw, including the likes of more modern-day First Nations players such as Craig Berube and Chris Simon.

And, of course, Cherry produced and mass marketed the Rock 'em Sock 'em home video series, which required him to study countless hours of professional hockey fights, and pick the very best.

According to Cherry, the toughest and best scrapper he ever witnessed, of any ethnic background, was the relatively unknown Ron Delorme—an Indian from Saskatchewan who played with the Colorado Rockies and the Vancouver Canucks for most of his career.

Cherry is full of hockey stories, and Delorme is one of his favourite all-time characters.

"I was coaching the Bruins against Vancouver the first time I saw Ronnie Delorme play... and what stood out about Ronnie was the way he stood up for himself and his teammates.

"We had a real tough team in Boston, with plenty of punching power in the lineup. Well, I never saw anything like what I saw the first time we played against Delorme. First period, this skinny Indian kid fights Terry O'Reilly to a standstill. Second period, he takes John Wensink on and holds his own. Finally, in the third period, he goes at it with Stan Jonathan. One guy, and he takes on our toughest guys, one by one, period by period. Ron Delorme was a good, clean fighter. No dirty stuff. Just straight up, blow for blow, and he wouldn't back down from any of them!

"Fighting takes a lot out of a player. To be able to keep going like that in the third period was incredible. I think Ronnie is the only guy who has ever done that."

★ ★ ★ ★ ★

That was a great story the first time I heard it during an interview with Don Cherry for the *They Call Me Chief* documentary. Cherry, of course, is one of Canada's most famous citizens, certainly the most popular on-air television personality in hockey nation-wide. Don is knowledgeable, opinionated and, when he "endorses" a player, you know there is some credibility behind it all.

Don Cherry's credentials are impeccable to some, questionable to others. Before we go on to tell our story of Ron Delorme's career, it is relevant to establish the credibility of Delorme's biggest backer, from our own direct experience with this icon who the Canadian public treasures like a vintage wine—or tolerates like too many other Canadian whines.

★ ★ ★ ★ ★

Prior to producing the documentary, the only experience I had with Don Cherry was the image I saw on my TV screen that he presented on his five-minute "Coach's Corner" show, which has become a mainstay of our typical Canadian winters of *Hockey Night in Canada*. My experience was basically the same as any other hockey fan in Canada has with Cherry, who offers his insight, experience and expertise about the latest goings-on in hockey every Saturday night. And I generally find myself in agreement with Don's point of view every second Saturday night.

During the production of our documentary, we desperately needed an interview with Don Cherry, because he had coached Stan Jonathan and we knew he could provide the best play-by-play or blow-by-blow analysis of the video footage of the Jonathan–Bouchard fight we had obtained from WSBK-Boston, because Don was behind the Boston bench that night.

Don's son, Tim, set up the interview in their restaurant in Mississauga, Ontario. When we arrived, Tim greeted us and showed us to the space where the interview would take place, and we started to set up. I could see Don Cherry moving about in a distant office. I was quite apprehensive because Don is much quicker mentally than he ever was on skates, and I'm not as bright as Ron McLean, who often gets skewered by Cherry in "the Corner." I was completely ready to just ask the questions that needed to be asked, get the content we needed to flow through our doc, and duck out.

Sincerely, I really, really did not expect the reception we got. As soon as were ready to start, Don walked onto our set and it was like we had known this guy all of our lives! Don put me and the crew at ease so easily and quickly, we were completely taken aback.

The simple truth was that this icon made me feel like a peer in absolutely no time at all, and that is no easy feat, given my limited background and experience.

We were using 30-minute beta videotapes and I figured we'd be lucky to fill one tape, considering Don's busy schedule—the CBC had made him a finalist in their series Top Ten Canadians of All Time—and other things, like perhaps me asking stupid questions. After rolling through a couple of tapes, and my camera operator saying "we have to change tape" for the second time, as well as my being completely out of questions, stupid or otherwise, Don said, "[Have you] got enough? You want some more stories? Is there anything else you'd like to ask? I can give you some more material if you'd like!"

Suffice to say that I deeply appreciated the cooperation Don gave to us. And there was more waiting for us back in our hometown of Winnipeg.

Throughout this book, I have mentioned the hockey stick we were carrying around to raise money for that charity for unwed teenage moms back home. Of course, we asked "Grapes" to sign the stick, and Don complied (even signing for Blue, his bull terrier, with a paw print.)

Yet there was more. When we got back to Winnipeg, there was a huge box of swag for us in our office that Don had arranged to ship immediately. There were *Rock 'em, Sock 'em* videos, T-shirts, pucks, pictures and all sorts of other memorabilia—accompanied by a note from Don Cherry that read, "Please feel free to sell or auction off any of this material to raise money for your wonderful program."

Don's public image is rough and tough and gruff, but really, he is a very nice guy, and obviously quite sentimental. You could even call him an "old softie."

★ ★ ★ ★ ★

But this chapter is about Ron, not Don, and I have to admit that Don Cherry, despite providing us with 90 minutes of material, did not provide us with the whole story about that night Ron Delorme took on those "three bears." We learned that Cherry was being rather gracious in his telling and Ron Delorme was no Goldilocks when it came to this particular incident. As a matter of fact, Cherry himself almost became the first man in during this fracas, and with good reason.

Delorme isn't particularly proud of his behaviour that night, but Cherry didn't want to cast a bad light on a bad night for a feisty little Indian who would eventually become a good friend.

So Don clammed up. Don Cherry! Honest!

★ ★ ★ ★ ★

Fortunately, Delorme was willing to tell the whole story about what happened on that night in Boston.

"I fought those guys, yeah, but there's another little story behind all that I'm kind of embarrassed to tell you, because, actually, I started the whole darn thing. You see, in those days, when I scored, I used to pull an arrow out of a make-believe quiver on my back and make it look like I was shooting it into their goalie or their bench, which is a real hot-dog move. Early on in that game, I scored against Gerry Cheevers or Gilles Gilbert and when I fired an arrow into their bench, Don Cherry was so upset he was actually coming after me. I was already going back to my bench and they were holding him back. He was taking his jacket off wanting a piece of me!

"So I got up, you know, I stood up on my bench like I'm going to 'go' with him and, all of a sudden, he says 'I'll get my guys after you,' to which I says, 'Go ahead!' And I didn't get much time to think about it until after and then I thought, 'Oh my goodness! I gotta face O'Reilly, Jonathan and Wensink and all these guys!' But, you know? When it came time, when it happened…I took them on.

"My first experience was not great. With O'Reilly, well, he was an experienced veteran, but I thought I was going to knock him out with the first punch and I swung so hard I spun all the way around but I missed and I fell down on my ass and O'Reilly just looked at me and he says, 'Well, get up!' He was laughing so hard! At first.

"But I did get up…and I think all three fights were pretty even. Yeah, I remember that game very well!"

Eventually, Cherry would become very impressed with Delorme when they were paired together in Denver (Cherry as coach of the Rockies and Delorme as a reliable third- or fourth-line player).

"Don believed in me, and I believed in him so much that I would go through a wall for him, and I did. My best years in hockey were playing for Don Cherry. He was a player's coach. He would give you a little bit of rope, just don't take too much. As long you gave Don your best effort, he would back you all the way. You can ask anyone who ever played for him.

"You know, when we were first paired together in Denver, Don was still mad at me about the bow-and-arrow thing, so the first thing he says to me is, 'Kid, you're gonna have to give up that quiver and arrow thing because all that does is get the other team mad.' I said, 'Okay. Not a problem.'

"After he had a taste of me for about a month and saw what I was doing for him—like I say, I went through walls for this man and I still would today—Don came back to me and he asked, 'Kid, do you want to do what you did in the past? Do you want to do that arrow thing? Go ahead!'

"But I couldn't do it. Because I knew what his true feelings about that matter were."

Cherry and Delorme soon developed a bond that became as strong as family. With an understanding so unique that few of us outsiders can understand it.

"Later on, I got into a scrap with Gordie Lane and he hit me with his stick and kind of punctured my cheekbone. We had two games we were playing, Philadelphia and Edmonton, and I didn't want to show two tough teams that I was afraid. I told Don I was going to play.

"I was scheduled to go into the hospital for an operation but I said, 'I'm gonna play…So, the one game I played, they put a special helmet on me to cover my jaw. And right away, what do I do? I was going to challenge Dave (Cement Head) Semenko for acting up against my teammates. I'd fought him a number of times before, but it probably would have been a mistake at this time because I was already caved in on this part [Ron points to a side of his face].

"Don asked how I was and I think I said, 'I can't hardly open my mouth' and I could see his respect for me as a guy who would play for him in those conditions. He stopped me from going over the bench for my next shift and told me to sit out and get the operation.

"Fighting Semenko at that time would have been tough, but you can never show that you are afraid in the NHL. Don saw what was going on and saved me from myself."

If Ron's version of Don's stories don't make sense, that's because there is so much about a "jock mentality" that doesn't seem to make sense to ordinary people.

Yet, I've seen it work. I've seen this jock mentality, in actual practice, preserve and promote sportsmanship and fair play, even during the most hellish of scraps. Accomplishing things that purists and pacifists can only dream about. Many of these athletes cannot articulate what they achieve. But unless they are bullies or braggarts, I salute them, because they are doing things we can only watch and try in vain to explain.

★ ★ ★ ★ ★

In the end, Don's faith in Ron would cost Don his job. Management in Denver wanted to keep another player, this rookie, first-round draft pick, on their roster. Don considered the kid to be a prima donna, and spoiled. Cherry sent the rookie down to the minors for seasoning.

But Don also sent that kid down because he wanted to keep a spot open on his roster for Delorme—a tireless worker who would bring the meat to the table of Don's lunch-bucket brigade. When Colorado's management was informed of Don's moves, they informed Don that he was no longer welcome behind the Rockies bench.

Don Cherry ended up in front of a CBC camera, where his popularity and legend now rivals Foster Hewitt's. And Ron Delorme was shipped off to Vancouver—where he achieved success off the ice as well.

★ ★ ★ ★ ★

The faith and brotherhood Don Cherry extended to Ron Delorme would be extended by Delorme to his Indian brothers in the NHL.

"After my fight with Stan Jonathan, Stan said, 'You know, Ron, Natives shouldn't be fighting Natives.' And I agreed. Brothers shouldn't fight brothers. Stan and I figured that there's 660 guys in the League out there, why should we fight each other? There's only 10 of us! I mean, there's 650 other guys to look after!

"Then again, I did go after Bryan Trottier once, only because it was playoff time and there is a time and place for everything. I thought, 'We'll just take care of this after the game when we can talk, but right now, we got to win!'"

★ ★ ★ ★ ★

We'll let www.hockeydraftcentral.com provide the background on Ron Delorme: "Ron Elmer Delorme. Born: September 3, 1955, North Battleford, Saskatchewan. Selected in fourth round, No. 56 overall by Kansas City

Scouts. Position Centre/Right Wing. Height 6-2. Weight 182. Part Cree Indian. Nicknamed 'Chief'."

Sigh!

When Ron Delorme was a "little chief," he started playing hockey in a little town in Saskatchewan. "Cochin was about 150 miles northwest of Saskatoon. It was school hockey and I also played 'lake hockey.' I got noticed by a scout from the New York Rangers who used to bring his kids to play on the lake, and he encouraged me to play in the city [Saskatoon].

"That was quite an experience for me, going into the city. I didn't grow up on a reserve even though I am treaty; I grew up in a resort town, but small, and we did things a certain way. When I first walked into a dressing room in the city, I just put my equipment on over my clothes, which was normal for me, but everybody else had hockey underwear. When I was done, my jeans and shirt were soaked with sweat. Everybody else showered after the game but that wasn't normal where I came from.

"But I got noticed and I ended up at St. Thomas College for two years. The program there was excellent, just like at Notre Dame [in Wilcox, Saskatchewan, home of the Hounds], where kids come from all over the world."

Delorme also benefited from the Indian hockey scene in Saskatchewan "on the side." In those Indian hockey circles, this scrawny kid was bouncing around the big time with the big boys by the time he was 15.

"I played with Fred Sasakamoose when I was just a 15-year-old. I got asked to join a team that went to a tournament in Kamloops, BC. It turned out to be a great experience for two reasons. One, I got listed by Vernon. Actually, four of us got listed. Charlie Shear, Brian Baptiste, myself and a guy from up north."

Getting listed meant a chance to get noticed by the mainstream junior teams. "And I got to play with Fred Sasakamoose, which was the ultimate for any Indian kid from Saskatchewan.

"Freddie was a great player, but in this tournament, he had to be more of an enforcer. He took care of me. I was a skinny little 15-year-old, and guys were coming after me and Fred took care of me. He was fighting for me. He was a very skilled hockey player, but he was fighting for me."

★ ★ ★ ★ ★

Ron Delorme was what NHL scouts would call a "late bloomer" and had to play as an overage junior and bounce around the minor leagues before making it to the "show."

Delorme slowly climbed the hockey ladder starting with the Prince Albert Raiders (when they were in the Tier Two Saskatchewan Junior Hockey League), and then moved up to Swift Current in the Western Junior League, a franchise that relocated to Lethbridge for Ron's final year of junior. Delorme played on a line with Terry Ruskowski and Tiger Williams in Swift Current, all of whom went on to successful NHL careers.

"What I remember most about my junior career was that it made my dad buy a car. Dad never had a car before because he said he didn't need one. So he walked five miles to and from work. But he finally bought a car because now he had to drive me to games 90 miles or more away."

Dad came in handy in another, more important, way. "That New York Rangers scout had recognized me because of my talent. But I was getting close to quitting because there were so many racial taunts directed towards me, and I started getting known as this 'wagonburner.' I really had a rough time to deal with it, but long talks with my dad really helped."

Delorme's dad, like many Indian dads, had plenty of first-hand experience with racism, and some sage advice to pass on: the seven sacred teachings of the Grandfathers—respect, love, goodness, truth, humility, courage and knowledge.

Ron began to practise the teachings his dad passed on, every day. But he maintains that wasn't quite enough. It took some "tough love" and practical advice from a real tiger to take him over the top.

"I still had been dealing with it all physically. The sad part is that I became an aggressive person from it. Guys on the ice were treating me based on my race all the time. Then, the best words of wisdom that was given to me came from Dave 'Tiger' Williams. He told me, 'You can't keep fighting every time they call you a name. You are what you are.' I thought about it and I decided to be proud of my heritage. If I was going to blame anyone, it could only be my parents, and that would be crazy!

"Tiger said, 'If you want to hurt these people, look at the scoreboard. Just score goals! That is the way to keep these people really, really quiet.' And that's what I did.

"It isn't like they report in the press where they say kids are protected from racial taunts. Or, at least it wasn't in my younger days. It was very difficult because I simply thought I was succeeding like everybody else, but there was always this negative stuff attached to me.

"Then, of course, there was the loneliness. And, being the only Aboriginal on my junior teams, we were different socially. I had never been told to watch a light before crossing a street or told what time to go to bed. There were all these rules. Fortunately, I was somewhat integrated because I didn't grow up completely in a reserve environment.

"And I started to realize there was this stigma against Native kids. I was watched carefully because for some reason they thought I might not behave like the other kids. And I quickly realized that I had to be better than a white kid who had the same skills as me if I wanted to stick.

"There was a Native kid who was way better than me, Charlie Shear, but he had a few discipline problems, and he didn't make it. I often wonder how big a star he could have become. Those discipline problems were minor things, but they turned out to be major if an Indian kid did it."

★ ★ ★ ★ ★

Delorme's professional hockey career began in the WHA with the Ottawa Civics, but after 22 games, he switched to Denver to play four seasons with the NHL's Colorado Rockies, who had drafted him when they were the Kansas City Scouts. Ron's best season was 1979–80 when he scored 19 goals and added 24 assists for 43 points in 75 games. His final totals were split evenly between 83 goals and 83 assists for 166 points in 524 games. The highlight of his career was when he played an integral role in helping a Cinderella Canucks squad from Vancouver, led by the stellar netminding of "King Richard" Brodeur, to the Stanley Cup finals, where they lost to the New York Islanders of Bryan Trottier.

The key statistic that defined Ron Delorme's career was the 667 minutes in penalties he racked up. This wrecked Ron's body, and his career was plagued by injuries due to his fearless style of play.

The write-ups in the media guides went like this: "Missed part of 1979–80 season with knee injury…missed part of 1980–81 season with separated shoulder…missed part of 1982–83 season with strained knee ligaments…missed most of 1984–85 season with a left knee injury [this one incurred during a collision with Calgary Flames defenseman Jamie Macoun which ended both Delorme's season and his career]."

Delorme followed up his playing career by scouting amateur players for the Canucks from 1986 to 2000, and then was named Chief Amateur Scout for three years. He eventually climbed the management ladder to become, ironically, Vancouver's Chief Scout.

"It was the first time in my life there was a valid reason for me to respond to people when they properly addressed me as a Chief. During my playing days, I got called Chief so often, I stopped responding to 'Ron.' It was only when I heard 'Chief' that I would turn around. Now I really was a Chief, but most people started calling me Ron or Mr. Delorme [shakes his head]."

★ ★ ★ ★ ★

Like the other Indians described in this book, there is another side to Ron Delorme. Like Fred and Reggie and Bryan and Stan, Ron Delorme is heavily involved in "giving something back."

We began to uncover the other side of Ron Delorme by the very way he handled our request for an interview for the documentary.

The time constraints of the documentary format caused us to dole out our available air time most preciously. We couldn't tell the complete story of every player's career, and, as a matter of fact, we had to focus on isolated aspects of each individual player's career to highlight subject areas of concern (for example, we focused on racism in our coverage of Fred Sasakamoose, and alcohol abuse with Reggie Leach, even though both were seriously affected by both issues). Ron Delorme was well-known for starting the

Aboriginal Role Model Hockey School in Saskatoon, therefore, our focus on Ron was the positive development of Native youth, not his career.

Ron understood, and he cooperated to the max.

We had scheduled an interview with Delorme for an evening in Regina well in advance. Then Ron got late word that he had to be in Saskatoon that evening because the NHL draft was pending. Most other people would have simply blown us off or rescheduled the interview, but not Ron Delorme.

Instead of conveniently changing his itinerary and taking a direct flight from Vancouver to Saskatoon, Ron stayed to our original plan and flew into Regina, rented a car, met us in the hotel room, allowed himself to be interviewed for as long as we needed or wanted (which turned out to be for three hours), and then drove up to Saskatoon in that rent-a-car.

Ron Delorme literally went out of his way because he had made a commitment to us and he proved to be a man of his word.

★ ★ ★ ★ ★

In Indian country, Ron is most famous for starting the Aboriginal Role Model Hockey School in Saskatoon.

"I remembered all those Native kids who were better than me at lake hockey, and at the Indian tournaments, and even in junior camps…and I started figuring out why I made it to the NHL, even though I wasn't as good a player. It was attitude. Two ways. Both the way I was being looked at, and the way I looked at things.

"I wanted more kids to live their dreams, just like I did, so I decided to start this hockey school with Kevin Tootoosis of the Federation of Saskatchewan Indian Nations. And the first thing we said to the kids was, 'Don't get cut because you are a discipline problem, or you relaxed, or you are lonely or you cut yourself in any way. You've got to at least try, and if you are going to get cut, make sure that it's because of your skill and ability.'

"And that is what the school was all about. To give these kids an idea of what it takes to be a player. No matter if they want to move on professionally or just feel better about themselves; there is a prescription, and I wanted to pass it along."

★ ★ ★ ★ ★

"I have learned so much as I moved on to scouting. And I've heard too much in the scouting rooms that bothers me. I don't like to name teams but at one time in the NHL, there was this perception of this one Native kid who scored 60 goals and had 100 points in junior; he could skate, he saw the ice, he had everything you could want in a player! But I heard the scuttlebutt in the scouts' room; I heard the guys talking about this kid, that he was drinking, he had problems off the ice drinking.

"Well, that kind of woke something up in me and I went to find out about this kid. I went snooping—scouts are sniffers—and I found out there was not a problem. He was no different than the guys I was sitting beside in that scouts' room, but that was the perception based on one guy stereotyping this kid. Somebody else hears that, and it just filters down the road. And I think that is so unfair. They say the kid has a drinking problem and I ask, does he drink seven days a week or just on weekends and they say they don't know but he has a drinking problem. I asked the kid if he drank and he said he had one or maybe two beer after a game, but that became five to this scout. I say that the 19 guys this kid is sitting beside in the dressing room probably have the same "problem".

"And then we would draft a guy from Russia and we know nothing about that guy. The perception of that Native kid was so unfair. So that kid ended up working at my hockey school for six years.

"And there are guys like Gino Odjick, who joined my school the very first year. Gino makes a million dollars a year. I can't give Gino no million dollars. I give him a couple of thousand for his time. He didn't come for money. He knows my dream to try and encourage and motivate kids to try and follow their dreams just like we did."

★ ★ ★ ★ ★

Ron Delorme cannot claim to have ever been a fan favourite in Denver or Vancouver, but his work ethic and feisty nature made him a popular player. When that knee injury ended his career, he became a mainstay in management on Canada's West Coast, starting out as a scout.

While making such "finds" as Gino Odjick, Delorme also found some adventures he didn't expect, travelling the trails a scout must traverse almost 365 days a year. "I had a very bad experience one time. It was based on a redneck situation in North Dakota. There was a big debate based on the Native people being called the Fighting Sioux and well, they don't want that. It's a big issue there and they were going to have a vote, but some gentleman from Las Vegas, who was alumni there and owns a casino, was building a new rink for the University of North Dakota hockey team."

Ralph Englestad, who owned the Imperial Palace in Vegas (which, by the way, contained a secret Nazi war room full of memorabilia from the Hitler era in Germany), was the UND alumnus Delorme is referring to. Englestad had committed the money to build a new arena for the hockey teams of his alma mater, but also threatened to cancel his commitment if the local Sioux nations got their way and stopped the university from using their name, likeness and image as a mascot for their sports teams. It was a hot issue between Indian and white people, one of many that have festered ever since the Battle of the Little Big Horn in Montana to the west and the Incident at Ulm in Minnesota to the east.

"They were getting a new rink but, well, apparently, if they change the name, he pulls the money. The people were going to vote and say they were at least debating it and, all of a sudden, the money came in and the people said 'no way,' we're going to stick with the name. So lots of these issues were going on.

"I was scouting the UND hockey team and when I was driving home, I stopped in a rest area and I went to the washroom. And I got attacked by three guys based on my race, based on what I am. They called me everything in the book, for being a red Indian drunk and everything else.

"I didn't do anything. I mean, there were three guys. I can take care of myself but I'm pretty smart, too, and I wasn't going to do anything stupid.

They had surrounded my car and they hauled me out of the car and started beating me up.

"But I was able to get back into the car and I headed for the highway. It was a four-laner (Interstate 29) going north and south, so I was going to head north to Winnipeg, but this guy got in his truck and blocked that road off, so I turned and made a big U-turn and I was going to try and make a hard left turn on the entry in but I couldn't make it. They chased me and hit my car and they chased me up the wrong way of the Interstate highway and I was going against traffic on the Interstate.

"Can you picture that? It was like a movie! They chased me up the highway, I mean, the wrong highway…but I got away. It seemed to be instinct on their part. Or maybe it was because there was the issue about using that name at the time. Maybe they were just picking on Canadians. Maybe I was just in the wrong place at the wrong time. But it was just sort of an uncomfortable place at the time…so I got it.

"If you look at my experiences growing up, they're still existing there today. Some of the bad experiences I had as a young guy, growing up defending what I was. And all of a sudden, here I am, in the wrong place at the wrong time, defending nothing really, based on what I had no knowledge about. I had just heard about the Fighting Sioux thing."

It amazes this writer how these accounts of racism and hatred that these warriors on ice like Ron Delorme relate seem to remain full of wonder and innocence. To this day, Ron Delorme doesn't study issues such as the use of a race of human beings as mascots. That is for academics. Ron doesn't really care that much about this issue, yet he had to deal with it directly.

Readers of books like this don't have to deal directly with these issues either, but it serves a purpose to pause here and try to guide the public gently to a higher understanding, hopefully without lecturing, preaching, creating guilt feelings or hitting people over the head about the use of Indians as sports mascots, in advertising and in the media.

★ ★ ★ ★ ★

First Nations people have been used as mascots by sports teams ever since sports teams started giving themselves names. Warriors, Braves, Chiefs and Indians are the most popular.

One of the most well-known and popular nicknames provides the essence to the reason Indians object to being used as mascots by sports teams.

The National Football League team in Washington goes by the name Redskins. If we take the time to learn the history behind the origin of this term, we begin to understand why it should not be used, just as the word "nigger" should never be used.

In the early days of pioneer settlement by Europeans in North America, settlers in New England had to clear the land of trees, boulders, wild animals…and Indians. Naturally, Indians were the most difficult to get rid of, being best able to fight back, and doing so fiercely since they had lived on this land for thousands of years. Therefore, a bounty of $100 was paid to any settler who killed an Indian. All the settler had to do was bring in the skull from the dead Indian.

With muskets being much more effective than arrows, the number of skulls piling up behind the bounty offices got way too high, so the bounty hunters were told that it was okay to just bring in the scalp of the "savage." But some of the white settlers got greedy and started killing off their black or brown-haired Caucasian brethren and bringing in those scalps. The solution to that problem was that every scalp that was turned in had to have a piece of "red skin" attached to it, or the hundred bucks was not to be paid.

And this is how the term "redskin" originated. Over the years, the term "dirty, thieving redskin" began to be used like terms such as "lazy, shiftless, nigger." This completely racist term, which celebrates the genocide of a race of people is loudly proclaimed and supported in the capital of the United States of America! Indians are told to "get over it" or "stop having such a thin skin," when these fans dress up in headdresses made of cardboard and chicken feathers, with "war paint" on their faces, and slap themselves in their mouths while yelling "Woo-Woo-Woo!"

An Indian bonnet adorned with eagle feathers is a highly revered political symbol in First Nations culture. Traditional Indian dances are often sacred celebrations of the lifestyle, history and spirituality of very proud nations. To infantilize this highly advanced culture, to somehow think it can be recreated instantly and cheaply, is obviously an insult to any thinking person.

We would certainly hesitate to name a sports team the New York Negroes or the Jacksonville Jews. And we would be hauled into criminal court, or before some human rights tribunal, if we called our home team the Nashville Niggers or the Hamilton Hebes.

Dexter Manley was a defensive lineman with the Washington Redskins. Manley became famous not only for his accomplishments on the football field, but also because he was drafted out of college despite the fact he was completely illiterate—he had the reading and writing skills of a child in Grade 5.

Dexter was once asked how he felt about the fact so many Native American groups objected to the name "redskin." His reply was simply: "Well, if the people whose names we are using don't like it, we shouldn't be doing it."

Dexter Manley should lead us on this issue?

★ ★ ★ ★ ★

The practice of using Indians as mascots may never stop because there is simply too much money invested in "sports traditions."

Take the Atlanta Braves (please!). Yes, the team did away with "Chief Knock-a-Homa" (an actor who would dance around a teepee every time a Brave hit a home run), but the fans in Atlanta still maintain a ridiculous cheer called the "tomahawk chop" (a rallying cry where 50,000 fans chop their hands in unison to a "hidden orchestra" (music we used to hear in Hollywood B westerns). I recall how embarrassed Jane Fonda (formerly known as left-wing fave "Hanoi Jane," and a supporter of the Vietnam War objector movement, who once did public service announcements for a draft counselling program I used to be involved with) used to look as she hacked her hand in the air by her right-wing hubby Ted Turner, owner of the Braves. But Jane, and Ted, and hundreds of thousands of fans, did the tomahawk chop.

There is a simple reason Turner rebuffed all requests by Native leaders, or activists, or militants, or warriors, or their bleeding-heart liberal supporters, to rename his team. The owners of the Atlanta Braves simply make too goddamn much money selling hats and uniforms and other trinkets with the Braves name and logo (as do the owners of the Washington Redskins). Turner deserves some credit for at least responding to overtures by Native American groups by financing a favourable movie about Apache legend Geronimo on his CNN cable television network.

But he gets away with using a race of people as mascots mainly because the debate is so very subtle in this case. After all, the logo of the Atlanta Braves is not "cartoonish" (like Chief Wahoo of the Cleveland Indians). And, on the surface, who could possibly object to being called "brave"? Being brave is a rather complimentary term in most instances. It seems very difficult for Indians to object to this without being called "overly sensitive" or "thin-skinned." But, once again, if one looks deeper, and searches for the real truth, we find that there is a valid argument against even the use of the word "brave" to describe Native Americans.

Now, I grant readers the right to consider this argument a stretch. I offer it as information for you to simply consider. Not that there is any absolute right or wrong. I just break it out for you and you can make up your own minds.

The way it goes is that, during the time of the so-called "Indian wars," the US Cavalry had to convince their troops of their superiority over the enemy, the Indian. Therefore, the word that was sent forward amongst the bluecoat troops was that, while Indians were very brave, they were also very stupid and disorganized. The American military force was more intelligent and organized, into privates, corporals, sergeants, lieutenants and so on up the ladder. Indians were just a bunch of "braves"—a pejorative term. An inferior class.

When former American President Jimmy Carter came to Winnipeg to help build homes for the Habitat for Humanity program and was presented with this argument, he steadfastly maintained that his home state's capital "honours" Indians by calling them Braves. So maybe the Indians are wrong. They might be right. Bottom line on this incident with President Carter is that a former president of the United States has a lot of influence. This is just one example of what the Indians are up against.

★ ★ ★ ★ ★

At the professional sports level, there seems to be little progress in the protests by Indians to stop being used as mascots. At the college level, there has been a lot of movement.

The NCAA has ruled that colleges must change the names of sports teams that Native Americans find objectionable. In other words, they must have the support of the First Nation whose name they choose to use. In New York, the St. John's Red Men have become the St. John's Red Storm out of general empathy. Teams that continue to use Indian names that are not sanctioned faced severe penalties.

The Florida State Seminoles will continue to be called that, because the Seminole Tribe has endorsed this usage, and will be consulted in all representations to insure that all appearances are culturally appropriate and not exploitative.

Meanwhile, back in North Dakota, the NCAA gave UND three years to gain the approval of the Standing Rock and Pine Ridge Sioux, or UND's team name must be changed, or they would face sanctions (such as loss of scholarships and ability to play in Bowl games). The Englestad family, along with many former players and alumni, are fighting vigorously to keep the name.

The so-called Indian wars are not over, after all. They certainly were not for Ron Delorme on that day, when he had to put the pedal to the metal the wrong way on I-29 facing high-speed traffic in North Dakota to escape a beating from some rednecks, about an issue he was not involved with and knew little about—just as much as the people who were chasing him, when you stop to think about it.

★ ★ ★ ★ ★

Author's Note: The author has been informed that the Board of Regents of the University of North Dakota, in order not to lose the funding offered by Ralph Englestad, decided to wait until Mr. Englestad, elderly at the time he offered his financial donation to build the Englestad Arena, simply passed on and then they could change the name of the UND team. Englestad, having learned of this, instructed the builders of the arena to incorporate the Indian head logo into every brick, tile and seat of the arena so that if they changed the name of the team, they would have to replace the entire venue. At last word, no agreement had been reached by UND and the Sioux Nation governing use of the Sioux name and image. And the owners of the Englestad Arena were preparing business plans and feasibility studies to see if they could operate their facility profitably without renting to the UND hockey team.

★ ★ ★ ★ ★

The Incident at Ulm

The Sioux Nation was facing severe hardship. The sacred Waken Tonka (buffalo) was all but gone, and Sioux leaders of this great nation who resisted being confined to a reservation appealed to the local agent from the Bureau of Indian Affairs for help with food to get through the hard winter.

"Until your people agree to live on the reservation we have set aside for you, let your people eat grass!" the agent said.

Two of the Sioux warriors returning from the Agent's comfortable lodgings, happened along a white settler's farm. They decided to help themselves to some eggs from the chicken house. The settlers wife shooed them away with her broom like some "racoons".

Humiliated, one of the warriors killed the farm wife, and a postman who happened to be at the farmhouse.

In retaliation, 3 Siousmen were hanged at Ulm, Minnesota.

7

"THEY CALL ME COACH"

"I'll never forget playing hockey on the same team as my brother, Steve. My mother [Rose] would drop us off in the morning at the rink in a town near our home in Garden River. We couldn't afford two sets of equipment so my brother would take the gloves and the stick and the helmet and go out for his shift on the ice, then he would come back to the bench and hand me the gloves and the stick and the helmet when it was my turn to go out there.

"All those people from the town must have been thinking, 'Awww! Look at those poor little Native kids, they can't even afford sticks and gloves.'

"After the games, Steve and I would skate around and practise while we waited for our mom to come and pick us up. Well, one time I fell down on the ice and my brother was using the gloves. Somebody accidentally skated over my hand and the blade sliced right across all of my fingers.

"None of those people from the town would offer this 'poor little Native kid' a ride to the hospital so I had to wait for my mother to come get me late in the afternoon. I needed a lot of stitches. It was a long wait."

★ ★ ★ ★ ★

Ted Nolan (born April 7, 1958) grew up in Garden River—a small rural First Nations community outside Sault Ste. Marie which was like so many other reserves in Ontario—tiny, overcrowded homes without running water, lack of employment or economic opportunity, and many of the social problems that plague poverty-stricken communities.

Ted handled it all with "attitude": "Growing up in Garden River was one of the best times in my entire life. When I tell people about my background, sometimes they say 'You didn't have indoor plumbing' or 'You didn't have too much money'...there was a lot of drinking, there was a lot of abuse once in a while, but you take that all away and you look at the good in the people.

"Most important, we focused on what we had, and not what we didn't have. We had what we had and we made do with what we had. Like, I couldn't afford to buy weights for working out and we didn't have a high school with a jogging track or anything like that. But we had a railway track running beside the house, and sometimes the crews would leave railway ties behind. I lifted those railway ties like a weightlifter uses barbells. And when I needed some road work, well, what better way to pace yourself than running down a railway track between evenly spaced railway ties for miles and miles?

"My mother created a rich life for us. She not only encouraged me in sports, but she instilled a strong sense of my Native heritage and culture within me. The community would be putting on a play about Hiawatha, I was 'little Hiawatha.' There would be a spiritual gathering taking place in Alberta, my mom would take us. She took us to all the powwows.

"You know, we always talk about the traditional way of life. As far as I'm concerned, hockey has always been part of that traditional life to our people. We have been playing hockey for a long time and we had a senior team right from the community called the Red River Braves...they were the Montreal Canadiens and the Toronto Maple Leafs to me as a child. Watching the Braves play and listening to the NHL on the radio was just as much a part of life as our powwows.

"Summertime was the moccasins. Wintertime was the skates. I Indian-danced until I was 16 or 17. I wasn't a very good dancer but I at least tried. I at least knew the meaning of the drum. Being Indian is not just growing long hair and putting braids in it and being an Indian that you see on TV. It's about being a First Nations person from within, I think.

"I owe a lot of that to my father, who was a very stern man. He told me to always be proud of who you are and don't let anyone push you around or be ashamed of who you are. Be strong and stand up for who you are.

"This is what our people had that made us rich. We didn't have racism in Garden River. So I didn't understand exactly what happened that day when my hand got cut."

★ ★ ★ ★ ★

The Creator works in mysterious ways.

On that fateful day that Ted's hand got sliced, Steve and Ted finally realized that sharing equipment simply could not continue. Ted and Steve also knew that, because goaltending equipment was very expensive, the local townspeople chipped in and supplied all the equipment for any kid who had the guts or patience to play goalie.

"Stevie and I flipped a coin and he lost. He turned out to be a pretty good goalie in his own right, but I got to 'play out' and I became a forward. That gave me the chance to try and stand out. Some people took notice and I was invited to try out for the Sault Ste. Marie Greyhounds. I didn't make the team, so I was assigned to the Kenora Thistles of the Manitoba Junior Hockey League."

Where perhaps "playing out" wasn't such a good thing. "I never seen anything like it. Guys would hit you from behind or spear you in the ribs with their sticks and call you 'Wahoo' or 'f' in welfare lines,' you name it.

"People were calling each other names right in the middle of Main Street. And there was a lot of fighting on Friday nights.

"They say there are turning points in your life and that was a definite turning point in my life, again, having never gone through any type of racism growing up. I used to think I was a playmaker, or a goal scorer. A stickhandler. I wanted to be like Bobby Hull or Bobby Orr. In Kenora, I had to learn how to fight. Luckily, I also started to grow."

Nolan's size provided him with physical protection, but emotionally, he was a wreck. The situation at school was pretty much the same so he stuck to himself.

"Wondering why people would treat people like that. When my brothers came to town, they had a tough time getting a hotel room. Kenora was like Alabama of the North. It's embarrassing to say that a big strapping boy like I had become was crying himself to sleep most nights. But I wasn't going to be known as a quitter. Or that somebody chased me out!

"So I stuck it out, and actually, by the end of the year, I made some good friends, white friends, and I kind of liked it at the end. I think it's kind of like with all people, once you know who they are, not their colour of skin or where they are from or their economic or social or religious background, it's who they are as people, and I made some pretty good friends by the end."

Nolan went on to play junior hockey (left wing) with the Sault Ste. Marie Greyhounds of the Ontario Hockey Association and then was drafted in the fourth round by the Detroit Red Wings. Despite the fact that few prospects, including first-round picks, crack an NHL lineup as rookies, Ted had high hopes for his first professional camp. This naivety caused a fall he had not foreseen to be that much harder and farther.

The Red Wings assigned Nolan to their farm team in the International Hockey League. In those days, the IHL was considered "red-headed cousin" to the American Hockey League.

Nolan was crushed. And he decided to give up. "I had also been considering a career in law enforcement. I was thinking about becoming an RCMP [Royal Canadian Mounted Police] officer. I went home to Garden River and I walked into the house where my mother was waiting. I will never forget what happened.

"You talk about turning points in your life. Usually, when I got home from hockey, it was kind of like, my mom would give me a big hug and 'I'm glad you're back home' type of thing. But this time, for whatever reason, my mother turned her back on me, just for maybe three seconds, but it seemed like three hours, and I knew she was upset. Because I had left something I had been thinking about and talking about forever and that was to play hockey. And here it was, my first pro camp, and I just left!

"As soon as she did that, I turned on my heel and got back on that bus. I knew that I couldn't just give up on what I had been working for my whole life. So I went down to Kansas City (IHL), and the rest is history."

That history included a gruelling climb up the minor league ladder, with the Adirondack Red Wings, the Rochester Americans and the Baltimore Skipjacks serving as rungs, before Nolan finally made the NHL. But his career was plagued by injuries, and Nolan managed to play just 78 regular season games over four seasons with the Detroit Red Wings and the Pittsburgh Penguins. Ultimately, a back injury sent him to the sidelines for good in 1985. His final NHL totals: 6 goals and 16 assists for 22 points in 78 games with 105 minutes served in the sin bin.

Ted Nolan was a gritty player who might have risen above the status of journeyman if not for the injuries which, ironically, were the unavoidable and inevitable result of the rugged style of play responsible for what success he achieved.

But, as a multitude of junior players, pros and youth from First Nations throughout Canada would find out, Ted was a teacher first and foremost. By becoming a coach, Ted Nolan would make his mark in the world. It would be a huge exclamation mark!

★ ★ ★ ★ ★

Nolan's alumni team from junior hockey gave him his coaching start. The Sault Ste. Marie Greyhounds hired Nolan as a mid-season replacement head coach in 1988 and Nolan ruled there for six years.

"I didn't get off to a very good beginning. We finished in bottom place. I heard the fans and the radio stations and the newspaper saying, 'Nolan can't coach.' It just stirred something inside of me, and I said, 'I'll prove to them I can.' My whole life has been proving to people."

And not being too proud to ask for help. From people you respect. It's an "old Indian trick"—you go seek wisdom from the Elders.

Growing up, Nolan had admired Philadelphia Flyers coach Fred Shero, whose teams won two Stanley Cups in the mid-1970s. Nolan asked Shero's son, Ray, for help.

"Ray sent me a box of material. At the top of one of Fred's notes, the best thing I read was, 'You have to learn to win with what you've got or you don't win at all.' I read it over and over and over again and I went, Man-n-n!

"It all started to come back to me from Garden River. 'You don't worry about what you don't have. You make do with what you do have.' You can't be saying 'I wish I had a better winger or I wish I had better goaltending.' I've got to work with what I've got. I have to make these athletes the best they can be."

It all ended up in an enormously successful run, considering there were almost 60 teams competing for Canada's major junior hockey championship. Nolan led the Greyhounds to the "final four" (a Memorial Cup championship berth) three straight years and capped it off with a title in 1993.

"It's extremely tough to get to the Memorial Cup Final once, and we were able to get there three times. A key to our success was recognizing and accommodating who the individual is when the sweater and the skates and the shoulder pads come off.

"Growing up in Garden River, we were taught that 'the person who collects the wood is just as important as the one who gets the deer.' My upbringing and background in a communal setting where harmony is essential to survival fit in perfectly with what's needed to make a sports team successful."

The greatest punishment in a traditional Indian community was banishment, because it was so difficult for an individual to survive in such a harsh environment as Canada's. Individual achievement was still recognized and appreciated, but there was a strong willingness to conform for the good of the whole, even by the great warriors, the protectors and the providers.

"Of course, I kept all this in the back of my mind as sort of an ingrained thing and my coaching mostly consisted of the usual 'Xs and Os' and 'rah-rah-rah' messages to the team, but we developed a kind of atmosphere—on the ice and on the bench and in the dressing room—with the Greyhounds that was successful."

The NHL took notice (who can ignore three appearances in Canada's nationally televised and nationally obsessed-over Memorial Cup?). Nolan's climb up the NHL ladder was as rapid as any river in, uh, Garden River. After spending just one season as an assistant coach with the Hartford Whalers, Nolan was named head coach of the Buffalo Sabres. To be given the responsibility of guiding an "original 14" NHL franchise with Nolan's relative inexperience was unprecedented.

Fortunately (or maybe not), expectations were low for the 1995–96 team in Buffalo. The roster was "blue collar" at best—basically 20 grunts and a superstar. The superstar was goaltender Dominik Hasek. It is widely claimed that a good goalie can take almost any team to the top, and the Sabres had the top 'tender in the world!

Dominik Hasek has accomplished everything a hockey player possibly can. The "Dominator" compares favourably with any superstar who played any position throughout hockey history. And on every stage that matters in this sport.

Hasek, a Czech, is a "foreign" player, which created a kind of love-hate relationship with North American hockey fans. But the respect and admiration for him is indeed universal—even if he broke your heart as an enemy from time to time.

Let's start with that. Nagano, Japan, 1988. The Czech Republic had a good team, but it was basically a bunch of "no-names" (after the 1998 winter Olympics, the scouting budget of every NHL team would go up and over to eastern Europe in an effort to put faces and personal histories to these no-names big time!).

Hasek had allowed only four goals during round-robin play and he faced a very hungry, and stacked, lineup of Canadian NHL superstars in the semifinal of the medal round. The game went to a shootout and five of Canada's best snipers had a shot at advancing the Canadian team to a gold medal for the first time in almost half a century. One by one, Hasek stopped Theoren Fleury, Raymond Bourque, Joe Nieuwendyk, Eric Lindros and Brendan Shanahan. The Czechs got the winning goal on their fifth try and advanced to the gold medal game against the hated Russians. Hasek blanked the Bear 1-0 and was named best goaltender at the Olympics.

Canadian hockey fans will always remember screaming "Find a way to beat this bastard!" as shooter after shooter failed to put the puck past Hasek. It was heartbreaking and frustrating and it made a lot of Canadian hockey fans angry at Hasek, but, of course, they all had to admit the guy had amazing talent, and Canadian hockey fans ended up with great respect for one Dominik Hasek, who had truly earned his nickname "The Dominator."

Hasek's play made him so popular in his home country that shouts of "Hasek to the castle" were heard throughout the Czech Republic, so much so that Hasek called the country's President Vaclav Havel and reassured him that his job was not in jeopardy. (This contact was indeed necessary as Hasek is more than just a "jock." He is a bit of a renaissance man, with a university degree in language and history; he is actively involved in numerous charities and has launched a number of high profile business enterprises. He would have been a most formidable political opponent.)

On this side of the pond, Hasek was the NHL's dominant goalie during the 1990s. He won six Vezina Trophies (top goaltender in the NHL) between 1993 and 2001, and he won consecutive Hart Trophies (most valuable player in the NHL), the first goaltender ever to do that. Wayne Gretzky, the Great One, has called Hasek "the greatest player in the game."

Thus was the situation in Buffalo when Nolan took over as a rookie head coach. Nolan recognized that you cannot treat every player equally (some need to be "guided gently to a higher understanding" and some need to be "kicked in the ass") and that superstars sometimes receive a touch of favour. But Nolan also knew what had made him successful "in the Sault." The word "team" would dominate the dialogue in Buffalo.

Okay, there is no "I" in "team" but there is the word "me." Most of the Sabres bought into Nolan's team "all for all" concept, but there was some friction between Nolan and Hasek. Neither has ever stated specifically what went wrong, but it became an integral part of a drama that would rival anything Shakespeare could come up with—complete with betrayal, beheadings and, the worst tragedy of all to an Indian person, banishment.

On the surface, everything appeared rosy, as Nolan followed up his "getting acclimatized and getting to know you" first season with remarkable, unexpected success in his second year behind the Buffalo bench. The Sabres battled their way to the top of the NHL's Northeast Division in 1996–97 and Nolan was awarded the Jack Adams Award as Coach of the Year in the NHL. Ted Nolan was on top of the world—the top coach in the top league in the world!

But voting for that trophy takes place right after the regular season (so that all coaches, including the ones who don't make the playoffs vie for the award on an equal basis). A lot would happen during the playoffs that same year that might have had voters reconsidering their choice for top coach, simply because awards such as this are not usually associated with conflict or controversy, and plenty of that surfaced in Buffalo during the post-season.

The soap opera that developed during the Sabres playoff run included all the required elements: gossip, rumour, deceit, backstabbing and eventually blacklisting. The element that would be required to turn the plot of this strange story around for Ted Nolan, revenge, would indeed be a meal best served cold—ten years cold.

Tension was already high between Nolan and Hasek from the regular season and there was a cliquish atmosphere in the Buffalo clubhouse. The Sabres opened the post-season against the Ottawa Senators. After being scored on in game three, Hasek left the game. That forced backup Steve Shields to substitute in net. Hasek claimed he felt a pop in his knee and the Sabres team doctor listed him as day-to-day.

But some of Hasek's teammates hinted that they felt he was "bailing out" on them. *Buffalo News* columnist Jim Kelley wrote an account in the next day's newspaper that detailed Hasek's injury, his conflict with Nolan, and questioned the goaltender's mental toughness. After the Senators won game five of the series, Hasek came out of the Sabres training room and responded to Kelley's request for an interview by physically attacking the reporter, tearing Kelley's shirt. Hasek issued an apology but the goalie was on his way down a very slippery slope.

After Shields starred in a big Buffalo rally to overcome Ottawa in seven games, the NHL announced that Hasek was suspended for three games for his attack on Kelley, prior to the Sabres' next Stanley Cup playoff round against the Philadelphia Flyers. The Sabres quickly fell behind the Flyers three-zip and hopes were pinned on Hasek turning around the series when he returned from his suspension. But Hasek told the Sabres training staff that he felt a twinge in his knee after the pre-game skate before game four and left the ice. Shields, who somehow seemed to shine in just these exact circumstances, managed to come up with a season-saving show to stave off elimination for one more night. But Shields was unable to duplicate that feat in game five, when Hasek duplicated his act of declaring himself unfit to play. And the Sabres season came to an end.

The accomplishments in Buffalo were recognized and well-appreciated during the off-season. General Manager John Muckler was named Executive of the Year for 1996–97 and, of course, in his second year as an NHL head coach, Ted Nolan was chosen the best in the land.

Naturally, Ted thought he would be rewarded for his achievements in Buffalo by the Sabres owners. Mostly, Ted wanted the three Rs: Respect, a Raise, and increased Responsibilities. But in an NHL organization, those things only come from the top, usually from the General Manager. And, strange as it might seem given all the success they were sharing, relations between Nolan and GM John Muckler were also strained.

There is normally no more important bond than between coach and GM; that's why one guy often assumes both positions—they must work so closely together that one guy sometimes just takes on both jobs himself. So Nolan was caught in the middle of a classic sports power struggle, starring the general manager, the head coach and the superstar. Things could only get bizarre with that kind of situation in place.

Hasek and Muckler teamed up against their mutual enemy. Hasek harmed his case by showing a lack of class (and common sense and timing) by stating, during the NHL Awards Ceremony (where Nolan was being honoured as Coach of the Year) that "it would be better for me if he [Nolan] did not return." Ironically, it was Muckler, who was himself coming off a "top dog" award (that Executive of the Year honour), who became the first fall guy. Muckler was fired prior to the 1997–98 season.

Some people claimed that Nolan had turned the players against Muckler. Nolan says that it was simply a matter of two strong-minded and strong-willed individuals having a few disagreements, and things got "blown up bigger than they should."

"I disagreed with John on some matters, and he disagreed with me, and that's the way it should be when a GM and a coach are trying to build a winning team. We depend on each other; for him to get me the players and for me to mould those players into a winning team. It's a two-way street. Unfortunately, at the time, I didn't know too many people in the business."

Muckler knew almost everybody "in the business" and, while at first it looked like Nolan would be the winner/survivor in the battle in Buffalo, Muckler's connections would win the war.

If firing Muckler seemed to make little sense, the next move that was made in Buffalo proved to be completely nonsensical. Muckler's replacement, Darcy Regier, was told that he would have the freedom to choose his own coach. Only Regier knows what went on in his own mind, but rather than replace Nolan, whose two-year contract had just expired, Regier offered Nolan a one-year contract extension, reportedly worth $500,000.

When you look at this a certain way, Regier was playing his cards artfully, or at least carefully, keeping all the options open only to him. Regier wouldn't have looked very smart getting rid of a Coach of the Year, but he had to make his own mark on the team and he might have been wary of a personality like Nolan, who couldn't seem to get along with his boss and his best player. Regier might have figured that his rather lowball offer would humble Nolan, sort of put him in his place, and the one-year length of it would buy sufficient time to sort things out.

Regier didn't account for the pride and simple sense of justice instilled in this Indian he was dealing with. Nolan knew that he had achieved a most rare feat, leading a "blue collar" team full of "grinders" to first place with only one superstar (Hasek). The five hundred grand was nowhere near the raise Nolan believed he had earned and he also had huge problems with the manner in which Regier was handling things.

"I got a call that there would be an announcement about a new contract the next morning and I didn't know the length of it, I didn't know the increase, whether that was an increase, or no increase. I think you should show the person you are negotiating with respect, and an opportunity to at least review the contract, to accept it, or even turn it down.

"You know, our people signed treaties that they didn't understand a long time ago. Now it was 1998. I was not about to sign a contract that I didn't see or didn't know what was in it. So I just turned it down before I even knew what was in it, because I didn't know what was in it."

Nolan says that Regier had never contacted his agent or revealed the contents of the contract in any form or manner. "It was one of those situations where you give something to somebody you know they are going to turn down and that is exactly what happened. But I just wished that…if you don't want me back, just tell me you don't want me back and move on, versus this process."

After rejecting Regier's offer, Nolan pitched the Jack Adams trophy down the stairs to the basement in his home. Yet it wasn't Regier's actions, or even Regier's reaction to Nolan's rejection, that would dictate the trail of torment that Nolan would endure for the next 10 years. It was Nolan's sour relationship with Muckler, a long-standing charter member of the NHL's old boys' club, that would cause Ted to toil outside of hockey's mainstream for a decade.

And, according to Ted Nolan the man, it didn't help that he was an Indian.

★ ★ ★ ★ ★

Following his departure from Buffalo, it has been reported that Nolan was offered NHL coaching jobs in 1997 by the Tampa Bay Lightning (head coach) and in 1998 by the New York Islanders (assistant coach). Nolan denies this. In any case, it would be eight years before Nolan acknowledged that he was offered an NHL coaching job again. Speculation as to why ranges from a perceived fear that Nolan was a "GM-killer" because of his acrimonious working relationship with former boss Muckler, to charges of outright racism.

Ted Nolan claims that racism played a major role in his exile from the NHL. Don Cherry doesn't agree. Now, despite Cherry's tirades and stereotypes of "chicken Swedes" and "frightened French guys," Don is not a racist. He simply points out "characteristics" in certain individuals who dominate the image of a certain race and then applies them generally to that race. The confusion over racism arises because there is always some truth to what Don says and he proves that with examples.

If a Paul Bunyan-like Swede were to sit down with Don and show him some serious log-lifting, Don would readily recognize the contrast between that tough Swede and some of the "chicken Swedes" Don, and other people, such as myself, see playing in the NHL. Then Don would (rightfully) point to examples that prove his point. Don is a difficult guy to argue with because he always has some specific examples (and almost always on videotape no less) that back up what he says and, as I said, there is always *some* truth to what he says.

Don Cherry doesn't believe that Ted Nolan was the victim of racism simply because Don doesn't believe in racism nor does he have any idea of what racism really is. That is because Don is a former player and coach in the minor and major leagues of professional hockey and racism does not make any sense at all in hockey or any other team sport. So it doesn't make any sense to Don that racism played a role in keeping Ted Nolan out of the NHL for eight years. Racism is a very complicated issue and Don Cherry doesn't have the time to study years of research and textbooks. He says what he says based on his personal experience and, in that regard, he is entitled to his opinion. To Don Cherry's credit, his opinions are based on what he knows from his experience and are always worthy of serious consideration.

Cherry maintains that Nolan's mistake was getting into a very public scrap with a respected GM like Muckler, who has friends throughout the NHL and all of the minor pro and junior leagues. Whether Muckler went out and badmouthed Nolan to all and sundry or not, hockey is a very high profile public business and the battle between Muckler and Nolan was known to all and sundry. And when it comes down to the basics, the NHL is a business, and business runs best when things run smoothly. Upsetting the apple cart is generally frowned upon, no matter who is right or who is wrong. The turmoil between Nolan and Muckler, and maybe some bad words to the good ol' boys network, may have been what kept Nolan out of the NHL.

In all likelihood, most of the NHL's business insiders would be expected to side with Muckler, age 74, since he was a known commodity who had been wheeling and dealing and caring and sharing for many more years than Nolan, age 40. Cherry maintains that Nolan should have backed off a bit, performed a little PR and made the effort to befriend (or even ingratiate) the powers that be.

Whether Cherry was right or wrong remains unanswered. But Cherry was right about one thing. Don steadfastly maintained that Nolan should get back into hockey in some way at some level. While Nolan claims there were no opportunities because he was blacklisted, and Cherry believed that Nolan was simply being stubborn, eight years passed.

"You also have to keep in mind that, if I went back to coaching junior or accepted a position in the minor leagues, I would have to make a commitment to whatever program I became involved with. That is the only way I know how to coach or play. Total dedication and loyalty. I hesitated to take a job because what if I did well and the NHL made me an offer after just a short period of time?

Eight years passed after Nolan said that; eight years before he finally ended up back behind a hockey bench

★ ★ ★ ★ ★

Those eight years were not wasted, by any means. The contract complications in Buffalo may have raised disappointment, anger, confusion and even sadness in Ted, but they also challenged his faith in himself, as much as when he almost turned his back on a hockey career when his mother turned her back on him.

But just as Rose Nolan turned an instant into a lifelong lesson for her son when it came to hockey, she would be responsible for steering Ted back to his roots, where he would change the lives of thousands of Native people throughout North America forever.

"We always talk about how important our men and our boys are in our communities, but I know the importance of Native women in our communities, our reserves and our homes," says Nolan.

"We men all walk around and we're big and macho and we pretend we're the bosses and we control the family. But when things get too tough, you ask them who they run to—they run to their mommies and ask for advice. Mothers are the birth-givers, they are the care-givers. There's certain points where fathers take them under their wing and teach them to shoot a puck or catch a ball. But as far as I'm concerned the ones that really care about the kid—you know, that rub the knee when they get bandaged up —is the mom. So there is a big, big, important role that mothers play in our homes. I don't think it's just the Native community. It's every community."

★ ★ ★ ★ ★

"My mother was killed one night by a drunk driver. I wanted to honour her memory. In a small way, I've been able to do that."

Nolan did that by forming the Rose Nolan Memorial Golf Tournament to raise funds to help other Native woman realize their dreams. To achieve goals that Native women identified for themselves, not what they were told was "good for them."

"Mom never went to university or was able to use her high school education towards a career or anything like that, but she changed the lives of a lot of other people. Mom was always there to support other women, and children, and men in the community, who wanted to improve themselves by going back to school, or maybe taking a training course, in something like carpentry, which by now would be like say, computer programming. Mom would even encourage people in the community to take ceramics lessons, something to keep them busy or productive and feeling better about themselves and bettering themselves.

"It costs money to go back to school or take courses and things like that. So, to honour my mom's memory, we set up the Rose Nolan Memorial Scholarship Fund, and began to raise money through an annual golf tournament. We've raised thousands and thousands of dollars to provide scholarships for people in the community who want to improve their lives. The tournament has spawned a number of different things, all for the betterment of the lives of the people in our First Nations."

The Ted Nolan Foundation was also established to become a vehicle for the positive social and economic change that Ted would like to realize in his community. Developed during his "time off," the Foundation is a registered charity promoting healthy lifestyle choices for young First Nations people.

Ted also became a "poster boy" for Canada's Assembly of First Nations. The image of a fit and mature adult leader like Ted Nolan, posed wearing a suit but carrying a hockey stick, is sure to stick in the minds of Native youth and motivate them to dream. And to fulfill those dreams, because after all, this Indian on the poster did it, so why can't I?

Ted soon found himself constantly on the road, visiting First Nations communities throughout Canada to speak to youth and children directly. The AFN supported his development of an Indigenous Hockey Program, which resulted in the formation of a junior team that competed in Finland.

"We hoped it would become something like Hockey Canada or USA Hockey. But that would require way more money and time and effort and resources that we could ever get. But we got players like Jonathan Cheechoo and Terence Tootoo involved and we all know how well Jonathan is doing. [Terence Tootoo, the brother of the Nashville Predators Jordin Tootoo, tragically committed suicide.]

"We've been walking around this country a long time, from reserve to reserve to community to community, and people talk about how much talent we have. Wouldn't it be great if we could assemble that talent into one team? So that's what we've been doing, and trying to find corporate funding, but that's a job itself."

Eventually, "politics" would derail Nolan's dream of forming a national indigenous team ("AFN put a guy in charge of the program who had no background in hockey and we lost our key organizers who were knowl-edgeable about the Native hockey scene," Nolan says).

It was the worst of times; it was the best of times. The high water mark came when Nolan's son Brandon saw a film clip of his Dad counselling Native kids about the dangers of sniffing glue. Brandon said, "Isn't it good that you're not in hockey anymore?"

Ted asked, "Why is that?" and his son said, "Because you wouldn't have had a chance to go see those kids."

"For him to say that…sometimes we lose sight of what matters. Brandon was right. Maybe this thing was a blessing. It showed me what was impor-tant in life.

"I loved getting up in the morning and driving my sons to school. I loved going to their hockey practices. I loved staying at home and playing my wife in stupid card games and going to a movie on Friday night. I had lost maybe a little bit of who I was.

"In eight years, you get that back. Family and home come back to you. As I travelled across the country, trying to pass on the values and the work ethic and the attitude that carried me to the NHL, I started to recall things like when I decided to make a rink in our backyard so my brother and I could practise. We didn't have running water and a hose or anything like that. I flooded that rink pail by pail and that's what I tell these kids when I talk about how to succeed in life: it's pail by pail. You do it pail by pail.

"And you make do with what you've got. You don't worry about what you don't have. And I don't just mean running water or a hose. I mean things like intelligence, or good looks, or athletic ability, or money, or status in the community, or prestige, or even fancy clothes. You make the best of what you've got!"

During his hiatus from the NHL, Ted had a lot of time and he made the best of it. He even found time to co-host a widely acclaimed and multi-award-winning television documentary series called *The Sharing Circle* with internationally renowned producer Lisa Meeches. All this was part of an effort to develop positive social, cultural, recreational, educational, economic and yes, even political initiatives that will enhance the future of Canada's First Nations.

Ted wasn't just keeping busy while he waited for his coaching career to resume. He was being productive in a very meaningful way. "To me, I wouldn't change it for nothing."

★ ★ ★ ★ ★

But change would inevitably come to him. No matter what the old boys might say, Ted was a proven master at motivating young players, one of the best at getting players to overachieve because—bottom line and despite the disputes with the likes of Hasek and Muckler—Ted Nolan is an incredible "people person."

Nolan knew he was a good coach and that he could succeed at any level if given the chance. While he didn't follow Cherry's advice and jump at whatever opportunity to get back in the game that came along, Nolan balanced those eight years re-establishing his roots in family and community with work to stay abreast of what was happening in the NHL.

"All the while, I was studying every team in the League, getting to know their personnel, their breakouts, their power play, and kind of going back to school, hopefully becoming a better coach for it all.

"The other thing is that some great coaches have gone through this. Scotty Bowman was unemployed in the coaching ranks for about four years…Pat Burns wasn't coaching and now he is. I'm not the first guy to go through this and I won't be the last. It's not an exclusive club that Ted Nolan was in. I think how you come out of it is the most important thing."

★ ★ ★ ★ ★

It wasn't a call from Don Cherry, or some heartfelt conversation with his family or friends, that finally convinced Ted to return to coaching, even though the offer he eventually received should have been beneath the notice of an NHL Coach of the Year. It was simply time to prove the powers that be wrong when he accepted the position of head coach of the Moncton Wildcats in 2005.

The Wildcats were rated 61st out of 61 major junior level teams when Nolan took over. By the time he was finished just over one year later, the Wildcats would finish one win short of winning the Canadian junior championship, falling in the Memorial Cup final to the Quebec Ramparts coached by Montreal Canadiens and Colorado Avalanche legend Patrick Roy on May 28, 2006. That success would pave Ted's path back to the "show."

But before we go there, the role of racism has to be examined, as much because it kept rearing its ugly head throughout Ted's life as out of respect for his claims that racism is real and rampant throughout the sport of hockey.

That was certainly evident during the time Ted spent coaching in Moncton. The most famous incident took place during a Quebec Major Junior Hockey League game against the Saguenéens in Chicoutimi.

During the game, some of the fans in the Centre Goerges-Vézina started making war whoops and tomahawk gestures at Nolan. Others pretended to shoot from a bow and arrow at the Moncton bench. It was all ignorant and cruel, and one would like to believe such actions do not represent the majority of fans in Chicoutimi, Quebec or anywhere in Canada. But it was done, and it is still being done in many rinks throughout the country.

Guy Carbonneau, vice-president of the Saguenéens, explained the actions with this: "It's a sporting event. There are people who go there, they're emotional, they drink, and sometimes people think they're being funny with their comments. But the comments are not funny for others."

Carbonneau's awkward apology reveals the lack of awareness, time or effort the Saguenéens had put into preventing racism. The public address system in the Vézina had exacerbated the situation by playing the "tomahawk chop" song during the game. Fans were not prevented from continuing their taunts as the Wildcats bus left the arena. For that, there is no excuse.

At first, Nolan took the "high road" in his response to the incident. "I don't know if they need better security here, but they do need better manners in this town," Nolan simply said.

But the situation escalated because of the massive publicity such incidents attract in this age of the Internet, and it ended with Nolan calling the

Chicoutimi region of Quebec the "Alabama" of the QMJHL. The commissioner of the Quebec League issued a formal apology and launched a new anti-discrimination policy. So, some good came out of it. Bill Schurman, GM of the Wildcats, was satisfied with the response from the Saguenéens, and pressed the QMJHL for more.

"We should adopt a zero tolerance rule in all of our buildings for any kind of abuse, including racial abuse. If someone suggests a racial comment, out they go. You have to have certain codes of conduct for your arenas. You can't smoke. You can't throw anything on the ice, and certainly abusive vocabulary and behaviour should become part of the rules of having a QMJHL game."

But the fact remains that racism is, in fact, present in hockey, if not in the dressing room or on the ice so much, but in the stands. Nolan claims that racism also exists in the boardrooms of the NHL and that is what kept him from returning to the NHL for such a long period of time.

★ ★ ★ ★ ★

That return begins in January, 2006, when the New York Islanders fired Head Coach Steve Stirling. Islanders owner Charles Wang, who would never be considered part of the old boys' network of the NHL, and obviously impervious to any hangovers from the Muckler episode, asked Nolan to "take over the team."

Notwithstanding Nolan's solid credentials, Wang is well-known for making moves that are at best innovative, courageous, if not adventurous, but have also been called unfamiliar, ignorant and downright stupid. The Islanders' track record of draft picks and trading away top draft picks and double troublesome trades under General Manager Mike Milbury have been seriously and repeatedly questioned. And straight away, Wang's move to hire Nolan was questioned, because it took place at the same time the Islanders were undergoing total uncertainly and transition at the level of general manager.

Nolan simply said, "This doesn't appear to be an accident, because I don't think there is any general manager who would have hired me."

Wang and the Islanders were always doing the unexpected, the unconventional, and maybe that is the simple reason Ted made it back to where he belongs as a head coach in the NHL.

The Islanders even bounced from mega-experienced General Manager Neil Smith to Garth Snow, a pretty good goaltender who had absolutely no experience as a GM. Wang was either going against the grain as usual, or perhaps he was living up to his promise to let Nolan play a large role in running the team. Whatever the reason, Ted Nolan once again found himself behind the bench of a team playing in the world's biggest and most prestigious league, the NHL.

His first two seasons coaching the Islanders have been a mixed success. The Milbury era had left the Isles with a mixture of veterans and prospects nobody expected to have much success, so the pressure to win wasn't too heavy a burden. But Nolan's teams performed better than expected (where have we seen that before?), making the playoffs in 2006–07, for the first time in three years, following an astounding 92-point season. The eighth-seeded Islanders threw a scare into Nolan's nemesis, the Presidents Cup-winning, top-seeded Sabres, before falling in five close games. And, while everybody keeps predicting the Islanders will go into the tank during Nolan's second year, they were keeping their heads above water (around the .500 mark) halfway through the season.

Wang seems to be living up to his promise to let Nolan have a strong say in the running of the team, and there haven't been any public reports about conflicts between GM Snow and Head Coach Nolan. The fact that Bryan Trottier was hired as executive vice-president of Player Development soon after Nolan was hired, and John Chabot was hired as an assistant coach, would seem to say that Nolan has a sway over the way things are run on the Island. Certainly, the Islanders are the NHL team influenced most by Indians.

But perhaps it was no coincidence that just as I was wrapping up this chapter on Ted Nolan, something would happen that may bring credence to claims Nolan has consistently made about racism in the boardrooms of the NHL.

In mid-December Chris Simon, an Ojibway Islander, snapped during a game and stomped his skate blade at another player's leg. The action could have resulted in a serious injury to the Achilles tendon or an artery, and Simon was suspended for 30 games.

Simon was just returning from a 25-game suspension for swinging his stick two-handed into the face of another player. The debate over Simon's actions, his punishment—indeed coverage of this entire incident—is not in the purview of this book. But something else happened during the Simon incident that does belong in this book.

As Colin Campbell, the NHL's disciplinarian, was handing down Simon's punishment, he also made mention of the fact that Simon would be receiving treatment from the NHL's "drug and alcohol doctors for his problem."

Chris Simon had a drinking problem during his youth and early adult days. But fortunately, at that time, he found himself under the coaching reigns of one Ted Nolan, and Ted steered Chris toward the right track. Chris Simon hasn't had a drink in years and alcohol is not an issue.

The claims of racism against Simon and Indians in general gained further support when Chris Pronger of the Anaheim Ducks, who has been suspended repeatedly for "dirty play," stomped on the leg of Vancouver Canuck's Ryan Kesler. Pronger was given an eight-game suspension.

"I think it's definitely not fair," Simon told the *Minnesota Pioneer-Press*. "My opinion is there's obviously two sets of rules. If you look at the tape and look at his history, you can't say we're different, other than he is a star player and I am not."

And Pronger is white and Simon is red.

Now perhaps Campbell simply made a mistake because the same "drug and alcohol doctors" who treat players for substance abuse also treat players for behavioural issues; treatment that Simon wanted, needed and was granted. Nolan, and National Chief Phil Fontaine of the Assembly of First Nations, saw Campbell's misrepresentation differently, and they came out swinging. They claimed that Campbell was stereotyping Native people. Since Chris was an Indian, Nolan claims that Campbell automatically assumed Simon's problems must be connected to alcohol abuse.

Native people have long suffered from the stigma associated with alcohol abuse. It manifests itself in the denial of opportunities to citizens of Canada's

First Nations. If people think that all Indians have drinking problems, they are discriminated against when it comes to finding a job, a place to live, and joining in as full and equal partners in the social, cultural, economic and political fabric of their country.

Is that what happened to Ted Nolan when he was denied the opportunity to coach in the NHL for over a decade? Did some of the "old boys" think that Ted's "problem" was somehow associated with the demon rum? (Recall that Nolan missed a practice on one occasion and media speculation was automatically that it was because of over-indulging in alcohol—it wasn't).

Ted Nolan claims that racism played a major role in holding him back in his career. Most white people who are not racist exist in denial, partly because they have never experienced outright racism, but mostly because they are simply decent human beings themselves and they have difficulty believing that other people (who look the same as them!) can actually behave like that. Thank the highest powers for good old Canadian naivety, decency and optimism.

But Ted has experienced racism and still does. Having to be two or three times as good as the white kid for somebody to take notice. Experiencing the spears to the ribs and the name-calling in Kenora. Walking down the streets in many of our Canadian cities and towns. From the stands in Chicoutimi.

"I sincerely believed that my status as a hockey coach meant that I would never be called a redskin again. The one thing you always fight for is respect. And I thought I had really reached it where they're not looking at the colour of my skin anymore. Four or five guys behind the bench doing the tomahawk chop and war cry and pretending to shoot the bow and arrow. All of a sudden, four turned into ten and ten turned into twenty. It really floored me. It was almost like you were verbally raped in front of 3,000 people who didn't do anything about it."

Ted Nolan has experienced racism so often he can sense it, perhaps even smell it. We should give him the benefit of the doubt when he claims that racism is behind certain things that happen.

After what has come his way, and how he has handled it, you can be assured that Ted Nolan is not the kind of person to cry wolf.

★ ★ ★ ★ ★

Ted Nolan was back in the NHL and the circle was mended, but before the year 2008 ended, "philosophical differences" between Nolan and rookie General Manager Garth Snow resulted in Nolan being fired on July 14th. The sacred hoop was not back in place, as Ted once thought.

"We would sit around a drum, round like Mother Earth. And we would pound the drum like the heartbeat of Mother Earth. Even the seasons, Black Elk said, form a Great Circle in their changing, and always come back to where they were. That goes for hockey seasons, too. I spent nine away. It feels good to be back. I feel like I belong."

★ ★ ★ ★ ★

Unfortunately, as this book was published, Ted Nolan was back out of hockey, despite having proven himself as a knowledgeable and successful "hockey man." At the same time, Ted Nolan has carried his Indian identity with pride and he has worked tirelessly to promote a better understanding of First Nations culture, history and lifestyle, both among Canada's Native peoples and this country's mainstream population.

Many people have asked if Nolan somehow incorporated his Native background, the culture and the teachings of Canada's First Nations, into the coaching he has provided so successfully at the major junior and NHL level. He's has been asked about this many times, and yes, there were times when his Native background enhanced the success his teams achieved on the ice. But mostly it was the communal philosophy of "all for one and one for all" that helped Nolan's teams the most, by building team spirit.

"I did some stuff in junior hockey, where I got them stretching in a circle. In our sharing circle, an eagle feather is passed around, and the person holding that feather is the only one who is allowed to speak. Everybody else must listen. But everybody gets a chance to speak. And the person who is holding that eagle feather must tell the truth.

"I got some sage and some sweetgrass and we burned it inside the dressing room. Sage is a good medicine for travellers and sweetgrass is used to cleanse one's spirit. Junior hockey players can use this, as can we all. The kids had a lot of fun with it in a good way, not in a demeaning way.

"You know, people have been asking me what my coaching philosophy is all the time and I found out that it is basically about respect, but reality as well. Our sacred teachings tell us that every one is important, no one is unimportant, so you don't treat your superstar a bit different from your fourth- or fifth-line player. Everybody deserves respect. I'm not saying that everybody's going to receive the same amount of ice time.

"One time, a medicine man I knew from home happened to be in Detroit when I was playing with the Red Wings. I brought the elder into our dressing room and he held a smudging ceremony [a cleansing wherein sweetgrass is lit and passed around, the smoke off the sweetgrass medicine is passed over the heart and mind of the person being smudged]. The Elder also rubbed some medicine on one player's stick. That player scored a goal that night. The next day, other players were looking for that medicine.

"It's all good. Look for the good. In yourself. In others. Do well with what you have and you will be well."

On February 2, 2008, Ted Nolan set up a visit between Chris Simon and youth who were incarcerated in the Manitoba Youth Centre. Simon passed on some of his positive values to the youth—how to overcome obstacles, how to deal with substance abuse and things like that—as a friend, not as a "role model," as Simon likes to say.

How to find the good in themselves. And to do well with what they have.

And isn't it ironic that after the "establishment" associated with John Muckler couldn't do well with what they had (Nolan), a completely inexperienced GM (Snow) and absentee foreign owner who didn't know a puck from a stick growing up, also think that they cannot do well with what they had.

8

AMERICAN CHIEFS AND OTHER NOTABLE WARRIORS

The territory of the Ojibway First Nation ranges from northern Ontario, east into Manitoba and south down to Minnesota. The creation of the 49th parallel, the geographic boundary that divides Canada and the United States, divided North America's First Nations into "Canadian Indians" and "American Indians." Of course, tribes whose territory straddles the border between Canada and the US will call themselves Indians first (or Ojibway, Sioux, Lakota, Dakota, Nakota, Mohawk, Oneida and so on). The Indians south of the 49th parallel are more likely to enlist in the American military and suit up in red, white and blue uniforms when it comes to playing hockey internationally. Their "northern" brothers and sisters are more likely to sport a maple leaf on their chests. This chapter is about the Indians who made their name and claim to fame as American Indians.

The Indian most well-known for supporting "Old Glory" was Henry Boucha, a full-blooded Ojibway, whose hockey journey carried him from "Hockeytown, USA…" to…"Hockeytown, USA" (this is because Warroad, Minnesota, where Boucha was born, and Detroit, Michigan, where Boucha spent most of his NHL career, both claim the name). There was a lengthy stint in service with the US national team in between.

Warroad is a border town famous for its fanaticism over hockey. This small town of almost two thousand souls (1,772) has produced some of the best high school hockey teams to ever compete in the world-renowned and enormously popular Minnesota High School Hockey Tournament (Warroad High School won the Class A crown in 1994, 1996, 2003 and 2005).

The town gets its name from the path it lay on, which was used by Indian tribes on their way to war. Christians have dominated ever since they arrived, Father Aulneau at the pulpit and the Christian Brothers in commerce (Christian hockey sticks are produced at their family plant in Warroad). Bill Christian (father to Dave Christian) was a member of the gold medal-winning American Olympic team in Squaw Valley in 1960, which Dave followed up by being an integral part of the team that performed the "Miracle on Ice" by winning the Olympic gold medal in hockey in Lake Placid, New York in 1980.

Henry Boucha first started to gain notice by leading Warroad High School to the championship final of the 1969 Minnesota state tourney. Unfortunately, Boucha got injured in that game and Warroad ended up losing to Edina, 5-4 in overtime.

Boucha moved up to Winnipeg to spend a year with the Jets junior franchise in the Western Hockey League. Henry then enlisted in the army (the mandatory two-year stint for Americans of draft age) and became the first member of the 1972 US Olympic team to sign an NHL contract (Boucha had been drafted by the Detroit Red Wings in the second round of the 1971 entry draft, 16th overall). After winning a silver medal for Uncle Sam in Sapporo, Japan, Boucha squeezed in 16 games with the Wings. Boucha notched a goal in his very first game in the NHL, and was chosen Detroit's Rookie of the Year the next season—his first full season in the NHL.

Boucha played centre and was a gifted playmaker most noted for his penalty-killing. Check that. Boucha was most noted for the Indian headband he wore as he flew around the ice. Boucha's career only lasted four years because of a severe eye injury, but he made it into the NHL record books with one of those obscure records that are most valued for their bragging rights in a bar (or to win a trivia bet in the same place anytime after midnight). Boucha is tied for the record for second-fastest goal scored from the start of a game, six seconds after they dropped the puck to start the first period at a game in Montreal in 1973.

It looked like Boucha was going to enjoy a long and prosperous career in the NHL, even though he was traded by the Wings to the Minnesota North Stars (for highly regarded sniper Danny Grant). But Boucha got involved in an ugly stick-swinging incident with Boston's Dave Forbes in just his fourth season in the NHL, and that left Henry with a cracked orbital bone and blurred vision. The trauma of that injury, and double trauma caused by a court case as the state of Minnesota tried to charge Forbes with assault, diminished Boucha, and he was never the same. Boucha bounced around, to the Minnesota Fighting Saints of the World Hockey Association, and then back to the NHL with the Kansas City Scouts (who moved to Colorado to become the Rockies) before retiring following the 1976–77 season.

Henry Boucha was elected to the United States Hockey Hall of Fame in 1985. He has been an active supporter of Native American causes and charities since retirement. He followed up his athletic career with a career in real estate and was named the 47th most important sports figure in Minnesota history by the *Minneapolis Star Tribune*.

★ ★ ★ ★ ★

Next Indian up stateside was another Ojibway, who just happened to be Henry Boucha's cousin.

Gary Sargent could have gone any number of ways in sports, because he was an all-around athlete who excelled in baseball and football. He followed his heart, which beat most to the rhythm of hockey.

Gary was born in Red Lake, Minnesota on February 18, 1954, and he was raised in Bemidji. He helped put this small Minnesota town on the map.

An outstanding baseball player, Sargent turned down an offer from the Minnesota Twins to play third base. He was such a star on the gridiron, he turned down 15 college football scholarships after making all-state as a fullback and linebacker in high school.

But Gary's first love was hockey, and he started out as a slick centre before switching over to defence, where he was just as slippery. Sargent played locally with Bemidji State and Fargo-Moorhead, but it wasn't long before he attracted national attention and was chosen to represent the United States at the first (unofficial) World Junior Hockey Championships in the Soviet Union (Leningrad). Sargent was chosen the most valuable defenceman at that tournament.

Gary was drafted in the third round of the NHL entry draft by the Los Angeles Kings (48th overall). Sargent's NHL career lasted eight years, but was dogged by injuries. From 1975 to 1983, he played in 402 games, notching 61 goals and adding 161 assists (222 points) with 273 minutes in penalties. Like his cousin, Henry Boucha, Gary was chosen his NHL team's outstanding rookie (Kings 1975–76). Sargent followed that up by being named the Kings' outstanding defenceman for the 1976–77 season. At one time, Sargent held Los Angeles records for single-season points (54), goals (14) and assists (40) by a defenseman, but of course those early marks were made to be broken.

The best indicator of the value that defined Gary Sargent can be found in a rather obscure, but vitally important statistic. While with the Minnesota North Stars, Sargent was on the ice for 53.1 per cent of his team's goals, the best percentage in the NHL that season (1978–79).

Gary Sargent was plagued with back problems throughout his career, missing parts of most seasons most of the time. When his knee flared up in November of 1982 and was reinjured the following season, Gary hung 'em up.

Oh yeah! Sargent has been inducted into the Bemidji High Hall of Fame. Natch!

9

OTHER NOTABLE CHIEFS

The most difficult decision a filmmaker or an author makes is what to include and what to leave out. As I wrote earlier, we produced over 100 hours of videotaped interviews for the documentary *They Call Me Chief*, and we could only use 46 minutes and 40 seconds of that material. And it was all good!

Same with this book—we have compiled binders and binders of interesting interviews and information about Indians who played in the NHL or made other contributions to hockey. I know that the players featured so far here warrant the space and attention, and I sincerely apologize for having to cut short the stories of many other remarkable and successful Indian athletes.

★ ★ ★ ★ ★

John Chabot was selected by the Montreal Canadiens in the second round of the 1980 NHL entry draft, 40th overall. A native of Summerside, Prince Edward Island, John played his major junior hockey in Hull and Sherbrooke before turning pro. As a QMJHL rookie, Chabot played 68 games, scoring 26 goals and 83 points. He followed that up with an 89-point season the next year. In 1981–82, he played for the Sherbrooke Beavers, scoring 34 goals and 109 assists for 143 points in just 62 games.

Chabot got his first taste of NHL action in 1983–84, playing 56 games with the Canadiens, scoring 18 goals and 43 points. Midway through the following season, he was traded to the Pittsburgh Penguins, where he played for three years before joining the Detroit Red Wings. He remained in the Red Wings' organization until 1991, when he joined the Canadian National Team, suiting up for eight games.

With his NHL career at a standstill, Chabot wanted to continue playing hockey at an elite level, so he joined the Berlin Prussians of the German League in 1992. The club's nickname was changed to Prussian Devils for the start of the 1994-95 campaign. Chabot's best season was 1995–96, when he scored 16 games and 81 points in 50 games. He continued to play pro hockey in Germany with the Berlin Polar Bears through the 2000–01 season.

John worked with Aboriginal social, political, cultural and business organizations to instill pride and offer a positive role model for Native youth throughout his career. In 2007, he was asked by fellow Native Ted Nolan to serve as an assistant coach with the New York Islanders. With Bryan Trottier serving the Isles in an executive position, and with Chris Simon on the ice, the New York Islanders became a popular team for First Nations people throughout North America (Simon was traded to the Minnesota Wild on February 26, 2008 for a sixth-round draft pick in 2009).

★ ★ ★ ★ ★

John Chabot will always occupy a high-water mark in my heart and mind, even though I have never met him personally. John is one of those guys who accomplishes things without attracting too much attention to himself. The guy in the boardroom who rarely speaks, while others argue back and forth. But when this man raises his hand politely to speak his turn, everybody else shuts up and listens, because they know what he has to say or do will be important.

I got this impression from working with John on the development of an Aboriginal NHL Alumni hockey team. John had been working on this idea, which would bring former Indian NHL stars together to play exhibition games for charity and to provide positive role models for children and youth, as well as boost the image of First Nations people in general, for quite a while before he came into contact with me. John's project was a great idea, which normally wouldn't involve a writer of debatable talent and a hockey player of definitely dubious skills.

So you can imagine how blown away I was when I received an e-mail one morning from John Chabot, asking me to provide my sweater and pant size because I was listed as a member of the NHL Aboriginal Alumni team. I know, for sure, that I lost my breath when I first read the e-mail. I swear to all that is higher than I that my heart started racing and I was approaching hyperventilating. How did this happen?

I have never played in the NHL, of course, or even in any hockey league above "beer league." Yes, I did play defence for the Scouts for 20 years—a skilled Aboriginal team (we once beat a combined team of UND and Minnesota Gophers). Nobody worked harder on that team, but everybody had more talent and skill. My main job was to stay at home and play within my game (that is, avoid being a pylon, get the puck and pass it to my defensive partner or a forward who knows what to do with it). I am not going to sink so far into false modesty as to state that my teammates only allowed me to play because I raised all the money to cover expenses that took our team to tournaments in Banff, Sun Valley, Los Angeles and Lake Placid. I maintained an okay plus/minus and my contribution on the ice was appreciated by my teammates. But I was nowhere near junior or semi-pro or pro calibre.

John Chabot was either an extremely nice man, or he had heard I might be able to raise money to cover costs, or perhaps it was because I was a producer of theatre, films and live entertainment shows. In any case, John put me on a roster that included names like Reggie Leach and Bryan Trottier and John Chabot. In the end, I was on the roster simply because John followed the principle that if Don Marks was going to work behind the scenes and help do all the work that goes into organizing a project like this, he deserves the chance to suit up and skate with the team if he wants to.

The development of this version of an NHL Aboriginal Alumni team got sidetracked as other commitments kept drawing John away and I got sidetracked by some personal and professional issues. The idea was revived when Bryan Trottier and I got together for breakfast in Winnipeg and we worked together to stage "Legends and Legacies" (described in Chapter 5).

But the attitude John Chabot showed by including me on the roster is a measure of the man. Yes, he may have been offering a carrot on a stick to a dumb donkey or simply being fair, but the main gist of his actions was "inclusive." John was fully prepared to defend his decision to include a guy who was not Aboriginal and who never played in the NHL on his NHL Aboriginal Alumni team, and that could not have been easy!

John had a checkered playing career, but he made the "bigs," and that in itself is a million-to-one shot. Throughout that career, John has gone out of his way to cooperate with autograph signings, skill development clinics and speaking engagements, which instill positive values and offer positive role models for First Nations—and all other—youth and children throughout North America. He continues to do that, working with Bryan Trottier and other Native players who keep "giving something back."

Bottom line, the man made a special effort to include me on the roster of his very special team. This was one of the biggest thrills in my life. So I believe that John Chabot is a great man.

★ ★ ★ ★ ★

The next notable Indian in the NHL (in no particular order) is another Maritimer. Everett Sanipass was born on February 13, 1968 in Big Cove, New Brunswick. A member of the Mi'kmaq First Nation, Everett was a very slick, very skilled hockey player, but he became best known for his fights (sigh!).

Sanipass started his NHL career with the Chicago Blackhawks in 1987 after being drafted 14th overall in the 1986 NHL Entry Draft. Sanipass also played for the Quebec Nordiques. His record is included in the "Player Records" appendix of this book.

Sanipass is most famous for his role in the brawl that would be called the "Punch-up in Piestany" during the 1987 World Junior Hockey Championships in Czechoslovakia. Because it was Sanipass who started the whole damn mess!

Back in the 1980s, the most bitter rivalry in international hockey was between Canada and the Soviet Union—a holdover from the infamous 1972 Summit Series. "CCCP" on sweaters meant "dirty, sneaky, red commies." Emotions, mostly tempers, were always at a feverish level whenever Canada faced off against the Soviets.

The USSR was showing poorly and was already out of medal contention by the time the final game of the '87 tournament was played. It was supposed to be a dream matchup between the Bear and the Beaver but only the Canadian squad had something more meaningful than a historical hockey rivalry to play for. If Canada beat the Russians by five goals, they would win the gold medal; if they beat the Bear by any less, Canada would settle for silver. A bronze for Canada was assured.

Canada was up 4–2 halfway through the game (with 6:13 remaining in the second period, to be exact). The Canadian juniors were surely pressing for 7-2 when all "H-E-double hockey sticks" broke loose. According to most reports, "A Russian punched little Theo Fleury without provocation." Fleury battled back and…"

Not so, according to Fleury: "I did not start this thing. I was simply sticking up for one of my Native friends, Everett Sanipass."

And that is the absolute truth. According to Sanipass, he was getting mugged by a Russian. According to Russian authorities, their player was, at most, "feathering this Indian" in accordance with the rules. Whatever, Sanipass took exception, Theo took greater exception and was obligated to "stick up for his Native friend" and the fight was on!

It was a pier one through ten brawl that included some of the most unusual events ever to take place in hockey's history of fighting. First of all, the reaction of the on-ice and off-ice officials in the former Czechoslovakia was bizarre at best. The referee and linesmen, faced with the prospect of breaking up a street fight between two "LA-style gangs like the Crips and the Bloods," simply fled the ice. Up in the officials' box, the powers that be figured that perhaps the best way to handle these "children" would be to turn out the lights and they would somehow fight or cry themselves to sleep. This was incredibly idiotic. Think about it. Let's help guys who are swinging blindly, by handicapping them with even less sight! It seemed that nobody was thinking clearly except for one of the back-up goalies—yes goalies, who got into their own little tiff. Canadian netminder Shawn Simpson ended up on top of his Russian counterpart for most of the match, wielding his blocker and shielded by his mask (obviously, Simpson was thinking enough to put on this equipment before vacating the bench).

It all resulted in both teams being booted from the tournament and the Canadian team coming home coloured in controversy, not gold, silver or bronze.

My recollection of this event remains vivid because I failed to lead with it on my Sunday night news show on local Winnipeg TV station CKND. I was responsible for writing and anchoring the Sunday night package of local news, weather and sports. Usually, this would consist of a small, local news package (weekend homicide wrap, traffic fatalities and a mix of picnics, parades and charitable fundraisers), a 30-second weather forecast, and a complete package of sports from all over the world.

So I did my usual bit, local news and weather, commercial break, and then I led off my sports report with the big punch-up. The next morning, I got a call from the big pooh-bah at CanWest Global Broadcasting, Don Brinton, berating me furiously for not leading off the entire package with the punch-up. This, after being told over and over and over again not to bring any sports into the opening local news package. The story was that big.

The reaction to the goings-on in Czechoslovakia was typically Canadian. Those in the know hockey-wise, that is, those who have actually played the game, celebrated the Canadian junior team for standing up for themselves. Others berated the team for being unsportsmanlike and gaining a stain on Canada's international reputation through thuggery. The debate got heated everywhere, even so far as a near-fistfight on the airwaves of the Canadian Broadcasting Corporation.

During an infamous CBC recap of the "Punch-up in Piestany," Host Brian Williams kept calling the Canadian team's behaviour a "black mark on Canadian hockey." Co-host Don Cherry was so incensed with Williams' remarks that, during a commercial break, he politely informed Williams that if he "called the Canadian team's actions a 'black mark' one more time, that he would have to hit him." A CBC director, in a futile attempt to diffuse, or at least lighten up the situation, suggested that they come out of a commercial break with Cherry's hands around Williams' neck in a joking gesture. Cherry declined because, as he said, "Once I got my hands around Williams' neck, I wouldn't be able to remove them!"

★ ★ ★ ★ ★

I never met Everett Sanipass, and I know that, if I phone him, the stories will flow and this book will become longer than an encyclopedia. But a chapter of my life included Everett Sanipass, and that chapter proved to be an indictment of attitudes carried by some members of the media, if that attitude is reflected by a certain member of Winnipeg's press corps.

I spent eleven years as a sportscaster with CKND-TV in Winnipeg, covering the Jets (as well as the Bombers and sports in general). One night, while covering a game between the Chicago Blackhawks and the Jets, I learned—and was naive enough be shocked—that so-called journalists carry racist attitudes and allow that to infect their so-called "objective" coverage of events and personalities.

The second period of the game had just ended and Sanipass was finishing off the period in a fight with some Jet. I was watching the fight with glee, when a local sports reporter, sauntered by and postulated "I wonder what Sanipass is sniffing tonight?"

I consider myself somewhat adept at comebacks, but even my big mouth was completely shut down. As this idiot (whom I choose not to name so as not to litter my index) headed off to the beer and buffet table a local hotel and brewery used to spoil the media with during Jets home games, I was simply in a state of shock. When I regained simple sight, I noticed that Les Lazurak of CJOB-Radio was hurrying after him.

Lazurak knew full well that I wrote, directed and produced the First Nations documentary series on CKND with Shingoose. He might have even known that I was the foster child of a Native family. I know that he informed the reporter that I was somehow "tight" with Indians and that perhaps his remark hasn't been taken that well. And that I might do damage to the reporter's career by letting it be known widely that he was a racist, ignorant bastard. Because, prior to the start of the third period, he came up to me and said, "Hey, man! I didn't mean anything by what I said about Sanipass. And I'm sorry." But then he went on to say: "But you know deep down that's what Indians are really like!"

Usually, by this point, I would be able to react, at least, physically. Give this guy a slap or tune him up or something! But I could only shake my head in amazement as he slobbered away.

"Revenge is a dish best served cold" being the mantra of all those who don't react quickly enough, I decided that I would report or broadcast this encounter on all the media outlets I was connected with, and expose this goof for what a fool he was.

The next day, over breakfast with Shingoose, I told him what had happened, and I told him what I planned to do. Goose wasn't impressed; more important, Goose simply did not care about the incident one way or the other. "This shit happens all the time," he said. "It's not worth the energy to summon up the anger it requires, and it's a waste of time to waste your time on people like that. The sediment always falls to the bottom of the river and the cream rises to the top of the cup."

Shingoose is not a passive man, and he has spent his life educating people all over the world about Indian culture, lifestyle and spirituality. But he doesn't have time to waste on the fringe. And that is where that idiot reporter resides, I realized.

The Ku Klux Klan is to Christians what al Qaeda is to Muslims. We have to target our efforts at the real, the organized and the powerful enemy.

People like him, who somehow find a place in the sun for a while, eventually get found out and eventually disappear.

Last I heard the reporter was hosting a radio call-in show on a local station that caters to the lowest common denominator. A Jerry Springer kind of thing. And that's where he belongs.

★ ★ ★ ★ ★

Blair Atcheynum is a Cree First Nation citizen who was born on April 20, 1969 in Estevan, Saskatchewan.

Atcheynum was a respectable 52nd overall draft choice by Hartford in 1989 after a junior career that saw him finish in 1988–89 with Moose Jaw in the WHL, scoring 70 goals in 71 games. But over the next three years the Whalers didn't use him even once, and in the summer of 1992 he was claimed by Ottawa in the expansion draft.

In 1992–93, Atcheynum got into his first four NHL games with the Senators, though he spent most of the year with the farm team in New Haven and all of the next four years buried in the AHL and IHL

The NHL never seemed so far away, but St. Louis signed him as a free agent in 1997 and his perseverance paid off. He played all the next year with the big team. Since then, though, his career involved much travel. Nashville claimed him in the expansion draft in 1998, but traded him back to the Blues near the end of the season, and in the off season he signed with Chicago.

Over the next three seasons, Atcheynum would see limited ice time with the Blackhawks while spending the better part of those three years with the team's AHL and IHL affiliates before calling it a career following the 2000-01 season.

Ordinarily, a player like Atcheynum would only be appreciated by his family and friends. We were interested in Blair because he is Aboriginal, but also because we had learned that he was one of the first players involved in the Aboriginal Role Model Hockey School that Ron Delorme and Kevin Tootoosis developed in Saskatoon.

Our problem was not only that Blair's career was so up and down and all over the place but that we only had 46 minutes and 40 seconds and we knew that, at best, we would only be able to fit in perhaps two 15-second sound bites from Blair in the entire documentary. It didn't seem worth the time, effort and money to track him down in some minor league town, which would cost way out-of-the-way airline (or train or bus or cab) money.

But we got lucky. We had to be in Edmonton to interview another player, and Blair just happened to get called up by the Chicago Blackhawks for the game against the Oilers we would be attending. We could kill two birds with one stone.

We bagged our first interview during the afternoon skate and tried to focus on Atcheynum during the game. Blair wasn't getting much ice time, but we were getting enough "bg" (background tape or b-roll) to cover edits in the interview. We were, of course, hoping that Blair would do something spectacular, perhaps even score a goal.

Well, as luck would have it, Blair was on the ice for an Edmonton goal near the beginning of the second period, and the Chicago coach had him riding the bench. Of course we were disappointed, but we kept on shooting, just in case.

Now, I have to set the next scene up for you. Pundits or those granted press passes are discouraged from showing support for one team or the other in the press box. No matter that we all know that reporters from this city or another are obviously biased in favour of their home team; they have to maintain a facade of neutrality.

My video crew and I could not care less who won the game we were videotaping between the hometown Oilers and the visiting Chicago Blackhawks. We were there to try to get some memorable video of Blair Atcheynum. And we were mired in the lowest of the low emotionally because Blair had been benched.

But, lo and behold, about five minutes into the third period, the Chicago Coach forgives Blair and sends him out for a shift. And, wouldn't you know it, he scores a goal! We couldn't believe our good fortune—or control ourselves! Even our camera operator, and those guys are really jaded—started hopping around, joining Clay and me, spinning in circles, and spilling our beer. "YES!"

It was the first NHL goal that Blair Atcheynum had scored in four years. And then…I get a tap on the shoulder. Grinning as wildly as a hyena, I spin around and suddenly I am face to face with Kevin Lowe, the general manager of the Oilers.

"Shit!" I realized immediately that I had broken the unwritten rule of neutrality in the press box. And Kevin was indeed upset with me, to put it mildly.

I really did have a good explanation, but it fell on deaf ears. "We're not from Chicago or Edmonton! We don't care who wins. We're doing a documentary on Indians who play in the NHL and Blair Atcheynum, he's an Indian, and he just scored, and he hasn't scored in over four years, and we didn't ever, never, mean no disrespect, like, we don't care who wins, and I'm really sorry and…"

Now, if I were a graduate of some school of broadcasting and/or even slightly known sports figure, I might have handled this better. But I'm a sports fan with some imagination and writing skills who has passed himself off. I'm always amazed and overwhelmed whenever I access a press box or score media credentials (and shit-scared I'll be found out and kicked out). On the one hand, this is good, because I retain my solidarity and perspective with the view of the common fan. On the other hand, my enthusiasm and sheer amateurism compromises my facade from time to time. And this was one of those times.

Lowe didn't kick us out, and even allowed us to interview Blair in the dressing room following the game. But we were under the eye of security the entire time, and I knew that the next time I requested media credentials for an Oilers game that denial would be on Lowe's lips and his hand would be on the "REJECTED" stamp.

Blair provided a very polite interview, careful to give credit to Delorme and Tootoosis for organizing the Role Model Hockey School in Saskatoon.

"I really only showed up to teach but it was a way of giving something back. I didn't grow up on a reserve but my father was full-blood Indian and he went through the whole thing, residential school and all that. My father played semi-pro hockey and he credits that for getting him off the reserve. Not that he didn't enjoy his family, and sometimes we spent six months at a time back in the Onion Lake area [in northern Saskatchewan]. It provided me with an idea of what it is like to live on a reserve, where the amenities are scarce and there is a lot of poverty. My father didn't want to wait for a house like he would have if he stayed on the reserve, because the waiting lists are always too long. Hockey provided the money for Dad to make a home for his family off the reserve. My connection with it all through him allowed me to relate better to the kids at the hockey school, and it provided me with motivation to give something back, because these kids need a positive boost to balance the poverty all around them back home."

10

HEART OF A LION

A more appropriate name for Theoren Wallace "Theo" Fleury would be Leo, because this small (five-foot-six) Métis man from equally tiny Russell, Manitoba displayed the heart of a lion throughout a hockey career that takes the phrase "twists and turns" out of the cliché heap and back into the genuine lexicon.

Considered by all to be too small to play in the NHL, Fleury proved them all wrong. Big time, as a matter of fact. Along the way, Fleury was at the centre of the most famous, bench-clearing hockey brawl in the world, the "Punch-up in Piestany." His career is dotted with suspensions for substance abuse, and incidents like getting sucker-punched and pounded on by nine bouncers in a bar late one night in Columbus, Ohio. Life's drama creeps in deeper when Theo is diagnosed with Crohn's disease. This takes place around the same time he learns his father is in failing health with cancer. There's another twist when Theo gets caught up in the middle of an Indian Chief's controversial dream to buy, oops! I mean win, the Allan Cup (Canada's historic senior hockey crown). Then another turn when a Canadian businessman tries to transform Theo into a Giant in Belfast. As if all that isn't enough, his life is touched by the infamous child sexual abuse scandal involving the sinister Graham James and his victim, Sheldon Kennedy, who was a childhood friend of Theo's before they become teammates in Swift Current, Saskatchewan. Unfortunately, he found himself in the position of being in the back seat during a car ride that James took Kennedy and himself in one time. Kennedy was sexually victimized by James in the front seat. At first, Fleury claimed that nothing happened, which doesn't reflect well on Theo when it comes to backing up a buddy. Later, Fleury stated that he was sleeping, and, while Kennedy's claims were proven in court, he could not corroborate them. Somehow, Fleury always seemed to end up in the wrong place at the wrong time.

Fortunately, Theo's path in life was somewhat smoothed out by a Stanley Cup win, an Olympic gold medal, a World Junior Hockey Championship, and a long list of NHL records.

One thing we found out for sure: Theo is not one to make excuses. For pretty much anything that happens, on or off the ice. Theo deals with what he is dealt straight up, and his explanation of events is the truth as he sees it. At times, this will get him into moose milk with the people who see things opposite. In the end, Theo has always accepted responsibility for the choices he's made in his life and we have already seen how he reacts to people who make wrong choices about him.

★ ★ ★ ★ ★

Russell, Manitoba is a small, agricultural supply town in northwestern Manitoba—kind of a gateway to Saskatchewan along Highway Number 4 (also called the Yellowhead Route).

Theoren Fleury was the fifth child of Harry and Jean Fleury. Harry was a proud Métis man and instilled a deep sense of pride in his family's Métis heritage.

Unlike most players with his level of skill and production, Theoren would end up playing four full seasons with the Moose Jaw Warriors in the Western Junior Hockey League while others with similar stats would be advancing to the pro level. Fleury displayed performance and leadership that would normally be enough to attract the attention of those responsible for calling juniors up for a look-see, but Theoren was always overlooked because so-called NHL brain trusts could not see past his diminutive stature.

So, despite point totals of 75, then 108, then 129, then 160 from 1984–85 to1987–88, it wasn't enough to warrant Fleury a serious chance at cracking the Calgary Flames lineup (Calgary drafted Fleury in the ninth round, 166th overall, in the 1987 entry draft). Even the fact that Fleury's 160 points (consisting of 68 goals and 92 assists) were accompanied by 235 minutes in penalties was not enough to convince professional pundits that Fleury could take care of himself and be injury-free while remaining productive. The tiny Fleury even developed a reputation for standing up for his teammates. As a matter of fact, Fleury attracted attention globally by sticking up for "a Native friend" during an incident that would rock the global hockey world—the "Punch-up in Piestany" which is described in Chapter 9.

★ ★ ★ ★ ★

The very next year, after the "PUP", Fleury and another squad of junior-aged players showed how our youngest and finest Canadian athletes do things right in the heart of the Russian Bear by winning gold at the 1988 World Junior Hockey Championships, smack dab in the middle of Moscow.

The disappointment—perhaps embarrassment, shame and loss from the previous year—was still fresh in Theoren Fleury's mind when he returned to the world stage in the Soviet capital. And Theo desperately wanted to prove to the Calgary Flames that he could compete, stand out, even shine, at the NHL level. The 1988 Canadian junior team was loaded with future NHL stars like Joe Sakic, Adam Graves and Mark Recchi. Trevor Linden was a bit player on this roster. The Soviets countered with superstars Sergei Fedorov and Alexander Mogilny.

But who should tie Rob Brown for most goals scored in the tournament? Theoren Fleury, with six. And who would be named to the World Junior All-Star team? Theo Fleury.

Despite all this, the Calgary Flames still figured Fleury's potential to be limited to "possibly a potentially entertaining" attraction for their International Hockey League franchise in Salt Lake City, Utah. Nobody in the Flames' dusty brain trust could be convinced that Theo was big enough to stand up to the rigours of the NHL.

This happens time and time again. Yes, it is true that more often than not "a good big man will beat a good small man." But all too often, so-called scouts are so rigid in their rules, or riding on too high a horse, or simply too afraid of making a mistake (how can that be with all the mistakes made every year in every draft?), that athletes like Theoren Fleury, who have proved themselves on the scoreboard and on the podium, aren't given a fair chance to show what they can do. From Camille Henry of the New York Rangers to Doug Flutie of the Canadian Football League, the sports world is full of small men with big hearts (and plenty of ability) who have had to endure a ridiculous trail of trials to get to where they should have started from.

The Flames didn't sign Fleury to a pro contract until late in the 1987–88 season, just in time to join the Salt Lake City Golden Eagles for the IHL playoffs. Theo was ready to seize whatever opportunity came his way and he scored 11 goals in just eight games to lead the Eagles to the Turner Cup (IHL championship).

But it was the same thing the next year. The Flames relegated Fleury to Salt Lake City out of training camp and again, Fleury didn't sulk or bitch or moan. Instead, he made the most of his first 40 regular season games in a pro uniform by scoring 37 goals and an equal number of assists for 74 points. And that finally convinced the Flames that this little bugger deserved a full-time shot at the NHL.

Fleury's NHL career began with the biggest bang of them all, and wouldn't end until 15 fun-filled and event-filled years later.

Not many players sip from Stanley in their first year, but Fleury, used at centre and at right wing, scored 31 goals in his first NHL season and was a big part of the Flames' NHL championship team of 1989. Two years later,

Fleury would crack the magic 50-goal mark (104 points) and make the NHL All-Star team. He was also selected for the Canada Cup tournament and was named Captain of the Flames in 1995. Fleury was a member of Canada's first Olympic gold medal-winning team in, quite ironically, Salt Lake City, in 2002.

Salt Lake City was where Theo began his professional career and also where he started to make real money out of hockey. Utah was founded by Mormons, and the people who live there follow a prohibition-style lifestyle. Fleury, who has battled the bottle ever since he was old enough to drink, was insulated from temptation during the time he played in Salt Lake City with the Eagles. Once he got called up to the NHL, beer was everywhere—in the dressing room following the game, on the plane, after practice, in the hotel rooms, at every public appearance. And what started out as a habit started turning into an addiction.

★ ★ ★ ★ ★

Theoren Fleury was the greatest player ever to wear a Calgary Flames uniform (as evidenced by the scoring records he holds as a Flame, surpassing players like Joe Nieuwendyk and Al MacInnis). But the NHL was structured to favour American teams financially during the 1990s. Not only could some Canadian teams like the Winnipeg Jets and the Quebec Nordiques not compete (the Jets became the Phoenix Coyotes and the Nordiques became the Colorado Avalanche), the Edmonton Oilers and the Flames were barely surviving, in small media markets and having to pay expenses in American dollars with loonies (the Canadian dollar) worth 60 cents. So it was that in 1999, the Flames were about to lose their star player, their marquee name, five-foot-six Theoren Fleury, to free agency because there was no way they could pay the going rate for this superstar on the open market. So the Flames did what they had to do and got whatever they could for a player they were going to lose anyway.

Fleury was traded to Colorado for Robyn Regehr, Wade Belak and Rene Corbet. Theo was an immediate hit in Denver, amassing 10 goals and 14 assists in just 15 games to end the season, then added 5 goals and

12 assists for 17 points in 18 playoff games. The Avalanche got what they wanted—a ringer for the playoffs but, of course, there is no guarantee when signing free agents at the end of a season that they will return for the following year, and Fleury moved on to New York. After three rather ordinary seasons with the Rangers (about 22 goals, 43 assists per year, and a big jump in PIM in year 3, Fleury signed with the Chicago Blackhawks for the 2002–03 season. This is where the Theo-meter began to burst over its top.

Already battling booze, Fleury's off-ice worries were exacerbated by the news his father would be undergoing an operation for cancer. Fleury was coming off a relapse of his addiction to alcohol in 1992, which had caused him to be suspended for six months and placed in the NHLPA/NHL Substance Abuse and Behavioral Health Program. He was taunted throughout the league by fans and began the 2002–03 season serving out a 25-game suspension. Just after he returned, Theo missed a practice (he claimed he overslept), and was suspended by the Blackhawks for a pair of games. The reason he overslept, or whether a faulty alarm clock could be a culprit at all, came into question midway through the season when Theo got involved in an incident at a nightclub in Columbus, Ohio. Details of this incident remain as foggy to this day as Theo's brain was that night.

The club was a "peeler place" called Pure Platinum, and Theo was doing his Pacman routine (simply spreading dollars amongst the strippers) when—and this is all that has been reported—he was punched out by up to nine bouncers. This was followed by the entry of some mysterious 'hawks, who swept in from some undetermined origin.

Two of Theo's teammates in Chicago, who were either with Fleury when he ventured into the bar, or simply happened upon the scene or were summoned to the scene, tried to calm things down and hustle Fleury away in a cab, when a squad car of the windy city's finest pulled up.

The two Blackhawks teammates are reported to have said to the police: "We play for the Blackhawks. Can you help us get out of here?"

From every angle, these two Blackhawk teammates were obviously not the sharpest shooting sticks in the rack. If they had accompanied Theo to the booze can originally, they are ignorant, because they knew full well their beloved teammate was in the NHL's substance abuse program and it was their duty as teammates, friends and Blackhawks to keep Theo out of bars and not encourage him to drink in any way, including by simply providing company. If they had just happened upon the scene or were summoned, well, they already had Theo in the cab, and the bouncers (and the owners of the bar) surely would not want any publicity about drunkenness, brawls or beatings. All the hockey players had to do was leave. Why would they approach an arresting force like the police, clearly represented in uniform and riding their painted horse (black and white), and identify themselves?

Many of those who were close to the scene claim that the Blackhawks and Fleury should have sued the night club and its bouncers for excessive use of force. "The Chicago police certainly had no problem with the players, but the players didn't want to charge other people," said Chicago coach Brian Sutter.

In any case, there was a lot of noise in the newspapers about the incident but the Blackhawks put a lid on it all. Chicago management maintained it was an "internal matter" and they managed to handle it internally. Outwardly, Theo didn't seem to receive any punishment. Except for the end of his NHL career. Inwardly, the Hawks had had it with him, and he was labelled persona non grata throughout the rest of the league.

All good things must come to an end, I guess, but Theoren Fleury still had the full heat of hockey rushing through his veins. Leagues like the AHL were just as out of reach as the NHL, and it started looking like the "beer leagues" were Theo's only option.

But this is Theo Fleury we're dealing with, and there is a twist at every turn. This one is a bit strange, as an Indian came riding to Theo's rescue just like the 7th Cavalry coming over the hill to rescue the wagon train in a Hollywood western B movie.

Chief Calvin Horse of the Horse Lake First Nation was a lifelong rabid hockey fan. Immensely proud of his nationhood, he cheered on all the Native stars of the NHL in particular. This Chief had an opportunity to raise his people to hockey glory by winning one of Canada's most historically cherished championships, senior hockey's Allan Cup, with his community's team, the Horse Lake Thunder.

Granted, the Allan Cup has lost a lot of lustre since the glory days of the 1950s (which I wrote about in the Introduction), when it was fought over by Olympic and Canadian National team stars who made up the Winnipeg Maroons and the Saskatoon Quakers. The current competition features highly skilled hockey, but it's mostly a matter of some guy in some town in some province having enough money to cobble together the best players outside of the NHL, AHL, ECHL, European leagues and so on, and then gather enough money to house and transport them to the annual Allan Cup competition held in whatever town or village where there's another hockey aficionado with deep pockets who can cobble together enough money to host the event. A village called Ile des Chenes (a "Timmie's" slurp of coffee just south of Winnipeg) won the Allan Cup in 2003 by coupling former NHL star Pat Falloon with a bunch of fine senior players from across Manitoba.

But it's all good, and if Chief Horse wanted to bring some glory to his nation and create some role models for his young people by winning a national hockey championship, then more power to him. Unfortunately (and especially in the case of Theoren Fleury), things never seem to turn out they way they were planned.

Fleury's start with Horse and his Thunder got off to a rocky beginning. The North Peace Hockey League tried to declare Fleury ineligible because he had an NHL contract (which, at the time, wasn't worth the paper it was written on). Theo's highly anticipated and widely announced debut with the Thunder was delayed from January 6, 2005 to January 22 and then only after two wrangling appeals. Frustrating, and perhaps agonizing as that was, it was nothing—and I mean nothing! compared to what would happen at the eventual showdown for the Allan Cup that took place in Lloydminster, Alberta during the spring of 2006.

Fleury was joined on the Thunder roster by some pretty fair country hockey players from Alberta, as well as NHL compatriot Gino Odjick and Fleury's cousin Todd Holt. They ran the regional table and qualified for the Allan Cup final.

The Allan Cup tournament in Lloydminster was completely sold out. The Thunder started off the tournament with two easy round-robin wins, but they lost to the eventual Allan Cup champions from Thunder Bay 6-5 in the semifinal. Thousands of Alberta hockey fans were extremely disappointed and demanded an explanation. Since Theo was the star attraction (and former Alberta star with the Flames) it was up to Fleury to explain.

It quickly became obvious that Fleury had forgotten his NHL media orientation sessions because what he said was brutally honest (the first lesson of media relations 101 is to never open up to the media but stick to clichés like "the better team won on this day" and "we'll get 'em next year," etc.). Fleury, who has always had disdain for referees, went into a tirade against the officiating during the Allan Cup tourney, declaring it not only incompetent but biased against his team, even pulling out the race card. That alone is enough to get any white backs in the crowd up and turn any white necks red, but Theo even managed to insult his biggest backers: the hard-working stiffs who came out to see and support him.

In response to a question about "letting down the locals," Fleury led with his ego instead of his egghead. "The only reason this tournament sold out was because of yours truly right here!" [The Allan Cup tournament was indeed sold out, well in advance of news that the Horse Lake Thunder had qualified for the finals, providing ammunition to detractors who claimed that the tournament would have been successful without Fleury.] But the Thunder were highly favoured to qualify, so a lot of Alberta fans bought their tickets in anticipation of cheering on the former captain of an Alberta-based, Stanley Cup-winning team as well as the locally based Thunder, so this argument ends up a "push."

About being criticized by certain fans, Fleury said, "Look at the source. A guy that carries a lunch bucket to work every day. A frustrated human being. He doesn't want to face his problems head to head. So who's the perfect target? Theo Fleury. He's had success. He's had fame. He's had fortune. Those people have to yell at me to make themselves feel better about themselves. You know what? I'll take the high road!"

Ouch! Talk about hitting the low road! Either Fleury wasn't thinking clearly, or maybe he was caught up in some star-status trip, but to insult the "lunch bucket," grassroots hockey fan is simply career suicide.

The media play ended with Fleury's admonishment of the paparazzi on hand. "You take another (bleeping) picture and I'll kill you!"

The Allan Cup ended up in Thunder Bay. The Chief of Horse Lake ended up in rehab (it seems that Chief Horse also had a problem with substance abuse) and Theoren Fleury ended up in…Belfast, Ireland!

★ ★ ★ ★ ★

"Let's do the Twist…" (Chubby Checker)

This turn involved a gentleman named Jim Jaworski, a Ukrainian, who happened to own the Belfast Giants of the British Elite Hockey League. Jaworski figured that the "little giant" would be a major attraction playing on his team.

More important, Jaworski is an avid member of Alcoholics Anonymous, and those whose lives were saved by that program feel a responsibility to help others out of their living nightmare. Jaworski recognized that Fleury could use a "year off" to find himself, to like himself again, to heal.

So Fleury was off to jolly old England, where he made his debut on October 15, 2006 against the Edinburgh Capitals a "simply smashing" one—scoring three goals and adding four assists while fighting some thug named Fredrik Oduya and being named "man of the match." This fun-filled or "fuelled" season of Fleury's circle of life included a hearing for entering the stands to fight with a fan of the Coventry Blaze who had been taunting him (Jaworski claims that Fleury simply turned around on the bench and waved his stick at the obnoxious fan and never left that bench). There was an ejection for threatening league officials for their "frustrating calls," which Fleury claims is the reason he would "never return to play here again." Again, Jaworski has another side to the story and it goes that, after a goal had been scored on the Giants, Fleury shot the puck down the ice in frustration, the puck never went near any officials or other players, Fleury was given a 10-minute misconduct and that was all there was to that incident.

And, while all this is happening, Fleury was chosen Player of the Year in the British Elite Hockey League. Most important, he was getting healed.

As they say in Ireland, home of "the Troubles," Belfast has a horrible past but a bright future. The same can be said now, for the time being, for Theoren Fleury.

At the time of publication of this book, Fleury had returned to Canada and settled down. A big reason for that, Fleury says, is having met Jennifer, his new wife. Along with Fleury's brother, Travis, they operate a concrete coating business and are trying to develop a reality TV series based on that enterprise. While concrete coatings may not sound interesting, Fleury certainly is, and I would bet that is what the producers of the TV series are counting on (and Fleury staying sober).

Did I mention that Fleury was also part owner of the WHL junior franchise in Calgary (the Hitmen) with wrestler Bret Hart and junior hockey teammate and close friend Joe Sakic at one time? Just another footnote in the flurry of activity that has defined the life of Theoren Fleury.

Perhaps the greatest and most representative accomplishment in Theo Fleury's career is the NHL record he holds for most shorthanded goals in a game—three. Quite simply, when Theo Fleury faces a challenge, when he is outnumbered and when the odds are stacked against him, he shines most. It's almost sad that it takes something uneven to bring out the best in him.

Theoren Fleury is winning the biggest challenge he ever faced in his life—addiction to drugs and alcohol. For now. But, as he says often these days, "This is a lifelong sentence."

Author's Note: Theoren Fleury had agreed to be interviewed for this book. In an e-mail to the author, Theo wrote, "I want to do anything I can do to help." I set up times for lengthy telephone interviews, but Theo later informed me that he had agreed to a deal with a publisher for a "no-holds-barred, tell-all, insider account" of Fleury's life in a book to be released in 2009. Fleury's publisher has instructed him not to grant any more interviews as this book was going to print.

We accept the decision that Theoren Fleury made in this regard, especially in light of what Fleury informed us: that he would be receiving a

$50,000 advance from his publisher (we certainly have no problem with a friend picking up 50K whenever he can).

Some of the material in this book is sure to provoke debate and disagreement, but it is what it is, straight from the heart. We didn't pay for any of the content. This is as much to avoid the pitfalls of chequebook or yellow journalism as to insure there are no written or unwritten obligations on anybody's part. Our goal here is to provide the history of Indian, Inuit and Métis athletes who played in the NHL, freely and honestly, with no expectations of sensationalism or controversy, legal or otherwise.

If there is any regret over these developments, it is that Theo could have provided us with his response to the quotes we have used and which have been widely publicized and attributed to him, especially the statements made at the Allan Cup, which shed some negative light on a little guy we think overcame *huge* obstacles.

11

THEY CALLED ME "BOY IN A MAN'S BODY"

"On the rink, they called me 'Chief.' That's what my teammates call me. On the reserve, they call me Chum Sa Bay. So as long as it's from the heart, I don't mind either name."

Chum Sa Bay is Algonquin for "Boy in a Man's Body." There is no other name that could describes Gino Odjick better.

"I remember one time I won a fight on the ice and then I was called a 'wagon burner.' I didn't like that too much. I just thought that wasn't right, so I went out and beat him up again."

Wayne Gino Odjick was also known as the "Algonquin Enforcer" during his 10-year career in the NHL.

★ ★ ★ ★ ★

Gino was born on September 7, 1970 on the Kitigan Zibi Anishinabeg Algonquin First Nation (formerly called the River Desert Band) in Quebec.

"Where I am from, Maniwake, it is cold in the winter so everyone plays hockey on the outdoor rinks. Softball in the summer. Growing up, the player I admired most was Stan Jonathan."

It wasn't only his admiration for "Little Chief" that caused him to average more than 200 minutes in penalties a season.

"When I was younger and playing at home, I thought I was a goal scorer. But when I left the community to play junior, I noticed right away how far behind I was. The people in the city practise on indoor ice three or four times a week and play more games; I just played in the Native tournaments for fun. I didn't even know the basics of the forecheck. They called it the two-on-two, where two guys go in and one guy stays high.

"One day in Hawkesbury, something happened. Somebody hit another player on my team and my instinct was to help out my teammate. I got into a fight and I guess everybody thought I did pretty good. And that was my job from that day on."

Odjick's junior stats certainly bear this out. During the 1988–89 season in Laval, Gino scored 9 goals and added 15 assists in 50 games, but piled up a whopping 278 minutes in penalties as well. During the playoffs, Gino didn't manage a single goal while verifying the old adage "you can't score from the penalty box," because Odjick spent 129 minutes there! It was a similar story the next year (GP 51, G 12, A 26, PIM 280/regular season, followed by 6, 5 and 110/playoffs).

Odjick was drafted by the Vancouver Canucks in the fifth round (86th overall) in the 1990 NHL entry draft. While he would certainly turn out to be a wise choice (after all, how many fifth-rounders play ten years in the NHL, if they make it to the big leagues at all?), Odjick would have slipped to the even later rounds if not for the efforts and enthusiasm of another Indian.

"Ron Delorme heard of me while I was playing in Laval. Me and him kind of went through the same process. He had children when he was young. I had three kids. I was playing in junior and working in the summer to support my family. He had gone through the same thing and we were both the same style players. When I went to the draft in Vancouver, and when Vancouver finally drafted me in the fifth round, Pat Quinn was the general manager and told me 'We had to draft you because Ron Delorme kept bothering us since the third round. We waited until the fifth and you were still available and we just did it. Ron thought you could help.'

"I was told that Vancouver management wasn't that high on me, but Ron, who was a scout for the Canucks at the time, kept bugging them every round to pick me. Finally, they put my name up in the fifth round just to shut Ron up."

Gino's professional career began in the International Hockey League with the Milwaukee Admirals (17 games, 10 points and 102 minutes in penalties, certainly in keeping with his trend). Then he became an immediate success in Vancouver. His NHL debut came against the Chicago Blackhawks on November 21, 1990. With the number 66 on his back, (Satan minus one six), Gino truly created hell on ice, getting into fights with three Hawks (and was acclaimed "victor" in all three bouts), including a scrap with leading NHL tough guy Stu Grimson. Odjick was named the game's "first star" and for the next eight years he was a regular in the Canucks' starting lineup.

Odjick's primary role in Vancouver was that of an enforcer. Gino fought so often there's a website called "Fight Card" that lists his bouts season by season. For example, in 1990–91, Odjick fought 22 times during the regular season and twice in the playoffs. The next year Gino fought 31 times, followed by seasons of 20 and 11, and then "rebounding" with 19 bouts in 1996–97.

On November 12, 1992, Odjick set a Canucks team record for most penalty minutes in a single game, albeit in a most comic fashion, by trying to destroy Warren Rychel of the Los Angeles Kings. The skirmish included a wild chase all over the ice, and the referees wore out their pencils writing up 47 PIMs, including roughing, cross-checking, a 10-minute misconduct and something called a "triple misconduct."

This toughness and willingness to stand up for teammates sometimes creates a situation that allows big, powerful players like Odjick, who also have fairly good skating and shooting skills, to pad their points on a line with a smallish superstar (like Marty McSorley or Dave Semenko being paired with Wayne Gretzky). In Vancouver, Gino was positioned on the left side of diminutive Pavel Bure, the "Russian Rocket." This not only protected Pavel from the pokes and punches of opponents trying to throw the Russian off his finesse game, it allowed Gino to post career-high totals of 16 goals and 13 assists for 29 points during the 1993–94 season (along with 271 minutes in penalties, natch).

Odjick and Bure became more than teammates or linemates. They ended up forming a friendship that defined unique, because they were "pale opposites of each other." Pavel was a Russian superstar transplanted to a new land, without a friend in that land, speaking a language nobody could understand. Nobody except for a "Native American" who most people weren't taking very seriously as a hockey player because he fought so well. Bure was white as the snow in Canada and Odjick was as red as communism. But there was a fateful connection that made the combination click.

"I'm French, English, Algonquin…and Russian. If I have to talk to the girls in Russian, I can get along pretty good! Same with Pavel, although, if I have to speak Russian, I would rather speak it with girls."

There is no doubt that Odjick and Bure got along on the ice. After scoring 15 goals in 185 NHL games over three seasons before being lined up beside Bure, Gino scored 16 goals in just one season with the Russian Rocket (creative nickname?).

And some of Gino's rough and toughness rubbed off on the Russian—in one game, Bure even knocked NHL tough guy Shane Churla out cold. (Bure's biggest fight, however, was reported to be off the ice with Russian compatriot Sergei Fedorov over tennis superstar Anna Kournikova.)

But the world of professional hockey is highly transient, and Odjick ("Mutt") and Bure ("Jeff") would eventually go their separate ways. Odjick was traded to the New York Islanders in the 1997–98 season and played there until 1999–00, when he was traded to the Philadelphia Flyers.

"Philadelphia was an interesting experience because I was reunited with Sandy McArthy, who I played junior with in Laval. Everybody feared that we would be some kind of wrestling tag-team match-up, which didn't happen. Actually, there were three of us Indians on the Flyers. With Craig Berube also on the team, now people were thinking the Flyers would dress an all-Native 'goon line,' which also didn't happen.

"We never thought to get a picture of us together even though you figure in your career that it's very rare to play on the same team with three

Aboriginal players. Then I left the Flyers for the Montreal Canadiens the next year and now I'm here with Aaron Asham and Sheldon Souray so maybe it's not so rare, but I'm going to get a picture anyways!"

★ ★ ★ ★ ★

Gino's career was ended by a bizarre series of events.

First of all, there was an incident off the ice when Gino chased a man who had tried to steal his car. Gino caught the thief but got stabbed in the stomach. This would lead to a series of abdominal injuries which would cause Gino to miss a lot of games during the late stages of his career.

And Gino's NHL career came to an end in Montreal because of blurred vision and headaches due to concussions. No, it wasn't a fist to the head that ended things for this man of many fights; the Algonquin Enforcer's professional days of playing and punching came to a halt because he was plucked square in the head by a puck!

But Wayne Gino Odjick was never one to forget his roots, and he always wanted to return to his community (and other First Nations communities) to help younger generations to pursue their dreams in the sport of hockey.

"Ron Delorme started talking about how important it would be for me to start giving back to our community. We met with Kevin Tootoosis during that first year and I could tell by the way they spoke they weren't in it to make money. They just wanted more kids to come out and play in the NHL.

"At that time [1990], I was alone but I had played with a lot of guys that I thought should be in the NHL. Delorme started talking about an Aboriginal Role Model Hockey School—somewhere where the kids can come and the players can just try to explain to them that it was possible for native players to make it.

"It was fun. We had a couple of good young students. We had Wade Redden, who may have been 14 or 15 years old. Sheldon Souray. It was nice to see them progress in junior and become prospects and then play in the NHL."

★ ★ ★ ★ ★

Sheldon Souray was sitting in a stall next to Odjick at the Bell Centre when interviews took place for the documentary. Sheldon's NHL career had started with mixed success with the New Jersey Devils, but eventually Souray's name would become synonymous with "superstar." But that started off the ice.

In New Jersey and the rest of the "tri-state area," which included New York and Pennsylvania, Souray quickly became more appreciated as a "handsome devil." Highly photogenic, Sheldon was featured in "eligible bachelor" photo spreads in such prestigious national publications as *Esquire* and *Gentlemen's Quarterly*. He also appeared in a cameo role in the hit soap opera, *One Life to Live* (which comedian Charlie Hill parodied from a Native perspective to be *One Land to Lose*).

This Métis child from Elk River, Alberta took it all in stride. "It was fun, mostly, and kind of funny. When some of my teammates in New Jersey teased me about doing fashion spreads, it was like I told Kenny Daneyko, 'Well, you could have been part of it, too, but the prerequisite was a full set of teeth and you didn't make the cut!'

"Those were things I never thought I would do but when the opportunities came up, it was all in fun. I'm not sure how long I'll be playing or I'll look like this so I'm having fun while I can!"

Following our "fun" interview, Souray went on to set an NHL season record for power-play goals scored by a defenceman (19, breaking Hall-of-Famer Denis Potvin's mark, which was shared by Vancouver's Adrian Aucoin). But the fun off the ice was reported to be tempered by an acrimonious divorce Sheldon was going through with his wife, a former *Playboy* playmate. Sheldon's performance on the ice indeed diminished during the time he was going through his marital breakup, but he recovered sufficiently to set that record, and to be able to dictate his own terms when he became a free agent.

With freedom looming both on and off the ice, everybody thought handsome playboy Sheldon Souray would sign with the Los Angeles Kings and melt into the mansions and minions of Beverley Hills. But Sheldon is, first and foremost, a "homeboy" and Alberta came a-calling.

"I'm from Fisher Lake, a Métis settlement in Alberta, but I was born in Elk River, which is the closest village to our community. I moved away from our settlement to play in Edmonton and the family moved. But all my uncles, my grandma and family are still in Fisher Lake."

It would be a stretch (using Hollywood lingo) to claim that Sheldon Souray passed on glamour and glitter in favour of Grandma. This superstar athlete had a more basic motivation to return to his home base to further his career. Despite having played in the holier-than-thou grail of hockey that is Montreal, home of the Habs, there was no more hallowed hockey ground to Alberta native Souray than Edmonton.

"More than anything, growing up in Alberta, with the Oilers winning all those Stanley Cups with Wayne Gretzky and Paul Coffey, Mark Messier, Glenn Anderson, Jari Kurri and Grant Fuhr and everybody else, I always wanted to be an Oiler, pure and simple as that."

On July 12, 2007, Souray signed a contract with the Oilers for $27 million over five years.

"As for Native role models who impacted on me growing up, I was able to identify with Fred Sasakamoose and Reggie Leach through my experience with the Aboriginal Role Model Hockey School. You see other Native people being successful at something you are trying to be successful at, and you identify with that. It's definitely people you look up to, people whose footsteps you want to follow in. They were the leaders and the pioneers in the sport, the way I see it. It's nice to have role models like that."

Q: And what is your nickname, Sheldon?
A: The Hammer! Or Chief!

Our camera panned from the tattoo of a magnificent buffalo on one of Sheldon's shoulders to an Indian headdress tattoo on Sheldon's other shoulder to a stall across the hall to Aaron Asham—another Métis, this one from the plains of Portage La Prairie, Manitoba.

Q: And your nickname is?"
A: Ash.

Q: Not Chief?
A: No, that's Gino's.

Souray and Asham are still in the prime of their careers as this book goes
to print, so we return to the Indian athlete who has hung up his skates, but
not his spirit.

★ ★ ★ ★ ★

Gino Odjick has moved on from the NHL in many, many ways. He now
spends much of his free time teaching Indian kids about the dangers of
drug abuse. Gino knows how hard it is to break out from a life in an
impoverished First Nation community and make it on the outside. One
does not need to add the obstacles of overcoming an addiction to drugs to
that effort.

Odjick also teaches at hockey schools throughout the country whenever he can. But at the end of his career, he didn't end up at home in Maniwaki. Odjick returned to his second home, where he's just as welcome,
Vancouver.

"I came here as a boy and I left as a man. So Vancouver feels like home.
During my NHL career, everywhere I went, I compared it to Vancouver.
So it is home."

Odjick returned to Canada's "lotusland" not only because it felt like
home, but because of a business opportunity he couldn't turn down. The
Musqueam First Nation, located in Vancouver, wanted to buy back a lease
on the Musqueam Golf Course, and needed a partner with deep pockets.
Gino made modern-day NHL money during his hockey career. He was
looking for a second career, and he loves golf, so the decision to invest was
a no-brainer.

"I thank God I've had the opportunity to go directly from hockey to
another job. A lot of hockey players don't have a college education. It's a
whole lot harder to make money in the real world."

The Musqueam Golf Course is already one of the most popular in Vancouver, arguably Canada's most popular metropolis. Like Stanley Park, the course is a rare survivor of the rush to development that has turned Vancouver from lotusland into condo-land.

"There is even a salmon-bearing creek running through the course. I'm told it is the only one left in the city and there used to be 50 of them at one time. We're not here to take our pay cut. We are cut out to leave this historic, natural setting in better shape than when we came."

It's kind of fun to picture tough guy Gino Odjick stroking a young salmon fingerling with loving care. And getting serious about improving his golf game, which is not generally considered to be one of your more macho sports.

Despite the mellow miles he's walking in his moccasins now, Gino Odjick will always be remembered as one of the toughest, yet skilled enforcers who ever played in the National Hockey League. Gino the Chief will never be inducted into the Hockey Hall of Fame, and the highlights of his career show why :

1992–93: Finished first on the Canucks with 370 PIM. Recorded first multiple point game of his career (0-2-2) Oct. 16 at Winnipeg. Had most productive NHL game (2-1-3, +3) Nov. 23 vs. Chicago. Set new Canucks record with 47 PIM in one game vs. Los Angeles Nov. 12.

1993–94: Registered a career high in goals (16), including five game winners. Led Canucks in PIM for 4th straight season with 271. Finished second on the team in plus/minus.

1994–95: Missed last 13 games of the season due to an abdominal strain suffered on April 17 vs. Winnipeg.

1995–96: Missed 24 games with torn abdominal wall suffered Nov. 22 vs. Dallas.

1996–97: Finished first on the Canucks and first in the NHL with a career high 371 PIM. Passed Garth Butcher on Nov. 16 to become the Canucks' all-time PIM leader with 1,946. Missed two games with a bruised finger and four games with an injured finger.

1999–00: Recorded 100 PIMs, giving him 100+ PIMs for 10th straight season. Ranked second on the Islanders with 3 game-winning goals.

And that's the story from Chum Sa Bay to the Algonquin Enforcer, with a lot of "Chiefs" and "wagon burners" in between.

12

FUTURE CHIEFS

This book tells the stories of just some of the Indians who played in the National Hockey League. We have limited our bios to, at most, a chapter each. So, once again, *They Call Me Chief*—the book this time—is missing a lot.

The complete stories may eventually be told in other books and films. Or perhaps to family and friends and the general public in other ways. Maybe around a campfire or a woodstove, maybe in a sharing circle, in a living room or rec room, perhaps more often in dressing rooms during the winter hockey tournament trail or during teepee-creeping evenings on the summer powwow trail.

Players like Rene Robert, Dale McCourt (George Armstrong's nephew), Sandy McCarthy, Craig Berube and many others haven't been covered at all. This is mostly because the players we did write about were so interesting and inspiring, there was no room to present an account of these other "warriors on ice" without being superficial, at best.

It was also important to include the history, culture and issues the players from First Nations raised because of their unique backgrounds.

We also couldn't write about present-day Native athletes who are currently starring in the NHL, because their stories are still unfolding year by year. Players like Jonathan Cheechoo, Jordin Tootoo and Carey Price will have long and outstanding (and interesting and meaningful) careers themselves, and I hope that someday their accomplishments will be recorded in future books.

All the players we featured in this book have achieved the highest honour—to play in the world's greatest and most elite hockey league, the NHL. From their stories we have learned how players like Bryan Trottier and Reggie Leach and Fred Sasakamoose accomplished what they did. We witnessed the obstacles they overcame, and we saw how they welcomed these challenges and proved themselves worthy to be called "warriors on ice."

★ ★ ★ ★ ★

All of this leaves us with just one subject that needs to be explored here: what needs to be done to increase the success of Native hockey players in North America in general? And how can the number of Native players in the NHL be increased? After all, the First Nations of the Americas may have invented the game of hockey in the first place. What can be done to help Natives develop to their utmost potential?

★ ★ ★ ★ ★

Perhaps a good place to start is by asking, "Do we need special programs to increase the number of Natives playing in the NHL?" And, if we do, why?

According to every player we talked to during the filming of the documentary and the writing of this book, there is a definite need to make a special effort, and to develop special programs. These guys are the experts and we'll just take them at their word. After all, who would know better than the guys who have been through it all and made it to the top?

But why do we need special programs? A major reason stems from the living conditions that many Native children and youth face growing up.

Poverty is a major factor in prohibiting Native kids, any kids, from achieving their full potential in hockey. Equipment is very expensive. Facilities and league registrations cost a lot. Even Canadian parents with middle-class and upper-middle-class incomes face difficulties, especially if they have more than one child enrolled in an organized hockey program. Low income parents simply cannot afford to pay for the equipment, uniforms, ice times, referees, registration and travel costs, which are estimated at $5,000 per season per child in 2008. Many Native children do not get to play organized hockey, even recreational hockey, simply because of the cost.

The prohibitive impact of expenses is exacerbated in First Nations communities, who are struggling to provide basic amenities such as housing, clean water, sewage treatment, roads and other community-wide needs. Recreation has long been a luxury in First Nations communities.

For the most part, Native children must learn their hockey skills outdoors, which is historically not a bad thing, but certainly puts them at a disadvantage against children who have access to modern indoor facilities. And, face it, many First Nations communities are located in the far north where it gets extremely cold in the winter, making it prohibitive to play outdoors—although a benefit can be gained from a longer playing season, as long as there are funds to maintain the outdoor rinks.

In addition to equipment and access to facilities, aspiring hockey players benefit greatly from good teaching. Sometimes there are skilled, experienced players in a community who can pass on what they know to the younger children, but this is hit-and-miss at best. Ideally, a child can learn from teachers who not only can demonstrate the skills of hockey, but who have also been trained in the art of coaching. There is a big difference between knowing something and passing that knowledge on to others effectively.

★ ★ ★ ★ ★

Through the years, there have been young Native players who have stood out, either because they simply possess overwhelming talent, or they were able to avail themselves of proper opportunities, equipment and coaching.

Yet many of these children and youth were failing to make the grade as well. This is because of another reason that Ted Nolan and others maintain remains a serious problem—and that is racism.

"You go to a triple-A camp and I can tell you that the Native kid doesn't have to be as good as the other kids to make the team. He has to be a lot better or he'll be cut," Nolan claims with absolute certainty. And he is supported by many of his compatriots.

So there is a need for a special effort and special programs to increase the number of Natives in the NHL.

Ron Delorme was a forerunner in the attempt to develop First Nations talent starting at a young age. Ron, along with Kevin Tootoosis of the Federation of Saskatchewan Indian Nations, formed the Aboriginal Role Model Hockey School in Saskatoon. Their goal was to identify Native kids with potential and hook them up with role models who could provide an example, advice, motivation and coaching that would enhance their chance for success.

The school was quite successful during the 1990s. Graduates included Sheldon Souray and Wade Redden. NHL players like Gino Odjick, Reggie Leach, Jamie Leach, Blair Atcheynum, Delorme and others lent their time to the school (basically for expenses). But the Aboriginal Role Model Hockey School faded away as organizers got busy with other things, and nobody picked up the puck with the enthusiasm of the original founders.

★ ★ ★ ★ ★

Another way to increase the number of Natives who might make it to the NHL is to take control over the leagues or teams that pick and choose the players.

Some Native coaches and community leaders have managed to exert influence over the peewee, bantam and midget-level leagues and teams, but there is no way any group can gain total or long-term control over community-based sports and recreation programs (although some may beg to differ).

At the junior level, many teams are privately owned, and "them that pays the bills, calls the shots." So there have been some efforts to buy junior franchises by First Nations and some individual Indian entrepreneurs.

First of all, the oil-rich Ermineskin Indian Band of Alberta founded the Hobbema Hawks of the Alberta Junior Hockey League. The Southeast Tribal Council in Manitoba developed the Southeast Thunderbirds in the Manitoba Junior Hockey League (later the Blades, which ended up being owned by National Chief Phil Fontaine of the Assembly of First Nations before he sold it to white interests), and the Waywayseecappo Wolverines also play in the MJHL.

The idea to develop an Indian-owned junior hockey team is basically the same no matter where it is attempted, therefore, we focused our attention on the two most visible Native-owned franchises in Canada: the Lebret Eagles of Saskatchewan and Manitoba's OCN Blizzard. Not only did these two teams provide answers to questions we were asking about how to increase opportunities for Native players in hockey, the history behind these two noble experiments is full of fascinating insights into the troubled relationships between First Nations and mainstream Canadian society that we can learn some important lessons from.

★ ★ ★ ★ ★

"Before the Starblanket First Nation bought the Lebret Eagles, there was one, maybe two Native boys playing in the Saskatchewan Junior Hockey League," claims Vern Bellegarde, former Eagles President. "Now there are two to three Native boys playing on almost every team in the league!"

Bellegard is telling the truth, but the ultimate fate of the Lebret Eagles was a mixed success. And, before the story of the rise and fall of the Lebret Eagles can be told, it's essential to provide some background into the setting and the history of the area, and the people who would ultimately determine the success or failure of this venture.

★ ★ ★ ★ ★

Lebret, Saskatchewan is a postcard town lying on the banks of Lake Qu'Appelle and the Qu'Appelle River. The Qu'Appelle valley is a most scenic interruption to the never-ending flatlands of southern Saskatchewan, a popular tourist area, with boating, fishing, even skiing.

The area gets its name from a trait more common to the area around the Swiss Matterhorn: echoes. The area is haunted by the echoes of Native people throughout history, the first explorers, settlers and now tourists, who get a kick out of calling out and hearing their voices ring so clearly back from the hills and valleys. In French, "qu' appelle" means "who calls?"

The valley is dominated by the town of Fort Qu'Appelle, a tourist town that also serves as an agricultural goods and supply centre for the hinterland. Lebret is a village seven miles east down a mildly winding lakeshore road.

Lebret is much smaller than Fort Qu'Appelle, but much larger, in a more powerful sense. Lebret was the centre of Catholicism in this area of Saskatchewan—home to a magnificent stone cathedral—and a "procession."

A procession is a very, very large hill, a steep climb marked with white crosses every 10 steps of the way. At the top is a large white cross and a shelter/shack for reflection. The procession dominates Lebret, just as the Catholic Church dominated the First Nations immediately upon its arrival in the Qu'Appelle Valley.

The most dominant feature of Lebret used to be the huge, three-storey, red brick Indian residential school, which was run by the Catholic clergy in concert with the Canadian government. A foreboding structure jutting out over Lake Qu'Appelle, the "Indian Residential School at Lebret" is said to have been home to some of the most horrific atrocities associated with the cultural genocide, general genocide, and physical, emotional and sexual abuse inflicted upon the children of Canada's First Nations. Some of that has been mentioned elsewhere in this book and detailed accounts can be found in the vastly accumulating research and documentation that is readily available through the Aboriginal Healing Foundation about this shameful period in North American history.

★ ★ ★ ★ ★

There's a statue outside that magnificent stone church in Lebret that grabs your eye, and then captures your total attention—and your imagination. You find yourself transfixed. You cannot take your eyes off this iron monument, or monstrosity, or whatever it is. It grabs your heart and your mind, fully, completely.

The statue is of an Indian child, three feet tall, who rests his head against the thigh of an eight-foot-high configuration of a "kindly" priest. The Indian child is full of awe and wonder. Deep affection and appreciation seems to emanate from the small, grateful red entity in his gesture towards the white priest, who reciprocates with knowing care and protection.

There is no work of art, no literature, no testimony created or yet to be created, that could so accurately portray the relationship between the Catholic Church in Lebret, and the First Nations that surrounded this village, as defined by the dominance the Church held over First Nations at the time the statue was erected. At the same time, there is no image that could so completely distort and misrepresent the actual relationship of hearts and minds that met in Lebret.

It's a complicated history. Some Indians embraced the teachings and religion of the Catholic and Protestant clergy who entered their lives. Others resisted with all the mind and might they could muster. Perhaps this conflict can best be symbolized by what exists on the road into the Peepeekisis First Nation, north of Lebret. There's no sign to tell you that you are entering Indian territory. You know because the paved road turns to gravel right at the border, and there is a Catholic church on one side and a Protestant church on the other. These institutions are not allowed to occupy Indian land, but they stand right next door, ready to welcome new members to their congregations, as some would say, or to proselytize, as others might claim.

This historical relationship between Indians and the Catholic Church would ultimately decide the fate of the Lebret Eagles junior hockey team. The valley simply ran too deep and wide.

★ ★ ★ ★ ★

The junior team in Lebret drew its name from the hockey team that used to be run out of that residential school—a team not unlike the one Fred Sasakamoose played for at the residential school in Duck Lake. The Lebret Eagles had a proud history (the residential school had access to a rink and, of course, whatever amount of time the priests wanted to devote to hockey so that their midget level players could develop "two on ones" and "three on twos"—at the expense of reading, 'riting and 'rithmetic, of course).

The Indians in the File Hills area (an area from Yorkton to Fort Qu'Appelle), had already become the first First Nations in Canada to throw the church administrators and their government backers out of a residential school by camping out, staging a legitimate protest and taking over operations of the school in Lebret, many years before the idea of developing a junior hockey team came to mind.

The organizers of the SJHL team in Lebret hoped to build on the pride and success and name associated with the Eagles school teams.

The junior Eagles franchise was owned by the Starblanket First Nation—one of four FNs—stacked upon each other on the map in the File Hills area (south to north it was Peepeekisis, Starblanket, Okanese and Little Black Bear, in that order). The residential school complex developed a dormitory in which the players could be housed at minimal cost. The school also owned an indoor ice hockey arena that provided facilities for home games at substantial savings. Neighbouring Fort Qu'Appelle is a relatively large and prosperous town, with dual industries of tourism and agriculture shielding it from boom and bust years, and it provided a base the junior hockey franchise of their neighbours in Lebret could tap into. The team got off to an okay start for a new franchise.

The overall record of the Lebret Eagles on the ice is posted in the "Records" section of this book. They ended up from first to last during the regular season, and never advanced past the semifinals in SJHL playoff action.

In the stands, success depended a lot on support from surrounding south Saskatchewan towns with names like Abernethy, Katepwa and Balcarres, but mostly, the Lebret Eagles needed the support from their immediate neighbour—the townspeople of Fort Qu'Appelle. This support was mixed at best—some citzens and businesses got rabidly behind the team, some were indifferent, and some completely rejected the concept of an Indian-owned anything.

It is very expensive to operate a junior hockey league franchise, even in Tier 2 provincial leagues like the SJHL. Players are paid a small stipend, but 20 times such stipends add up. Then there's the cost of equipment, travel, facilities and accommodations. Under ordinary circumstances, the cost of operating an SJHL team like the Eagles was way beyond the resources of the tiny Starblanket First Nation. Despite the support of their geographic hinterland, and the support of every Indian in southern Saskatchewan, every year was a struggle to survive financially for the Lebret Eagles.

As for providing opportunities for Indigenous players to showcase and develop their talent, the Lebret Eagles were a most viable option for youth from First Nations communities. The talent pool was certainly not sufficient to ice an all-Indian team, and the Eagles very wisely scouted and recruited athletes from all ethnic groups to try and assemble the most competitive lineup possible, just like any other SJHL team. Bottom line is that Indigenous players were given an absolutely fair and equal, if not preferential chance to play in the SJHL, which had never existed before.

It took a while for that attitude to spread throughout the league.

"I had to miss the first day of the SJHL evaluation camp because of a funeral," says Don Chesney, the 1997 head coach in Lebret. "I figured that all the best players would be picked over by the second day but I noticed this Native kid from up by Beauvalle who was head and shoulders above every other player at that camp. Boy! Was I surprised when I got back to Lebret and found out that the other teams had passed on him and I got him for the Eagles.

"I get credit for being an excellent scout but, really, my mother could have picked that kid out. I don't know why the other SJHL teams didn't grab him. Maybe they didn't want to take a chance on a Native kid."

From 1993–94 to 2000–01, the Lebret Eagles did the best they could to provide opportunities for Native youth to play junior hockey. And the number of players from First Nations in the SJHL increased year by year.

But then the ugly history of the past, and the ever-present petty politics of our times rose up and the Lebret Eagles folded their wings in failure.

★ ★ ★ ★ ★

The Lebret Indian Residential School was an imposing structure. Rising three storeys high over the lake and the tiny village, built of solid, square, red brick, the facility looked as much like a prison as it did a school. The entire image was one of reformatory instead of advancement, Alcatraz versus Harvard.

I can vividly recall the first time I saw the bright white windows of the school, surrounded by red bricks and topped off with a dark roof. I was viewing this scene from a distance, down by the shore from the deck at the Lebret Hotel.

At first, the school structure reminded me of the Anderson family home from that popular 1960s sitcom *Father Knows Best*, or the mini-bricks I played with as a child.

But then "shadows" appeared. Nothing specific. Just a dark shadow that wafted over the entire scene. I didn't hear any voices, or see any ghostly images of the priests or the children or the horrendous activities that we all know took place in this, and many other residential schools throughout Canada.

I just saw a shadow, a huge shadow, that made me stop and step back, shake my head and then, the image cleared. I ducked back into the bar at the Lebret Hotel and had another beer.

I had been drinking beer with Doc Swanson, Harry Bird and George Poitras from Peepeekisis. Nothing serious, in terms of alcohol, and we had been discussing the development of an ethanol plant on their First Nation.

Please allow me to digress for a moment. The ethanol plant would buy all of the grain the people of Peepeekisis, the other three File Hills First Nations and any other grain farmer in the area could produce; the plant would convert it to alcohol; Mohawk Gas would buy all the alcohol to make gasohol; the byproducts of the fermentation process were animal feed to support a cow-calf operation and CO_2 to fuel a greenhouse. What an ideal economic development project to create wealth and employment for a rural community like an Indian reserve!

But the gasohol project didn't happen for the same reasons many other great ideas don't happen in Indian country: there was no money available for capital investment. That was 25 years ago. Ethanol plants are springing up all over the country now.

But the gasohol project brought me to Lebret and my first experience with the school and the fact of the matter is that I got chills looking up at the Lebret Indian Residential School. Those shadows were real. And the feelings that I experienced were real.

So why am I telling you all this? Well, it's important to note that, to a white kid from Manitoba, who had no idea what the school was, or anything about its sordid history, the image of the school was unsettling, to say the least. And those feelings were similar to the reasoning that brought down that building and contributed to the end of the Lebret Eagles.

★ ★ ★ ★ ★

Some influential members of the Starblanket First Nation (owners of the Eagles) claimed that the Lebret Indian Residential School was an eyesore, a symbol of a history of rule and repression, and a vivid reminder of the horrors of physical and sexual abuse that had taken place within its walls. It created and recreated nightmares for the citizens of all the First Nations of File Hills. They demanded that the institution be taken out of view, torn down, and for good reason.

The demolition contracts would also create jobs for local First Nations people who were facing high unemployment. In any case, the Lebret Indian Residential School was indeed torn down, and with it went any savings that association with it provided. There was an accompanying negative impact on already testy relations between Fort Qu'Appelle, Lebret and the File Hills First Nations, as educators and labourers from Fort Qu'Appelle felt they had been treated unfairly in the deal.

At least, that's one side of the story I was told about why the Lebret Eagles folded in 2002 (after a one-year "leave of absence" granted by the SJHL to get their affairs in order failed). Others claim that the costs of operating an SJHL franchise were simply too much for the market in Lebret, Fort Qu'Appelle and surrounding areas to bear.

Unfortunately, the original goals—to provide opportunities for Native hockey players to play and excel to the best of their ability—got lost because of economic (and perhaps political) reasons. But the number of Native players in the SJHL has remained constant, so perhaps the Eagles accomplished that goal.

The statue of that priest and child from in front of the nearby church was also taken away, as part of the "renewal by removal" process. I'm told that the Indians had that statue melted down into scrap metal.

★ ★ ★ ★ ★

An interesting side note to the Eagles story is the use of this sacred bird as a mascot by the Indians. The eagle is a most powerful animal in the spirituality of Native people throughout the Americas. The eagle flies high and has extremely keen vision. It is the eagle that carries the prayers of the people to the Creator and it is the eagle that brings the answers to their prayers, as well as teachings from the Creator so that they may have foresight. With all of the controversy surrounding the use of Indians as mascots by white sports teams, it is interesting to note that Indian people themselves face a debate about their use of mascots for their own sports teams. Many elders objected to using a sacred animal such as the eagle to represent a sports team, which sometimes involves cheating, unsportsmanlike conduct, frivolity and even the fact that some vulgar language, as well as blood, can spill out of a player's mouth, over the image of an eagle on his chest. (The Indian-owned Southeast Thunderbirds of the Manitoba Junior Hockey League would change their name to "Blades" for these very reasons, the Thunderbird being another sacred animal).

This proves that the use of Indian symbols, names, culture and spirituality is much more complicated and controversial than most people think. And that should stop some people from simply telling Indians to stop having such thin skin when it comes to this matter.

★ ★ ★ ★ ★

The most successful Indian-owned junior hockey team in Canadian history is the OCN Blizzard of the Manitoba Junior Hockey League. The fact that this success was achieved in one of the most racist environments in all of Canada makes this accomplishment all the more remarkable.

The Pas, Manitoba, is a northern logging town that butts up against the south shore of the Saskatchewan River. To many townspeople in The Pas in the 1970s, the real "butt" was the Opasquiak Cree Nation, which sits opposite The Pas on the north side of the Saskatchewan. To say that this close geographic proximity created an uneasy relationship between the two communities would be an understatement that would rival "Hitler doesn't think too highly of Jews." There was outright hatred between the white people of The Pas and the Indians over in the OCN.

White folks did not like their "spear-chucking, wagon-burning, prairie nigger" neighbours to the north and the Indians felt the same way towards their "moonyash, honky crackers" across the creek. These ill feelings were exacerbated by programs such as "affirmative action," which Indians said they needed to overcome discrimination in hiring practices at the local logging plant, and by the development of an Indian-owned shopping mall in the OCN, which not only stopped the one-way flow of money spent on goods and services from the OCN to The Pas, but started to draw money away from The Pas to the OCN—along with hundreds of other issues, major and minor, individual and collective.

And then there was the murder of Helen Betty Osborne.

★ ★ ★ ★ ★

There have been incidents of violence, rape and murder of Indians by white people in northern Manitoba towns in the past, but few could compare with the murder of this petite Indian high school student by four white men in The Pas. That is partly because of the sheer brutality of this despicable act, but mostly because nobody was brought to justice for this crime for well over a decade, even though almost everybody in The Pas knew who did the deed. And it wasn't so much a cover-up, because local townspeople gossiped openly about the incident; the real crime became the fact nobody lifted a finger to point out and prosecute the perpetrators.

Helen Betty Osborne was a child of Joe and Justine (née McKay) Osborne of the Norway House First Nation. As a teenager, Helen dreamed of getting a college education, and the only way to do that was to move to The Pas, because there was no high school in her home First Nation.

Helen was placed with a white family in The Pas, who were paid for her room and board. She was a good student, described as "typical"; she liked movies, the popular music of the day and she had a boyfriend, Cornelius Bighetty.

Saturday, November 13, 1971 was a typical late fall day in The Pas. Local weather had already given away to brutally cold winter, and the ground was covered in snow. On this evening, Helen had decided not to attend a movie with her friends, and was walking home down Third Street, when a car driven by Pas resident James Robert Paul Houghton, who was accompanied by Dwayne Archie Johnston, Lee Scott Colgan and Norman Bernard Manger, pulled up beside her.

Many young white men in The Pas carried an ignorant, stereotypical attitude towards Indian women during the 1970s. Houghton and Colgan, both from upstanding middle-class homes, probably figured that Osborne would simply "put out" for them because Indian girls were "known" to do that.

Johnston was a biker type from the wrong side of the tracks. Tough, or just plain ignorant and nasty, he had a mean streak of hatred toward Indians in him that flowed naturally on this night.

Manger was indeed a mangy guy, a drunk, who by all accounts was so drunk on this occasion, he barely realized what was going on.

Houghton stopped the car beside Osborne, and Johnston got out. At first, he asked Helen to "come party," but she declined. When he persisted, she refused. Helen was then dragged off the street, forced into the car and driven away. As Houghton drove, Johnston and Colgan began to assault Helen, Johnston ripping at her blouse, despite her screams and cries, her pleas for help and her attempts to escape.

They took Helen Betty Osborne to the Houghton family cabin near Clearwater Lake, the local and tourist resort spot that serves The Pas. At the cabin, Helen was pulled from the car and beaten by Johnston while the other three men stood watching and drinking wine they had stolen earlier. Because Helen continued to scream, the men became afraid they might be overheard, so they forced her back into the car and drove her further from town to a pumphouse at Clearwater Lake.

More of Helen's clothing was removed in the car and then she was completely stripped, except for her winter boots, outside by the pump house. The beating continued, so viciously that her face was smashed beyond recognition. Helen Betty Osborne was stabbed over 50 times, apparently with a screwdriver. Evidence indicates that her body was dragged into the bush and her clothes were hidden.

There is a reason why I have described this assault in such detail. It is to let readers of this book know exactly what the townspeople of The Pas knew. Such an unfair, brutal and cruel assault would most certainly move most decent people to seek justice, no matter who the victim was, or what personal prejudices they might be carrying. But for the longest time, nobody in The Pas cared enough, or was moved deeply enough, to do anything about the murder of Helen Betty Osborne.

★ ★ ★ ★ ★

The body of Helen Betty Osborne was discovered the next day by a teenager who was out hunting rabbits. Initially, the investigation by the RCMP centred on Helen's friends, all of them Indian, especially her boyfriend Cornelius. All were cleared; Cornelius by a lie detector.

Police had no suspects until the following spring, when an anonymous letter was received in May, 1972, implicating Houghton, Colgan and Manger. It turned out the letter was written by Catherine Dick, who had been told about the murder by Colgan shortly after it took place.

Police seized the Colgan family car, which had been used in the abduction, and found traces of blood and hair, as well as a piece of a brassiere strap. An informant also told police about the involvement of Dwayne Johnston but, on the advice of their lawyer, D'Arcy Bancroft, all four men were instructed not to talk to police, and there was insufficient evidence to support a charge of murder. By the end of 1972, the investigation had stalled, even though rumours were circulating widely throughout The Pas about the specific identities of the men involved in the incident.

And so it remained for over 10 years. The four men lived with the knowledge of what they had done, and it appears their relatives and friends also knew. But nobody would come forward in the name of simple justice.

The entire sordid story can be found on the Internet, and a movie, *Conspiracy of Silence* was produced about it. The upshot is that, after a lengthy and extensive review of the case by RCMP Constable Robert Urbanoski, and a broad public appeal, some people finally came forward. Colgan and Johnston were arrested and charged with murder.

In the end, Colgan was granted immunity for his testimony against Houghton and Johnston. Johnston was found guilty of murder and sentenced to life imprisonment with no eligibility for parole for 10 years. Houghton was acquitted.

Many Manitobans asked why it took 16 years to bring the perpetrators to trial for this high-profile murder, when it was well known that many people in The Pas knew who was responsible. It was suggested that, because Helen Betty Osborne was an Indian, the townspeople considered the murder insignificant, not worthy of notice.

The murder of Helen Betty Osborne led to an Aboriginal Justice Inquiry, which examined all aspects of the way First Nations citizens are treated by the justice system. But over a thousand pages of recommendations to address, redress or correct this social situation sit collecting dust on the shelves of government bureaucracies.

The atmosphere of racism, mistrust and hatred simmered on the streets of The Pas through to the 1990s because there was nothing to bring these people together to deal with and overcome this division.

FUTURE CHIEFS

★ ★ ★ ★ ★

It's not that there were shootouts at high noon every day in The Pas or the OCN. Some individuals maintained friendships that transcended racial barriers, and there was some commerce between the two groups. The Town Council and the Band Council would meet and suggest some initiatives that might foster positive exchanges (a festival here, a powwow there), but the bad feelings festered. And while you might find some Indians and whites having a blast competing in a flour-packing contest during the afternoon at The Pas Trappers Festival, the fun and frivolity often spilled over into a fistfight by the evening.

And that's the way it was in January, 1996, when the Opasquiak Cree Nation wrapped up a deal they had been working on for years to build pride for their community and develop role models for their children and youth. They were going to try their hand at operating a Canadian Tier Two Junior A hockey franchise in the Manitoba Junior Hockey League.

There were precedents for Indians to own and operate a Junior A hockey franchise, like the Hobbema Hawks, the Lebret Eagles, and the Southeast Blades.

The Hawks and the Eagles had been competitive, making the playoffs from time to time, but neither ever won a championship to advance out of their province. The Blades generally lived in last place in the MJHL.

That doesn't mean these efforts at hockey ownership by First Nations were unsuccessful. Indians are known to view that proverbial glass as half full and the Hawks, Eagles and Blades had accomplished some good things. These franchises provided opportunities for Native players to develop and showcase their talent in a top-notch scenario, plenty of players had advanced to minor professional leagues such as the ECHL (which, bottom line, gave them a chance to travel, play the game they love, and earn a decent living), and many other players managed to earn scholarships at Canadian and American universities. The latter accomplishment is the greatest of them all, because these players who weren't quite NHL or AHL level were able to get an education and become productive citizens who set a standard for the folks back home. Their glass was indeed half full; they drank from it, and enjoyed every drop of the fruits of their labours together with the First Nations organizations and individuals who put in the time and effort to develop these hockey teams.

★ ★ ★ ★ ★

The OCN Blizzard, whether it was a matter of learning from what went before, or simply having more smarts than everybody else, were a smash success right from the get-go. The franchise was expected to endure a few losing seasons before developing a talent base that would be competitive, but there was none of that. In their first year, the OCN Blizzard advanced all the way to the championship final of the MJHL, and they made it to the semifinals in their second year. After those "growing pains," the franchise went on a tear that made everybody in Canadian hockey, from the MJHL to the NHL, take notice, if not stand up in awe.

From the 1998–99 season until 2002–03, the Blizzard won five straight Manitoba Junior Hockey League Championships. While it was a thrill to make the Opasquiak Cree Nation home for the Turnbull Cup (emblematic of MJHL supremacy), that act soon grew old, because the MJHL had been playing the part of "little brother" to their counterparts from the Prairies to the immediate west for way too long.

The Saskatchewan Junior Hockey League is an extremely well-organized league with experience and expertise up the wahzoo throughout the administration of the league and within individual clubs. A lot of the best players available to Tier Two junior hockey clubs choose the SJHL because they know they will be able to compete at a top level and they will be watched by scouts from minor and major professional leagues, as well as Canadian and American universities. The SJHL is stable and professionally run, and has a lot going for it when it comes to enticing players to play in its league.

What all this means for teams in the MJHL is that they have long been the red-headed stepchild when it comes to attracting the kind of players needed to advance out of the prairies and competing for the national Tier Two junior hockey championship. Champions of the MJHL and the SJHL face off each year in a best-of-seven series for the Anavet Cup; the winner gets to advance to the national Tier Two junior championship playdowns.

Most times, it is the representative of the SJHL that gets to play for the Royal Bank Cup (formerly the Centennial Cup), which is given to the top Junior A team in Canada after a round-robin playdown leading to a championship final. Actually, four teams fight it out in the final, three of which survive regional playdowns, and they're joined by the team from the host city.

The Blizzard, after they began blowing by their competition in Manitoba year after year, were, of course, saddled with the responsibility of restoring prairie pride to the province of the bison, but wresting it away from the gopher proved to be a difficult task.

From 1998–99 to 2000–01, the OCN Blizzard's record reads like the script from the movie *Groundhog Day*. "Won League, Lost Anavet Cup" [or AC] (to the Estevan Bruins), "Won League Lost AC" (Battleford North Stars), "Won League, Lost AC" (Weyburn Red Wings). Even if you were a member of another MJHL team and you hated the Blizzard, and especially if you were a fan of MJHL hockey, you were getting tired of the same old story, and you were doubting whether the MJHL was on the same level as the SJHL.

But finally, the Blizzard broke through. After six years, two falling just short of the MJHL championship, the next three years falling in the final of the Anavet Cup, the Blizzard beat the Red Wings from Weyburn, Saskatchewan 4 games to 1, to win the Anavet and advance to the Royal Bank Cup Championship.

At first, it seemed that advancing past the Anavet was tougher than advancing through the competition at the national level, because the Blizzard won their way into the championship final by defeating Chilliwack of the British Columbia Junior Hockey League 4-3 in the semifinal. But hockey is a game of bounces, and the Blizzard fell in the final game showdown to the Halifax Exports 3-1.

Of course, the thinking back home was that now that the Blizzard had gotten past that first hurdle and sipped from the Anavet Cup, they would overcome the next obstacle and be slurping from the RBC Cup soon enough, if not next year.

But it was not to be. The Blizzard's brethren in the MJHL had been watching, and they started to catch on, and catch up. And the SJHL wasn't going to go away.

The Blizzard won the Turnbull Cup in 2002–03 but went down 4-1 in the Anavet, and that started a downhill spiral that has seen the team eliminated in MJHL quarter-finals the next two seasons, then a defeat in the MJHL final in 2005–06 and then—horrors—the OCN Blizzard did not even make the playoffs for the first time in the history of the franchise in 2006–07.

This reversal in fortune is hard to explain, because whoever is responsible is certainly not going to claim responsibility. Actually, there is really nobody to blame. In sports, there are winners and losers, and there are some pretty damn sharp people in Portage La Prairie and Selkirk, Manitoba and let's just give credit where credit is due. The Terriers and the Steelers and the Flyers (Winkler) and the Winnipeg South Blues and the Winnipeg Saints are run by some very dedicated and knowledgeable hockey people, and every dog has his day.

★ ★ ★ ★ ★

The Hobbema Hawks, Lebret Eagles, Southeast Thunderbirds/Blades, the OCN Blizzard and the Waywayseecapo Wolverines were all successful at providing opportunities for their graduates to advance to pro, semi-pro and college ranks. The Blizzard, because of their phenomenal success on the ice, may have achieved the most in this regard. Therefore, in keeping with the positive focus of this book, we'll talk about the OCN results, recognizing that the other Native-owned junior teams achieved similar success.

The list of accomplishments by the OCN Blizzard is long and lofty. First of all, there are the Tootoos. Jordin Tootoo, of course, is famous for feistiness, which has carried him to regular employment with the Nashville Predators of the National Hockey League. Jordin only played one season with the Blizzard before moving on to the Brandon Wheat Kings of the WHL, and then on to the AHL before gaining a regular role as a sparkplug in Nashville. Jordin, the first Inuit to play in the NHL, signed a new contract in 2008 for just under $1 million a year (he got security and stability). Most important, Tootoo is a great role model for all Native youth, year after year. He returns to his home community of Iqaluit to conduct hockey skills clinics and pass on the values of hard work, sobriety and kindness, and is also in demand throughout the rest of Canada and the United States during the off-season.

Sadly, Jordin's brother Terence is one of the young Native people who didn't make it. Terence played four years with the Blizzard and is the sixth leading scorer in that franchise's history (217 GP, 109 G, 113A, 222 Pts, 849 PIM). Terence was getting ready to work his way through the minor professional leagues when tragedy struck. He got arrested by the RCMP for driving while impaired and, upon release, was found later, in the bush around Brandon, dead of a self-inflicted gunshot wound.

The circumstances surrounding Terence's death are confusing at best, suspicious at worst. The rate of suicide amongst Native youth in Canada is 10 times the national average. The RCMP, who are provided with all sorts of Native awareness training, must have been aware of this statistic. Terence was reportedly very distraught when he was arrested, because he thought the impaired driving charge was going to prevent him from crossing the border and working in the United States in the East Coast Hockey League. If this trauma was exacerbated by the effects of alcohol, one would think the RCMP would be sharp enough not to release him to his own custody, but rather, have Terence sleep it off in the "drunk tank."

But Terence was released and somehow he made it to his home and then into the bush, where his body was found. First Nations people and many Canadians throughout the country were shocked and saddened by Terence's death. Jordin and the OCN Blizzard pay tribute to the memory of Terence Tootoo whenever the opportunity to do so with respect arises.

When we produced the television documentary *They Call Me Chief,* we wanted to include interviews from young Native athletes who were benefiting from the opportunities being provided by their community leaders, and we interviewed as many Blizzard players as we could.

Shyness is a common trait shared by Native people, and we found it very difficult to get what we would call a good "sound bite" from OCN players. After going through all of our videotape, which was shot in the OCN dressing room, Terence Tootoo provided the only clip we could use (and remember, the Tootoos were not well known when we made the documentary, so we weren't searching for "star quality").

We didn't place the name of Terence Tootoo when our chosen clip of an OCN player appears in the documentary (both because the clip is so short and also because we just wanted Terence to represent a "typical player"). But he's the one you will see when you watch our coverage of OCN in the doc. Terence simply says: "Greatest fans in the world!"

Terence was summing up his appreciation for the fans who were packing the Gordon Lathlin Arena in the OCN every time the Blizzard played.

★ ★ ★ ★ ★

Those fans in OCN were treated to the most successful streak of championships by a junior team in Canada. Five straight provincial championships! And junior hockey, in general, is incredibly entertaining.

It may not feature the top level of skill of the NHL, but for the price, which is cheap, very cheap compared to an NHL ducat, junior hockey is an incredible bargain. First of all, these kids are at the age where they have no fear. They almost believe they're indestructible. And they are truly playing for the love of the game, the spirit, the adventure. They are free spirits, not bogged down by the worries of mortgages and marriage, raising a family and paying the bills. Players fly over the boards and skate their balls off, flying up and down the ice and sending bodies flying every which way with reckless abandon. A junior hockey game is full value for your money.

The Blizzard not only provided fast-paced, exciting hockey, but they sent their fans home happy most nights, because their teams won most of the time. MJHL teams from southern Manitoba dreaded the prospect of facing the Blizzard in front of their rabid fans, jam-packed into every nook and cranny so tightly they were literally and figuratively right on top of the players. I can recall one unfortunate member of the Winnipeg South Blues, who got into a scrap with a Blizzard player near the end boards one game. This poor chap not only faced a fired-up opponent firing fists at him like a piston in a car engine, fans were hanging over the boards screaming at this kid and calling him down. It must have been like taking on Godzilla, King Kong, Mothra and Muahmmed Ali all at once.

And the Blizzard provided plenty of colourful characters for the fans to follow. The best came first in the person of one Konrad McKay—a scrappy little Indian who was also one of the most skillful stickhandlers and playmakers in the MJHL during his time (1996–99, the first three years of OCN's play in the MJHL).

Konrad played 159 games, averaging much better than a point a game on the scoresheet (78 goals, 182 assists for a total of 260 points) and more than six minutes a game in penalties (McKay served a whopping total of 937 minutes in the sin bin in those three seasons). The most attractive (thrilling? entertaining? crazy? fun?) thing about Konrad was that he barely topped five-and-a-half feet in height, and he couldn't have weighed more than 150 pounds, but he would take on anybody, anytime, anywhere.

Yet there was a "theatrical" quality to Konrad. There was a "script" that Konrad liked to follow whenever he could. And it went like this:

FADE UP–WIDE SHOT: Gordon Lathlin Arena.

The venue is filled with fans watching the OCN Bizzard play the St. Boniface Saints. We ZOOM IN on a FULL BODY SHOT of Konrad McKay. CAMERA FOLLOWS ACTION as McKay gets speared by a Saints player, who skates away and quickly heads to his bench where he hops over the boards. McKay follows the Saints player but then one of his teammates yells, "Konnie" and passes McKay the puck. McKay accepts the pass, dekes a St. Boniface defenceman, then the goalie, both to the ice, and then rips a shot into the top centre of the net.

CUT TO: The goalie's water bottle goes flying up in the air. We PULL OUT to a WIDE SHOT and again, CAMERA FOLLOWS ACTION as, first McKay exchanges high fives with his teammates on the ice, then skates along the boards of the OCN bench, tapping gloves with his other team-mates in turn. But then McKay turns abruptly and skates over to the St. Boniface bench and points at the player who speared him. Konrad makes a gesture with his thumb for the player to join him, then skates to centre ice, where McKay takes off his helmet, places it on the centre ice dot, and starts it spinning in a circle on the ice, while raising his fists in challenge.

CAMERA FOLLOWS ACTION, etc.

The script above could have been written for a documentary because it describes exactly what Konrad McKay would try to do before every fight he got into. Imagine a skinny, little Indian with *cojones* large enough to remove his protective head-gear and start spinning it wildly at centre stage, home or away, challenging a member of the opposition—any member, and the bigger the better—to "put up your dukes" for a classic fist fight. And Konrad always gave as good as he got.

Konnie went on to bounce around the minor leagues (he failed a tryout with the Manitoba Moose of the AHL) and gain the experience of travel and some pretty healthy paycheques playing the game he loves. That's the bottom line, but many more OCN alumni went on to play college hockey and earn a degree that would provide them with a career and a fulfilling life.

OCN provided opportunities for both Native and non-Native players because there certainly weren't enough top-level players being developed in Indian country to stock a complete junior team roster. But when you examine the list of OCN franchise leaders as of May 23, 2007, the top 10 of OCN's grad list is dotted with Native names (Aaron Starr, Cliff Duschesne, McKay, Terence Tootoo and Jamie Muswagan). Teams that have picked up OCN graduates include the Milwaukee Admirals, Hartford Wolfpack (AHL), the Charlotte Checkers and the Roanoke Express (ECHL), the Lubbock Cotton Kings and Laredo Bucks (Central Hockey League), the Richmond Renegades (Southern Professional Hockey League), Bemidji State University, Cornell and Maine (NCAA) and the University of Manitoba (CIS).

Lebret, the Waywayseecapo Wolverines and Southeast can provide similar lists. First Nations-owned junior franchises have achieved their goals—to increase the number of opportunities for players from First Nations to play elite junior hockey, and for those players to advance to college and professional ranks

★ ★ ★ ★ ★

But what about the big story that dominated the headlines like no other in the history of The Pas? The murder of Helen Betty Osborne, and the racial divide which separated the side-by-side communities of The Pas and the OCN? Has anything happened to heal the wounds of that brutal tragedy?

"Before we didn't have much in common," says Gordon Hopper, then mayor of The Pas. "Now we have something in common. And that is a darn good hockey team."

"And if you look at the crowd, you'll see a mosaic. People of all ethnic backgrounds and all incomes attend the games, because junior hockey is affordable as well as entertaining and fun," says Hopper.

"It's better now," said Edwin Jebb, Director of Education for OCN in 2002 at the height of the Blizzard's success. "It's not perfect, but it's better now."

Come game night, the streets of The Pas and OCN are deserted, and the Gordon Lathlin Arena is packed. Every seat is filled with a fanny, and the standing room areas around the ice are full, as well as the side and end concourses.

"Yeah, it brings us together," Jebb concurs. "We celebrate the victories and suffer through the losses. And it spills over to the board rooms and the streets. The game sponsorships, advertising in the programmes, rink-board advertising, individual players sponsorships, you'll see a lot of businesses from The Pas, as well as the town government itself, are putting their money behind the team because it is a win-win situation. The businesses market their goods and services to pretty much the whole community, which gathers for every game, and supporting the Blizzard generates a lot of corporate goodwill.

"And the Bizzard are a handy ice-breaker," adds Jebb, with a slight smile because he has used this "ice-breaker" joke many times before. "Whenever our Councils get together to discuss business, joint ventures, festivals, our shared museum and the like, the meetings start off with hockey talk. It's what we share, like the weather, but the Blizzard "weather" reports are a helluva of a lot more interesting."

It's well-known that sports and recreation provide tremendous benefits to the individual—fitness, teamwork, task and time management, discipline and so on. In The Pas, Manitoba, a sports team helped to heal a hatred that ran deep. The Blizzard proved to be the only way to calm the storm, and brought two communities, two races, two nations together, in a spirit of friendship and cooperation.

★ ★ ★ ★ ★

As for how to increase the number of Indian, Metis and Inuit in the NHL? The answers are well-known. Provide better opportunities, find a way to pay for equipment and facilities, better coaching, cut down on the racism, and the list goes on.

But you know what? Most of the players whose careers are portrayed in this book didn't have all this. Fred Sasakamoose may have had some good coaching and access to facilities, but he had to cope with a lot of loneliness. Ted Nolan couldn't afford equipment and had to overcome racism to fight his way onto teams at an early age. Jim Neilson was raised in an orphanage. Reggie Leach's peers placed a bottle of beer in front of him at the age of 12.

When it comes right down to it, it's up to the individual. Yes, it helps when there are good role models; proper instruction; easy access to ice; safe, light and proper-fitting equipment and all the rest, but if somebody really wants to succeed they can overcome pretty much any obstacle and make it. Do you think all of that is too harsh? Or too simple? Well, it's also called "tough love." And there are just as many social scientists who will tell you that tough love works as often as it doesn't.

★ ★ ★ ★ ★

Better coaching, greater access to facilities and equipment, changes in attitudes and so many other things will have to be accomplished to increase the number of Natives playing in the NHL.

To end this book, we present a list of the top prospects who come from a First Nations background in western Canada and have overcome whatever obstacles they encountered, to stand on the verge of stardom—at least from where they stood in February, 2008. The list was compiled by NHL player agent and scout Jeff Edwards, who goes out of his way to represent and/or help Native players, and Scott Taylor, the sports editor of *Grassroots News*—Manitoba's largest Aboriginal newspaper.

It will be interesting to follow the careers of these players—some will make it big, some will benefit from playing hockey at the highest level they could achieve—whether that be minor professional or university—and the hockey careers of some of them may come to an end rather quickly, sometimes by choice (some kids, for example, choose to devote more time to their studies leading to a profession such as doctor or lawyer; some choose family over an outside chance at a hockey career, and some simply fail). Here's that list:

Brenden Biederman: A 20-year-old offensive forward with the Sudbury Jr. Wolves, he's a versatile player on the NOJHL's top team. He has all the tools to play at the next level, whether he decides to play in college or minor pro.

Kyle Birch: A 17-year-old No. 2 goaltender with the Tri-City Americans of the Western Hockey League, he has a nice butterfly style and led the Manitoba Triple A midget league in goals against average and shutouts last season. In fact, he set a league record for shutouts. He'll be Tri-City's goalie of the future and is seen by some to be the next Carey Price. His dad is from Island Lake First Nation in Manitoba.

Chris Cloud: A 19-year-old forward with the Vancouver Giants, this former star with the MJHL's Waywayseecappo Wolverines is starting to establish himself as a league heavyweight. Despite having only average size, he has a mean right hand. He will likely take his game to the minor pro ranks after his junior career is over.

Joe Cook: A 20-year-old forward with the Laronge Ice Wolves who is big and is very physical. He is considered by many to be one of the toughest players in the SJHL this season.

Winston Daychief: A 20-year-old freshman with the University of Alaska, Anchorage, in the Western Collegiate Hockey Association (WCHA), he played his junior hockey for BCJHL's Cowichan Valley Capitals. He's 6-foot-1, 190 pounds and can score. Last season he had 31 goals and 74 points in 59 games with Cowichan Valley. He's expected to be a terrific U.S. college player. He's a Native of the Kanai (Blood) First Nation of Standoff, Alberta.

Harley Garrioch: A big, strong 19-year-old defenceman from the Flin Flon Bombers, who just happens to be one of the SJHL's toughest players this year. To his credit, he plays the role of enforcer with good hockey skills, making him a crowd favourite at the Whitney Forum.

Colton Yellow Horn: A 20-year-old sniper with the Tri-City Americans, Yellow Horn is known as the Brocket Rocket. A little undersized, he's hard-nosed and intelligent and has a nice touch around the net. Should play pro at some level. Just might be the best player in the WHL this year.

Justin Michaud: An 18-year-old rookie from the MJHL's Selkirk Steelers who can play with a real mean streak. He has decent hockey skills, skills that will develop over his junior career. Fans could see him playing a similar role to that of Jason Bone (enforcer) in the minors.

Ken Neufeld: A 20-year-old veteran from the SJHL's Laronge Ice Wolves. He's a big, stay-at-home defenceman who has continued to improve throughout his junior hockey career. He should have the tools necessary to play pro.

Casey Pierro-Zabotel: A 19-year-old Métis forward with the WHL's Vancouver Giants, Pierro-Zabotel was drafted by the Pittsburgh Penguins in the third round (80th overall) in the 2007 NHL entry draft. He played the past two-and-a-half seasons with the BCHL's Merritt Centennials where he put up 116 points last year and has won two gold medals playing for Team West at the World Junior A Hockey Challenge. He decided to forego a scholarship offer to Michigan Tech and join the Giants in order to try to fast-track his path to the pros. He's an extremely good player now, who will only get better.

Jeff Ratt: A 20-year-old forward teammate of Neufeld and Cook. He's a little guy who plays a crash-and-bang style of game and is not afraid of the rough stuff. He'll take on all the SJHL's heavyweights.

Scott Restoule: Another 20-year-old forward with the Sudbury Jr. Wolves, he's a very good player at the Jr. A level and currently leads the NOJHL in scoring. He has OHL experience and has what it takes to play in the CIS or minor pro level next year.

Jordan Sinclair: An 18-year-old righthanded-shooting defenceman with the MJHL's OCN Blizzard, Sinclair is a slight (5-foot-11, 150 pounds) rearguard with a great scoring touch who will only get better and bigger as his junior career goes on. He came out of the Triple A Midget League's Norman North Stars and has done a lot for OCN's rebuilding program this season.

Myles Stevens: This 18-year-old forward, who plays with the Swan Valley Stampeders, could be the very best First Nations player in the MJHL. Chosen "rookie of the month" for January/08 for scoring 8 goals and adding 12 assist in 11 games, Myles was also selected "player of the game" at the Prospects Game held in conjunction with the MJHL All-Star Celebration on the Waywayseecappo First Nation.

Riel Thompson: He's a tough, physical, 19-year-old defenceman from the SJHL's Nipawin Hawks. Acquired from the Flin Flon Bombers, he has good size, puck movement skills and doesn't shy away from the rough stuff. He will get better with another year of junior, but scouts say he needs more focus.

Kalib Thunderchief: An 18-year-old rookie forward with the SJHL's Kindersley Klippers. He was acquired from the Selkirk Steelers earlier this season and is known more for his willingness to drop the gloves than for scoring goals. With his size and continued development, he has a future in pro hockey.

★ ★ ★ ★ ★

Along with existing stars such as Jonathan Cheechoo, Jordin Tootoo and Carey Price, we hope that the the players identified above star or carve out a career in the National Hockey League or in other national and international leagues and competitions. The projections are dotted with possibilities in minor pro and college ranks, in keeping with the original goals of the people who dreamed of creating opportunities for the talented young people they saw all around them in the First Nations communites.

We hope that Cheechoo, Tootoo and the parade of up-and-comers provide us with stories that will fill a sequel to the documentary *They Call Me Chief*, and a sequel to this book.

★ ★ ★ ★ ★

A major goal of this book is to provide hope and inspiration from "those who have gone before" to those who will follow. In keeping with that, we chose to accentuate the positive and downplay the negative throughout these pages. Maybe we should be spending more of our time finding solutions to build on, instead of running around looking for problems to solve, anyway.

I suppose there are negative aspects to the lives of these "warriors on ice" that we could have focused more attention on. But when you're summarizing someone's life in 20 pages, it's very difficult to be balanced and fair. We hope that readers understand why we chose to take the high road. Not only is it more safe, but this book is by no means an exercise in investigative journalism. All too often, anyway, in-depth reports or behind-the-scenes looks at people and personalities, with inside scoops or "exclusive" stories, turn out to be more full of sensationalism, rumours, exploitation and exaggeration than substance. Fact and fiction combine to form some kind of weird entity we could call "faction."

But the word "faction" exists, and it is defined as "backing one side over the other." If we have taken the Indian side on many occasions in this book, we hope that we provided enough facts that our writing doesn't appear as fiction. And besides, the Indian side hasn't been reported that often in textbooks and media throughout our history, so maybe we're providing a service by providing some balance that has so often been missing in the past.

It's always difficult to cover history and events we didn't actually attend or witness firsthand. Sometimes it's like shooting pucks blindly into the corner of a rink. Sure, we're going to get nailed into the boards from time to time, but I hope we've managed to keep our heads up most of the time.

We had no set format (or even set of questions) to follow during our interviews. So some of the stories are short and some are long. We just went wherever the stories and the people who were telling them led us. I think this was better because it created a relaxed atmosphere/forum; interviews usually ended up being just "two guys shootin' the breeze."

This "method," which starts out as swapping stories about sports with our Indian and Metis subjects, almost always led us to topics such as racism, treaty rights, culture, lifestyle, spirituality and other major (and often controversial) subjects of interest and/or concern. Some opinions on these issues were presented for all to see. Feel free to disagree.

And, of course, the process we went through to gather and compile this information was often unusual or fun. Stuff happened, and we let you in on it whenever we thought you might find it interesting.

★ ★ ★ ★ ★

The mission statement of our company, "Marks on Things" is "to empower people with information through communications so that they can make balanced and fair choices about social and economic justice."

I hope this book stands beside some of the films we have made that have helped us to achieve our mission statement (it's always been a hit-and-miss kind of thing).

★ ★ ★ ★ ★

Che Meegwich, or "thank you" for reading this book.

GEORGE ARMSTRONG

Center
Born Jul 6 1930 -- Skead, ONT
Height 6.01 -- Weight 204 -- Shoots R

			Regular Season					Playoffs				
Season	Team	Lge	GP	G	A	Pts	PIM	GP	G	A	Pts	PIM
1947-48	Stratford Kroehlers	OHA	36	33	40	73	33					
1949-50	Toronto Maple Leafs	NHL	2	0	0	0	0	--	--	--	--	--
1950-51	Pittsburgh Hornets	AHL	71	15	33	48	49	13	4	9	13	6
1951-52	Pittsburgh Hornets	AHL	50	30	29	59	62	--	--	--	--	--
1951-52	Toronto Maple Leafs	NHL	20	3	3	6	30	4	0	0	0	2
1952-53	Toronto Maple Leafs	NHL	52	14	11	25	54	--	--	--	--	--
1953-54	Toronto Maple Leafs	NHL	63	17	15	32	60	5	1	0	1	2
1954-55	Toronto Maple Leafs	NHL	66	10	18	28	80	4	1	0	1	4
1955-56	Toronto Maple Leafs	NHL	67	16	32	48	97	5	4	2	6	0
1956-57	Toronto Maple Leafs	NHL	54	18	26	44	37	--	--	--	--	--
1957-58	Toronto Maple Leafs	NHL	59	17	25	42	93	--	--	--	--	--
1958-59	Toronto Maple Leafs	NHL	59	20	16	36	37	12	0	4	4	
1959-60	Toronto Maple Leafs	NHL	70	23	28	51	60	10	1	4	5	4
1960-61	Toronto Maple Leafs	NHL	47	14	19	33	21	5	1	1	2	0
1961-62	Toronto Maple Leafs	NHL	70	21	32	53	27	12	7	5	12	2
1962-63	Toronto Maple Leafs	NHL	70	19	24	43	27	10	3	6	9	4
1963-64	Toronto Maple Leafs	NHL	67	20	17	37	14	14	5	8	13	10
1964-65	Toronto Maple Leafs	NHL	59	15	22	37	14	6	1	0	1	4
1965-66	Toronto Maple Leafs	NHL	70	16	35	51	12	4	0	1	1	4
1966-67	Toronto Maple Leafs	NHL	70	9	24	33	26	9	2	1	3	6
1967-68	Toronto Maple Leafs	NHL	62	13	21	34	4	--	--	--	--	--
1968-69	Toronto Maple Leafs	NHL	53	11	16	27	10	4	0	0	0	0
1969-70	Toronto Maple Leafs	NHL	49	13	15	28	12	--	--	--	--	--
1970-71	Toronto Maple Leafs	NHL	59	7	18	25	6	6	0	2	2	0
NHL Totals			**1188**	**296**	**417**	**713**	**721**	**110**	**26**	**34**	**60**	**52**

Coaching

Season	Team	Lge	Type	GP	W	L	T	OTL	Pct	Result
1974-75	Toronto Marlboros	OHA	Head Coach	70	48	13	9	0	0.750	
1976-77	Toronto Marlboros	OHA	Head Coach	66	31	23	12	0	0.561	
1988-89	Toronto Maple Leafs	NHL	Head Coach‡	47	17	26	4	0	0.404	Out of Playoffs

‡ Midseason replacement

Awards

1947-48 Eddie Powers Memorial Trophy 1972-73 Coach of the Year

BLAIR ATCHEYNUM

Right Wing
Born Apr 20 1969 -- Estevan, SASK
Height 6.02 -- Weight 210 -- Shoots R
Selected by Hartford Whalers round 3 #52 overall 1989 NHL Entry Draft

			Regular Season					Playoffs				
Season	Team	Lge	GP	G	A	Pts	PIM	GP	G	A	Pts	PIM
1985-86	Saskatoon Blades	WHL	19	1	4	5	22	---	--	--	---	---
1986-87	Saskatoon Blades	WHL	21	0	4	4	4	---	--	--	---	---
1986-87	Swift Current Broncos	WHL	5	2	1	3	0	---	--	--	---	---
1986-87	Moose Jaw Warriors	WHL	12	3	0	3	2	---	--	--	---	---
1987-88	Moose Jaw Warriors	WHL	60	32	16	48	52	---	--	--	---	---
1988-89	Moose Jaw Warriors	WHL	71	70	68	138	70	7	2	5	7	13
1989-90	Binghamton Whalers	AHL	78	20	21	41	45	---	--	--	---	---
1990-91	Springfield Indians	AHL	72	25	27	52	42	13	0	6	6	6
1991-92	Springfield Indians	AHL	62	16	21	37	64	6	1	1	2	2
1992-93	New Haven Senators	AHL	51	16	18	34	47	---	--	--	---	---
1992-93	Ottawa Senators	NHL	4	0	1	1	0	---	--	--	---	---
1993-94	Columbus Chill	ECHL	16	15	12	27	10	---	--	--	---	---
1993-94	Portland Pirates	AHL	2	0	0	0	0	---	--	--	---	---
1993-94	Springfield Indians	AHL	40	18	22	40	13	6	0	2	2	0
1994-95	Minnesota Moose	IHL	17	4	6	10	7	---	--	--	---	---
1994-95	Worcester IceCats	AHL	55	17	29	46	26	---	--	--	---	---
1995-96	Cape-Breton Oilers	AHL	79	30	42	72	65	---	--	--	---	---
1996-97	Hershey Bears	AHL	77	42	45	87	57	13	6	11	17	6
1997-98	St. Louis Blues	NHL	61	11	15	26	10	10	0	0	0	2
1998-99	Nashville Predators	NHL	53	8	6	14	16	---	--	--	---	---
1998-99	St. Louis Blues	NHL	12	2	2	4	2	13	1	3	4	6
1999-00	Chicago Blackhawks	NHL	47	5	7	12	6	---	--	--	---	---
2000-01	Chicago Wolves	IHL	7	1	0	1	0	---	--	--	---	---
2000-01	Norfolk Admirals	AHL	37	12	8	20	16	4	0	0	0	6
2000-01	Chicago Blackhawks	NHL	19	1	2	3	2	---	--	--	---	---
	NHL Totals		**196**	**27**	**33**	**60**	**36**	**23**	**1**	**3**	**4**	**8**

HENRY BOUCHA

Center
Born Jun 1 1951 -- Warroad, MN
Height 6.00 -- Weight 185 -- Shoots R
Selected by Detroit Red Wings round 2 #16 overall 1971 NHL Amateur Draft

			Regular Season					Playoffs				
Season	**Team**	**Lge**	**GP**	**G**	**A**	**Pts**	**PIM**	**GP**	**G**	**A**	**Pts**	**PIM**
1969-70	U.S. National Team	Intl	13	4	3	7	8					
1969-70	Winnipeg Jets	WCHL	51	27	26	53	37					
1970-71	U.S. National Team	Intl	49	30	27	57	12					
1971-72	U.S. Olympic Team	Intl	53	39	56	95	82					
1971-72	Detroit Red Wings	NHL	16	1	0	1	2	--	--	--	--	--
1972-73	Virginia Wings	AHL	7	3	2	5	9	--	--	--	--	--
1972-73	Detroit Red Wings	NHL	73	14	14	28	82	--	--	--	--	--
1973-74	Detroit Red Wings	NHL	70	19	12	31	32	--	--	--	--	--
1974-75	Minnesota North Stars	NHL	51	15	14	29	23	--	--	--	--	--
1975-76	Minnesota Fighting Saints	WHA	36	15	20	35	47	--	--	--	--	--
1975-76	Kansas City Scouts	NHL	28	4	7	11	14	--	--	--	--	--
1976-77	Colorado Rockies	NHL	9	0	2	2	4	--	--	--	--	--
	WHA Totals		**36**	**15**	**20**	**35**	**47**					
	NHL Totals		**247**	**53**	**49**	**102**	**157**					

JOHN CHABOT

Center
Born May 18 1962 -- Summerside, PEI
Height 6.02 -- Weight 195 -- Shoots L
Selected by Montreal Canadiens round 2 #40 overall 1980 NHL Entry Draft

			Regular Season					Playoffs				
Season	Team	Lge	GP	G	A	Pts	PIM	GP	G	A	Pts	PIM
1979-80	Hull Olympiques	QMJHL	68	26	57	83	28					
1980-81	Hull Olympiques	QMJHL	70	27	62	89	24					
1980-81	Nova-Scotia Voyageurs	AHL	1	0	0	0	0	2	0	0	0	0
1981-82	Sherbrooke Beavers	QMJHL	62	34	109	143	40	19	6	26	32	6
1982-83	Nova-Scotia Voyageurs	AHL	76	16	73	89	19	7	1	3	4	0
1983-84	Montreal Canadiens	NHL	56	18	25	43	13	11	1	4	5	0
1984-85	Montreal Canadiens	NHL	10	1	6	7	2	--	--	--	--	--
1984-85	Pittsburgh Penguins	NHL	67	8	45	53	12	--	--	--	--	--
1985-86	Pittsburgh Penguins	NHL	77	14	31	45	6	--	--	--	--	--
1986-87	Pittsburgh Penguins	NHL	72	14	22	36	8	--	--	--	--	--
1987-88	Detroit Red Wings	NHL	78	13	44	57	10	16	4	15	19	2
1988-89	Adirondack Red Wings	AHL	8	3	12	15	0	--	--	--	--	--
1988-89	Detroit Red Wings	NHL	52	2	10	12	6	6	1	1	2	0
1989-90	Detroit Red Wings	NHL	69	9	40	49	24	--	--	--	--	--
1990-91	Adirondack Red Wings	AHL	27	11	30	41	4	2	0	1	1	0
1990-91	Detroit Red Wings	NHL	27	5	5	10	4	--	--	--	--	--
1991-92	Canadian National Team	Intl	8	1	3	4	0					
1991-92	Milan	Italy Statistics Unavailable										
1992-93	Berlin Prussian	1.GBun	20	10	17	27	14					
1993-94	Berlin Prussian	1.GBun	32	9	29	38	27					
1994-95	Canadian National Team	Intl	3	1	2	3	0					
1994-95	Berlin Preussen Devils	DEL	43	20	48	68	48	12	5	7	12	14
1995-96	Berlin Preussen Devils	DEL	50	16	65	81	20					
1996-97	Zug	Swiss Statistics Unavailable										
1996-97	Berlin Capitals	DEL	45	12	34	46	43					
1997-98	Frankfurt Lions	DEL	47	12	46	58	72					
1998-99	Frankfurt Lions	DEL	49	7	52	59	44					
1999-00	Frankfurt Lions	DEL	38	10	33	43	16	5	1	3	4	10
2000-01	Berlin Polar Bears	DEL	47	11	24	35	37	--	--	--	--	--
	NHL Totals		508	84	228	312	85	33	6	20	26	2

Coaching

Season	Team	Lge	Type	GP	W	L	T	OTL	Pct	Result
2001-02	Hull Olympiques	QMJHL	Head Coach‡							
2002-03	Hull Olympiques	QMJHL	Assistant Coach							
2003-04	Gatineau Olympiques	QMJHL	Assistant Coach							
2004-05	Gatineau Olympiques	QMJHL	Assistant Coach							

RON DELORME

Right Wing
Born Sep 3 1955 -- North Battleford, SASK
Height 6.02 -- Weight 185
Selected by Kansas City Scouts round 4 #56 overall 1975 NHL Amateur Draft
Selected by Denver Spurs/Ottawa Civics round 3 #34 overall 1975 WHA Amateur Draft

Season	Team	Lge	Regular Season					Playoffs				
			GP	G	A	Pts	PIM	GP	G	A	Pts	PIM
1972-73	Prince Albert Raiders	SJHL	Statistics Unavailable									
1973-74	Swift Current Broncos	WCHL	59	19	15	34.	96					
1974-75	Lethbridge Broncos	WCHL	69	30	57	87	144	6	1	7	8	20
1975-76	Lethbridge Broncos	WCHL	26	8	12	20	87	7	3	6	9	24
1975-76	Tucson Mavericks	CHL	18	2	5	7	18	--	--	--	--	--
1975-76	Denver Spurs/Ottawa Civics	WHA	22	1	3	4	28	--	--	--	--	--
1976-77	Baltimore Clippers	SHL	25	4	6	10	4					
1976-77	Tulsa Oilers	CHL	6	1	2	3	0	--	--	--	--	--
1976-77	Colorado Rockies	NHL	29	6	4	10	23	--	--	--	--	--
1977-78	Colorado Rockies	NHL	68	10	11	21	47	2	0	0	0	10
1978-79	Colorado Rockies	NHL	77	20	8	28	68	--	--	--	--	--
1979-80	Colorado Rockies	NHL	75	19	24	43	76	--	--	--	--	--
1980-81	Colorado Rockies	NHL	65	11	16	27	70	--	--	--	--	--
1981-82	Vancouver Canucks	NHL	59	9	8	17	177	15	0	2	2	31
1982-83	Vancouver Canucks	NHL	56	5	8	13	87	4	0	0	0	10
1983-84	Vancouver Canucks	NHL	64	2	2	4	68	4	1	0	1	8
1984–85	Vancouver Canucks	NHL	31	1	2	3	51	--	--	--	--	--
	WHA Totals		**22**	**1**	**3**	**4**	**28**					
	NHL Totals		**524**	**83**	**83**	**166**	**667**	**25**	**1**	**2**	**3**	**59**

THEOREN FLEURY

Right Wing
Born Jun 29 1968 -- Oxbow, SASK
Height 5.06 -- Weight 180
Selected by Calgary Flames round 8 #166 overall 1987 NHL Entry Draft

Season	Team	Lge	GP	G	A	Pts	PIM	GP	G	A	Pts	PIM
				Regular Season					Playoffs			
1984-85	Moose Jaw Warriors	WHL	71	29	46	75	82	--	--	--	--	--
1985-86	Moose Jaw Warriors	WHL	72	43	65	108	124	13	7	13	20	16
1986-87	Moose Jaw Warriors	WHL	66	61	68	129	110	9	7	9	16	34
1987-88	Moose Jaw Warriors	WHL	65	68	92	160	235	--	--	--	--	--
1987-88	Salt Lake Golden Eagles	IHL	2	3	4	7	7	8	11	5	16	16
1988-89	Salt Lake Golden Eagles	IHL	40	37	37	74	81	--	--	--	--	--
1988-89	Calgary Flames	NHL	36	14	20	34	46	22	5	6	11	24
1989-90	Calgary Flames	NHL	80	31	35	66	157	6	2	3	5	10
1990-91	Calgary Flames	NHL	79	51	53	104	136	7	2	5	7	14
1991-92	Calgary Flames	NHL	80	33	40	73	133	--	--	--	--	--
1992-93	Calgary Flames	NHL	83	34	66	100	88	6	5	7	12	27
1993-94	Calgary Flames	NHL	83	40	45	85	186	7	6	4	10	5
1994-95	Calgary Flames	NHL	47	29	29	58	112	7	7	7	14	2
1994-95	Tappara Tampere	FNL	10	8	9	17	22	--	--	--	--	--
1995-96	Calgary Flames	NHL	80	46	50	96	112	4	2	1	3	14
1996-97	Calgary Flames	NHL	81	29	38	67	104	--	--	--	--	--
1997-98	Calgary Flames	NHL	82	27	51	78	197	--	--	--	--	--
1998-99	Calgary Flames	NHL	60	30	39	69	68	--	--	--	--	--
1998-99	Colorado Avalanche	NHL	15	10	14	24	18	18	5	12	17	20
1999-00	New York Rangers	NHL	80	15	49	64	68	--	--	--	--	--
2000-01	New York Rangers	NHL	62	30	44	74	122	--	--	--	--	--
2001-02	New York Rangers	NHL	82	24	39	63	216	--	--	--	--	--
2002-03	Chicago Blackhawks	NHL	54	12	21	33	77	--	--	--	--	--
2005-06	Belfast Giants	EIHL	34	22	52	74	270	7	1	12	13	34
	NHL Totals		1084	455	633	1088	1840	77	34	45	79	116

STAN JONATHAN

Left Wing
Born May 9 1955 -- Oshweken, ONT
Height 5.08 -- Weight 175 -- Shoots L
Selected by Boston Bruins round 5 #86 overall 1975 NHL Amateur Draft
Selected by Indianapolis Racers round 8 #103 overall 1975 WHA Amateur Draft

| Season | Team | Lge | Regular Season | | | | | Playoffs | | | | |
			GP	G	A	Pts	PIM	GP	G	A	Pts	PIM
1972-73	Peterborough Petes	OHA	63	14	35	49	107					
1973-74	Peterborough Petes	OHA	70	19	33	52	127					
1974-75	Peterborough Petes	OHA	70	36	39	75	138					
1975-76	Dayton Gems	IHL	69	26	47	73	192	15	13	8	21	54
1975-76	Rochester Americans	AHL	6	1	1	2	0	--	--	--	--.	--
1975-76	Boston Bruins	NHL	1	0	0	0	0	--	--	--	--	--
1976-77	Rochester Americans	AHL	3	0	0	0	7	--	--	--	--	--
1976-77	Boston Bruins	NHL	69	17	13	30	69	14	4	2	6	24
1977-78	Boston Bruins	NHL	68	27	25	52	116	15	0	1	1	36
1978-79	Boston Bruins	NHL	33	6	9	15	96	11	4	1	5	12
1979-80	Boston Bruins	NHL	79	21	19	40	208	9	0	0	0	29
1980-81	Boston Bruins	NHL	74	14	24	38	192	3	0	0	0	30
1981-82	Boston Bruins	NHL	67	6	17	23	57	11	0	0	0	6
1982-83	Baltimore Skipjacks	AHL	48	13	23	36	86	--	--	--	--	--
1982-83	Boston Bruins	NHL	1	0	0	0	0	--	--	--	--	--
1982-83	Pittsburgh Penguins	NHL	19	0	3	3	13	--	--	--	--	--
1985-86	Flamboro Mott's Clamato's	OHASr	3	3	1	4	2					
1986-87	Brantford Mott's Clamato's	OHASr	Statistics Unavailable									
	NHL Totals		**411**	**91**	**110**	**201**	**751**	**63**	**8**	**4**	**12**	**137**

REGGIE LEACH

Right Wing
Born Apr 23 1950 -- Riverton, MAN
Height 6.00 -- Weight 180 -- Shoots R

			Regular Season					Playoffs				
Season	Team	Lge	GP	G	A	Pts	PIM	GP	G	A	Pts	PIM
1966-67	Flin Flon Bombers	MJHL	0	67	46	113	118					
1967-68	Flin Flon Bombers	WCJHL	59	87	44	131	208					
1968-69	Flin Flon Bombers	WCHL Statistics Unavailable										
1969-70	Flin Flon Bombers	WCHL	57	65	46	111	168					
1970-71	Oklahoma City Blazers	CHL	41	24	18	42	32					
1970-71	Boston Bruins	NHL	23	2	4	6	0	3	0	0	0	0
1971-72	Boston Bruins	NHL	56	7	13	20	12	--	--	--	--	--
1971-72	California Golden Seals	NHL	17	6	7	13	7	--	--	--	--	--
1972-73	California Golden Seals	NHL	76	23	12	35	45	--	--	--	--	--
1973-74	California Golden Seals	NHL	78	22	24	46	34	--	--	--	--	--
1974-75	Philadelphia Flyers	NHL	80	45	33	78	63	17	8	2	10	6
1975-76	Philadelphia Flyers	NHL	80	61	30	91	41	16	19	5	24	8
1976-77	Philadelphia Flyers	NHL	77	32	14	46	23	10	4	5	9	0
1977-78	Philadelphia Flyers	NHL	72	24	28	52	24	12	2	2	4	0
1978-79	Philadelphia Flyers	NHL	76	34	20	54	20	8	5	1	6	0
1979-80	Philadelphia Flyers	NHL	76	50	26	76	28	19	9	7	16	6
1980-81	Philadelphia Flyers	NHL	79	34	36	70	59	9	0	0	0	2
1981-82	Philadelphia Flyers	NHL	66	26	21	47	18	--	--	--	--	--
1982-83	Detroit Red Wings	NHL	78	15	17	32	13	--	--	--	--	--
1983-84	Montana Magic	CHL	76	21	29	50	34	--	--	--	--	--
1997-98	Madison Monsters	UHL	1	0	0	0	0	--	--	--	--	--
	NHL Totals		934	381	285	666	387	94	47	22	69	22

Awards

1975-76 Conn Smythe Trophy

JIM NEILSON

Defense
Born Nov 28 1941 -- Big River, SASK
Height 6.02 -- Weight 205

Season	Team	Lge	Regular Season					Playoffs				
			GP	G	A	Pts	PIM	GP	G	A	Pts	PIM
Prince Albert Mintos		SJHL Statistics Unavailable										
1961-62	Kitchener-Waterloo Beavers	EPHL	70	9	33	42	78	7	2	3	5	2
1962-63	New York Rangers	NHL	69	5	11	16	38	--	--	--	--	--
1963-64	New York Rangers	NHL	69	5	24	29	93	--	--	--	--	--
1964-65	New York Rangers	NHL	62	0	13	13	58	--	--	--	--	--
1965-66	New York Rangers	NHL	65	4	19	23	84	--	--	--	--	--
1966-67	New York Rangers	NHL	61	4	11	15	65	4	1	0	1	0
1967-68	New York Rangers	NHL	67	6	29	35	60	6	1	1	2	4
1968-69	New York Rangers	NHL	76	10	34	44	95	4	0	3	3	5
1969-70	New York Rangers	NHL	62	3	20	23	75	6	0	1	1	8
1970-71	New York Rangers	NHL	77	8	24	32	69	13	0	3	3	30
1971-72	New York Rangers	NHL	78	7	30	37	56	10	0	3	3	8
1972-73	New York Rangers	NHL	52	4	16	20	35	10	0	4	4	2
1973-74	New York Rangers	NHL	72	4	7	11	38	12	0	1	1	4
1974-75	California Seals	NHL	72	3	17	20	56	--	--	--	--	--
1975-76	California Seals	NHL	26	1	6	7	20	--	--	--	--	--
1976-77	Cleveland Barons	NHL	47	3	17	20	42	--	--	--	--	--
1977-78	Cleveland Barons	NHL	68	2	21	23	20	--	--	--	--	--
1978-79	Edmonton Oilers	WHA	35	0	5	5	18	--	--	--	--	--
	WHA Totals		**35**	**0**	**5**	**5**	**18**					
	NHL Totals		**1023**	**69**	**299**	**368**	**904**	**65**	**2**	**16**	**18**	**61**

Awards

1961-62 Best Rookie

TED NOLAN

Left Wing
Born Apr 7 1958 -- Sault Ste. Marie, ONT
Height 6.00 -- Weight 185
Selected by Detroit Red Wings round 5 #78 overall 1978 NHL Amateur Draft

			Regular Season					Playoffs				
Season	Team	Lge	GP	G	A	Pts	PIM	GP	G	A	Pts	PIM
1975-76	Kenora Thistles	MJHL	51	24	32	56	86					
1976-77	Sault Ste. Marie Greyhounds	OHA	60	8	16	24	109					
1977-78	Sault Ste. Marie Greyhounds	OHA	66	14	30	44	106					
1978-79	Kansas City Red Wings	CHL	73	12	38	50	66	4	1	2	3	0
1979-80	Adirondack Red Wings	AHL	75	16	24	40	106	5	0	1	1	0
1980-81	Adirondack Red Wings	AHL	76	22	28	50	86	18	6	10	16	11
1981-82	Adirondack Red Wings	AHL	39	12	18	30	81	--	--	--	--	--
1981-82	Detroit Red Wings	NHL	41	4	13	17	45	--	--	--	--	--
1982-83	Adirondack Red Wings	AHL	78	24	40	64	106	6	2	5	7	14
1983-84	Adirondack Red Wings	AHL	31	10	16	26	76	7	2	3	5	18
1983-84	Detroit Red Wings	NHL	19	1	2	3	26	--	--	--	--	--
1984-85	Rochester Americans	AHL	65	28	34	62	152	5	4	0	4	18
1985-86	Baltimore Skipjacks	AHL	10	4	4	8	19	--	--	--	--	--
1985-86	Pittsburgh Penguins	NHL	18	1	1	2	34	--	--	--	--	--
	NHL Totals		**78**	**6**	**16**	**22**	**105**					

Coaching

Season	Team	Lge	Type	GP	W	L	T	OTL	Pct	Result
1988-89	Sault Ste. Marie Greyhounds	OHL	Head Coach‡							
1989-90	Sault Ste. Marie Greyhounds	OHL	Head Coach	66	18	42	6	0	0.318	
1990-91	Sault Ste. Marie Greyhounds	OHL	Head Coach	66	42	21	3	0	0.659	
1991-92	Sault Ste. Marie Greyhounds	OHL	Head Coach	66	41	19	6	0	0.667	
1992-93	Sault Ste. Marie Greyhounds	OHL	Head Coach	66	38	23	5	0	0.614	
1993-94	Sault Ste. Marie Greyhounds	OHL	Head Coach	66	35	24	7	0	0.583	
1994-95	Hartford Whalers	NHL	Assistant Coach							
1995-96	Buffalo Sabres	NHL	Head Coach	82	33	42	7	0	0.445	Out of Playoffs
1996-97	Buffalo Sabres	NHL	Head Coach	82	40	30	12	0	0.561	Lost in round 2
2005-06	Moncton Wildcats	QMJHL	Head Coach	70	52	15	0	3	0.764	
2006-07	New York Islanders	NHL	Head Coach	82	40	30	0	12	0.561	Lost in round 1

‡ Midseason replacement

Awards

1996-97 Jack Adams Award

GINO ODJICK

Left Wing
Born Sep 7 1970 -- Maniwaki, PQ
Height 6.03 -- Weight 215 -- Shoots L
Selected by Vancouver Canucks round 5 #86 overall 1990 NHL Entry Draft

Season	Team	Lge	Regular Season					Playoffs				
			GP	G	A	Pts	PIM	GP	G	A	Pts	PIM
1988-89	Laval Titan	QMJHL	50	9	15	24	278	16	0	9	9	129
1989-90	Laval Titan	QMJHL	51	12	26	38	280	13	6	5	11	110
1990-91	Milwaukee Admirals	IHL	17	7	3	10	102	--	--	--	--	--
1990-91	Vancouver Canucks	NHL	45	7	1	8	296	6	0	0	0	18
1991-92	Vancouver Canucks	NHL	65	4	6	10	348	4	0	0	0	6
1992-93	Vancouver Canucks	NHL	75	4	13	17	370	1	0	0	0	0
1993-94	Vancouver Canucks	NHL	76	16	13	29	271	10	0	0	0	18
1994-95	Vancouver Canucks	NHL	23	4	5	9	109	5	0	0	0	47
1995-96	Vancouver Canucks	NHL	55	3	4	7	181	6	3	1	4	6
1996-97	Vancouver Canucks	NHL	70	5	8	13	371	--	--	--	--	--
1997-98	Vancouver Canucks	NHL	35	3	2	5	181	--	--	--	--	--
1997-98	New York Islanders	NHL	13	0	0	0	31	--	--	--	--	--
1998-99	New York Islanders	NHL	23	4	3	7	133	--	--	--	--	--
1999-00	New York Islanders	NHL	46	5	10	15	90	--	--	--	--	--
1999-00	Philadelphia Flyers	NHL	13	3	1	4	10	--	--	--	--	--
2000-01	Philadelphia Flyers	NHL	17	1	3	4	28	--	--	--	--	--
2000-01	Montreal Canadiens	NHL	13	1	0	1	44	--	--	--	--	--
2001-02	Quebec Citadelles	AHL	13	2	1	3	40	--	--	--	--	--
2001-02	Montreal Canadiens	NHL	36	4	4	8	104	12	1	0	1	47
	NHL Totals		**605**	**64**	**73**	**137**	**2567**	**44**	**4**	**1**	**5**	**142**

EVERETT SANIPASS

Left Wing
Born Feb 13 1968 -- Big Cove, NB
Height 6.02 -- Weight 204 -- Shoots L
Selected by Chicago Blackhawks round 1 #14 overall 1986 NHL Entry Draft

Season	Team	Lge	Regular Season					Playoffs				
			GP	G	A	Pts	PIM	GP	G	A	Pts	PIM
1984-85	Verdun Junior Canadiens	QMJHL	38	8	11	19	84	12	2	5	7	66
1985-86	Verdun Junior Canadiens	QMJHL	67	28	66	94	320	5	0	2	2	16
1986-87	Verdun Junior Canadiens	QMJHL	24	17	36	53	175	--	--	--	--	--
1986-87	Granby Bisons	QMJHL	11	17	12	29	45	8	6	4	10	48
1986-87	Chicago Blackhawks	NHL	7	1	3	4	2	--	--	--	--	--
1987-88	Chicago Blackhawks	NHL	57	8	12	20	126	2	2	0	2	2
1988-89	Saginaw Hawks	IHL	23	9	12	21	76	--	--	--	--	--
1988-89	Chicago Blackhawks	NHL	50	6	9	15	164	3	0	0	0	2
1989-90	Indianapolis Ice	IHL	33	15	13	28	121	--	--	--	--	--
1989-90	Chicago Blackhawks	NHL	12	2	2	4	17	--	--	--	--	--
1989-90	Quebec Nordiques	NHL	9	3	3	6	8	--	--	--	--	--
1990-91	Halifax Citadels	AHL	14	11	7	18	41	--	--	--	--	--
1990-91	Quebec Nordiques	NHL	29	5	5	10	41	--	--	--	--	--
1991-92	Halifax Citadels	AHL	7	3	5	8	31	--	--	--	--	--
1992-93	Halifax Citadels	AHL	9	1	3	4	36	--	--	--	--	--
	NHL Totals		**164**	**25**	**34**	**59**	**358**	**5**	**2**	**0**	**2**	**4**

GARY SARGENT

Defense
Born Feb 18 1954 -- Red Lake, MN
Height 5.10 -- Weight 200
Selected by Los Angeles Kings round 3 #48 overall 1974 NHL Amateur Draft
Selected by Indianapolis Racers round 13 #179 overall 1974 WHA Amateur Draft

			Regular Season					Playoffs				
Season	Team	Lge	GP	G	A	Pts	PIM	GP	G	A	Pts	PIM
1972-73	Bemidji State University	NCAA	30	23	24	47	0					
1973-74	Fargo-Moorhead Sugar Kings	MidJHL	48	37	46	83	78					
1974-75	Springfield Indians	AHL	27	7	17	24	46	--	--	--	--	--
1975-76	Los Angeles Kings	NHL	63	8	16	24	36	--	--	--	--	--
1976-77	Los Angeles Kings	NHL	80	14	40	54	65	9	3	4	7	6
1977-78	Los Angeles Kings	NHL	72	7	34	41	52	2	0	0	0	0
1978-79	Minnesota North Stars	NHL	79	12	32	44	39	--	--	--	--	--
1979-80	Minnesota North Stars	NHL	52	13	21	34	22	4	2	1	3	2
1980-81	Minnesota North Stars	NHL	23	4	7	11	36	--	--	--	--	--
1981-82	Minnesota North Stars	NHL	15	0	5	5	18	--	--	--	--	--
1982-83	Minnesota North Stars	NHL	18	3	6	9	5	5	0	2	2	0
	NHL Totals		**402**	**61**	**161**	**222**	**273**	**20**	**5**	**7**	**12**	**8**

FRED SASAKAMOOSE

Center
Born Dec 24 1934 -- Debden, SASK
Height 5.09 -- Weight 165 -- Shoots R

			Regular Season					Playoffs				
Season	Team	Lge	GP	G	A	Pts	PIM	GP	G	A	Pts	PIM
1950-51	Moose Jaw Canucks	WCJHL	0	0	0	0	0					
1951-52	Moose Jaw Canucks	WCJHL	42	19	22	41	59					
1953-54	Chicago Blackhawks	NHL	11	0	0	0	6	--	--	--	--	--
1954-55	Chicoutimi Sagueneens	QHL	22	4	4	8	2					
1954-55	New Westminster Royals	WHL	21	3	8	11	6	--	--	--	--	--
1955-56	Calgary Stampeders	WHL	2	0	0	0	2	--	--	--	--	--
1956-57	Kamloops Chiefs	OSAHL	0	0	0	0	0					
1965-66	Saskatoon Quakers	WCSHL	0	0	0	0	0					
	NHL Totals		**11**	**0**	**0**	**0**	**6**					

BRYAN TROTTIER

Forward
Born Jul 17 1956 -- Val Marie, SASK
Height 5.11 -- Weight 195

Season	Team	Lge	GP	G	A	Pts	PIM	GP	G	A	Pts	PIM
				Regular Season					Playoffs			
1971-72	Moose Jaw Canucks	SJHL Statistics Unavailable										
1972-73	Swift Current Broncos	WCHL	67	16	29	45	10					
1973-74	Swift Current Broncos	WCHL	68	41	71	112	76					
1974-75	Lethbridge Broncos	WCHL	67	46	98	144	103	6	2	5	7	14
1975-76	New York Islanders	NHL	80	32	63	95	21	13	1	7	8	8
1976-77	New York Islanders	NHL	76	30	42	72	34	12	2	8	10	2
1977-78	New York Islanders	NHL	77	46	77	123	46	7	0	3	3	4
1978-79	New York Islanders	NHL	76	47	87	134	50	10	2	4	6	13
1979-80	New York Islanders	NHL	78	42	62	104	68	21	12	17	29	16
1980-81	New York Islanders	NHL	73	31	72	103	74	18	11	18	29	34
1981-82	New York Islanders	NHL	80	50	79	129	88	19	6	23	29	40
1982-83	New York Islanders	NHL	80	34	55	89	68	17	8	12	20	18
1983-84	New York Islanders	NHL	68	40	71	111	59	21	8	6	14	49
1984-85	New York Islanders	NHL	68	28	31	59	47	10	4	2	6	8
1985-86	New York Islanders	NHL	78	37	59	96	72	3	1	1	2	2
1986-87	New York Islanders	NHL	80	23	64	87	50	14	8	5	13	12
1987-88	New York Islanders	NHL	77	30	52	82	48	6	0	0	0	10
1988-89	New York Islanders	NHL	73	17	28	45	44	--	--	--	--	--
1989-90	New York Islanders	NHL	59	13	11	24	29	4	1	0	1	4
1990-91	Pittsburgh Penguins	NHL	52	9	19	28	24	23	3	4	7	49
1991-92	Pittsburgh Penguins	NHL	63	11	18	29	54	21	4	3	7	8
1993-94	Pittsburgh Penguins	NHL	41	4	11	15	36	2	0	0	0	0
	NHL Totals		**1279**	**524**	**901**	**1425**	**912**	**221**	**71**	**113**	**184**	**277**

Roller Hockey

1994	Pittsburgh Phantoms	RHI	9	9	13	22	2					

Coaching

Season	Team	Lge	Type	GP	W	L	T	OTL	Pct	Result
1993-94	Pittsburgh Penguins	NHL	Assistant Coach							
1994-95	Pittsburgh Penguins	NHL	Assistant Coach							
1995-96	Pittsburgh Penguins	NHL	Assistant Coach							
1996-97	Pittsburgh Penguins	NHL	Assistant Coach							
1997-98	Portland Pirates	AHL	Head Coach	80	33	33	12	2	0.500	Lost in round 2

1998-99 Colorado Avalanche NHL Assistant Coach
1999-00 Colorado Avalanche NHL Assistant Coach
2000-01 Colorado Avalanche NHL Assistant Coach
2001-02 Colorado Avalanche NHL Assistant Coach
2002-03 New York Rangers NHL Head Coach†   54 21 26 6   1 0.454
† Replaced midseason

Awards

1975-76 Calder Memorial Trophy   1978-79 Art Ross Trophy 1978-79 Hart Memorial Trophy
1979-80 Conn Smythe Trophy 1988-89 King Clancy Memorial Trophy

INDEX

A

Aboriginal Role Model Hockey School, 124, 127, 154, 203, 206, 221, 223, 230, 243
addiction, 41, 45-46, 61-65, 69-70, 85, 109-110, 184-85, 224
    workshops, 50, 63, 73, 82
alcoholism. *See* addiction
American Hockey League, 41-42, 56, 92
Anderson, Glenn, 223
Armstrong, George, 17, 30, 51-57, 89
    early years, 54-56
    hockey years, 56-58
    honours, 56-57, 60
    photo, 126
    stats, 56, **259**
Asham, Aaron, 119, 221, 223-24
Atcheynum, Blair, 201-204, 206, 230
    early years, 203, 204
    photo, 127
    as role model, 235
    stats, **260**
Aulneau, Father, 190

B

Baggataway, 16
Baun, Bobby, 56
Berube, Craig, 143, 220, 227
Biederman, Brenden, 253
Bill C-31, 17
Birch, Kyle, 253
Boucha, Henry, 189-93
    injury, 191
    photo, 128
    stats, 19, **261**
Broad Street Bullies, 63, 92
Brophy, John, 56
Bury My Heart at Wounded Knee, 54, 100

C

Canadian Hockey Hall of Fame, 10, 51, 57, 64, 69, 126, 192, 225
casino revenue, 116-17, 120, 156
Chabot, John, 124, 183, 193-98
    hockey years, 195-96
    photo, 129
    Players Association, 194
    stats, 193, 195, **262**
Cheechoo, Jonathan, 18, 178, 228, 256
Cherry, Don, 5, 31, 91-97, 98, 143-49, 175-76, 180
    Piestany punch-up, 199
Chesney, Don, 235
Chicago Blackhawks, 17, 31, 37, 39, 40, 41, 42, 44, 56, 92, 140, 196, 198, 199, 201, 202, 210, 211, 219
Chief Crazy Horse, 53, 54
Chief Peguis, 53
Chief Sitting Bull. *See* Resting Monarch of the Plains
Chief, The. *See* Armstrong, George
Chief Thunderstick. *See* Sasakamoose, Fred Christian, Bill, 190
Christian, Dave, 190
Clarke, Bobby, 66, 68, 84, 113
Cloud, Chris, 254
Coffey, Paul, 223
Conspiracy of Silence, 242
Cook, Joe, 254, 255
Crazy Horse, 53, 54
"Cuppa coffee" gang, 31

D

Daychief, Winston, 254
Delorme, Ron, 10, 18, 59, 130, 143-57, 230
    assault in North Dakota, 156-57, 161
    Boston fights, 143-44, 146-48
    challenges, 151-52
    early life, 149-50

fights, 148–49, 153
injuries, 153
Odjick and, 218
photo, 130
role model, 201, 203, 221
Sasakamoose and, 150
stats, 152–53, **263**
Tiger Williams and, 151–52
drugs. *See* addictions
Duschesne, Cliff, 250

E
eagle, as Indian symbol, 238–39
Eagleson, Alan, 112–13
Edwards, Jeff, 253

F
Fleury, Theoren, 18, 131, 169, 205–216
Allan Cup fracas, 212–14
Belfast experience, 214–16
challenges, 205, 209–10, 215
early years, 206
hockey years, 207–208
Ohio nightclub fracas, 210–11
photo, 131
Piestany punch-up, 197
Sheldon Kennedy and, 206
stats, 207, **264**
Fleury, Travis, 215
Flin Flon Bombers, 66, 67, 254, 256
49th Parallel, 189–90
Fuhr, Grant, 223

G
Garrioch, Harley, 254
Ginnell, Pat, 66
Grassroots News, 253
Gretzky, Wayne, 18, 60, 79, 92, 170, 219, 223

H
Hasek, Dominik, 169–73, 180
Hayes, Ira, 53

Hewitt, Foster, 32, 38, 149
Hobema Hawks, 243
hockey
creating opportunities, 229–47, 252–53
name origin, 16–17
Native prospects, 253–55
spiritual health and, 40, 238–39
Hockey Night in Canada, 27, 32, 38, 42, 144
hockey teams with Native players, 250–51.
See also hockey, Native prospects
Holt, Todd, 212
Hoop Dance, 35, 181, 186
Horton, Tim, 55–56
Howe, Gordie, 18
Hull, Bobby, 18, 39, 56

I
in Deo, 49
Indian
vs "Aboriginal", 23–24
name origin, 22, 49
Indian agents, 35
International Hockey League, 166, 208, 219

J
Jonathan, Stan, 10, 18, 87–103, 145, 218, 228, 256
Don Cherry and, 91, 92, 93, 95, 96, 97, 145
early years, 88–89, 95
fight with Bouchard, 92–96, 97
fights, 92
hockey style, 97–98
hockey years, 90–98
Neilson on Jonathan, 95
1978 playoffs, 96
photo, 132
post-professional hockey, 102–104
Sinden and, 98–101
stats, 92, 95, **265**

K
Keon, Dave, 56
Kurri, Jari, 223

L
lacrosse, 10, 16, 88
Lalonde, Edouard, 20
Leach, Jamie, 230
Leach, Reggie, 10, 11, 18, 30, 63-86, 89,
110, 195, 223
    challenges, 64-65, 69-72, 252
    early years, 64-66
    hockey years, 67-86, 223
    honours, 63-64, 69, 73
    photo, 133
    role model, 228, 230
    sobriety, 71-83
    stats, 63-64, 68, 69-70, **266**
Lebret Eagles, 4, 13, 134, 231-36, 243, 246
    photo, 134
Lebret Indian Residential School, 236-38
Lebret, Saskatchewan, 232
Lemieux, Mario, 18
Lerat, Dutch, 49
Little Chief. *See* Jonathan, Stan

M
Mahovlich, Frank, 56
Manitoba Junior Hockey League, 13, 137,
231, 238, 239, 243-45
Maple Leaf Gardens, 38, 39
Marks, Don, 10-14, 119, 195, 200
mascots. *See* Racism, tribe names
McCarthy, Sandy, 227
McCourt, Dale, 227
McDonald, Ab, 17
McKay, Konrad, 249-50
Messier, Mark, 223
Michaud, Justin, 254
Moose Jaw, 35
Moose Jaw Canucks, 35, 37
Moose Jaw Warriors, 201, 206
Muckler, John, 172-76, 182, 186, 187

Musqua, Felix, 49
Muswagan, Jamie, 250

N
National Hockey League, 4, 15, 16, 28, 31,
37, 43, 44, 51, 53, 88, 110, 111, 140, 141,
166, 225, 227, 246, 256
    early years, 41-42
    Native-owned Canadian franchises, 231-33
Neilson, Jim, 17, 53, 57-61
    early years, 58-59, 252
    hockey years, 59-60
    photo, 135
    stats, **267**
Neufeld, Ken, 254-55
New York Rangers, 17, 31, 51, 58, 110,
150, 151, 208
Nolan, Ted, 18, 163-87, 194
    challenges, 252
    Don Cherry on Nolan, 175
    early years, 163-66
    Hasek and, 169-72, 174, 180
    hockey years, 166-67
    initial coaching years, 167-68
    later coaching years, 180
    Muckler and, 172-74, 175, 180, 187
    photo, 136
    on racism, 175, 181-82, 230, 250
    Regier and, 173-74
    stats, 167, **268**
    throwing trophy, 174
Norris Trophy, 60, 135
Northern Ontario Hockey
Association, 55

O
OCN Blizzard, 4, 13, 135, 231, 239,
244-55
    photo, 137
Odjick, Gino, 18, 59, 155, 156, 212,
217-26, 230
    Delorme and, 218-19
    early years, 217-18

fight stats, 219
hockey years, 219
injuries, 221-22
junior stats, 218
Musqueam Golf Course, 224-25
stats, 225-26, **269**
oral history, 34-35
Osborne, Helen Betty, 239-40, 251

P
Park, Brad, 60
Peguis, 53
Pierro-Zabotel, Casey, 255
Pilote, Pierre, 17
Players Association (NHL), 111-14, 141
Poitras, George, 6, 30, 49, 236
poverty, 204, 229
Price, Carey, 18, 228, 253, 256

R
racism in hockey
alcohol stigma, 185-86
early, 52-53
healing, 252
Indian team names, 157-62
nicknames, 20-22, 59
sacred symbols and, 238-39
slurs, 45, 59-60, 67, 151, 185-86,
201-202
systemic, 36, 155, 176, 181-82,
230, 257
Ratt, Jeff, 255
Redden, Wade, 18, 221, 230
Reggie Leach Classic Hockey
Tournament, 83
Regier, Darcy, 173-74
residential school
abuses, 33-34
Lebret and, 232
Stephen Harper apology, 34
Resting Monarch of the Plains, 52, 54
Restoule, Scott, 255

Richard, Maurice, 18
Riverton Rifle. *See* Leach, Reggie
Robert, Rene, 227
Robinson, Bill, 17, 31
Rose Nolan Memorial Golf
Tournament, 177
Rose Nolan Memorial Scholarship
Fund, 178

S
sacred teachings, 187-88
Sanipass, Everett, 129, 131, 196-200
hockey years, 197-200
photo, 138
Piestany punch-up, 136, 197-98
stats, **270**
Sargent, Gary, 191-94
baseball, 192
early years, 192
hockey years, 192-94
photo, 139
stats, 192, **271**
Sasakamoose, Fred, 7, 10, 17, 18, 23,
27-50, 223, 234
Bobby Hull and, 39
challenges, 36, 41, 45-48, 252
early years, 31-33
hockey years, 33-42
legends, 42-43
loneliness, 40, 252
photo, 140
in politics, 48
role model, 223, 228
stats, 27, 36, 39, **271**
Sasakamoose, Tyler, 46-47
Saskatchewan Junior Hockey League, 35,
134, 151, 231, 244-45
Saskatchewan northern midget hockey, 34
Saskatchewan Rough Riders, 29, 30
Saskatoon Quakers, 41, 212
Sather, Glen, 57
Sharing Circle, The, 179

Shear, Charlie, 150, 152
Shingoose, Jonnie, 5, 19, 21, 122, 200
Simon, Chris, 143, 183, 184, 187, 194, 196
    suspension, 183-84
Sinclair, Jordan, 255
Sitting Bull. *See* Resting Monarch of
the Plains
Souray, Sheldon, 18, 119, 221-24, 230
Southeast Blades, 13, 243
Stanley, Allan, 56
Starr, Aaron, 250
Stevens, Myles, 255
suicide, 118, 247

T
Taylor, Scott, 5, 253
Ted Nolan Foundation, 178
The Chief. See Armstrong, George
They Call Me Chief documentary, 15, 18,
24, 118, 195, 247, 256
Thompson, Riel, 256
Thorpe, Jim, 53
Thunderchief, Kalib, 256
Thunderstick. *See* Sasakamoose, Fred
Tom Longboat trophy, 30
Tootoo, Jordin, 228, 246-48, 256
Tootoo, Terence, 178, 247-48, 250
Tootoosis, Kevin, 154, 201, 203, 221, 230
Topazzini, Gerry, 39
Toronto Maple Leafs, 17, 51, 126, 164
treaty rights, 17, 24, 31, 64, 98-101,
115, 257
Trottier, Bryan, 5, 10, 18, 19, 30 105-125,
194, 195, 196, 198, 228
    bankruptcy, 117-18
    challenges, 109-110
    early years, 105-107, 113
    fights, 111
    hockey years, 111-25
    music and, 107-108, 122-23
    photo, 141
    Players Association, 111-12, 183
    stats, **272**

U
Ulm incident, 162-63
United States Hockey Hall of Fame, 191

WXYZ
warrior, definition, 15-16, 86
Warroad, Michigan, 189-90
Winnipeg Blue Bombers, 29, 199
Winnipeg Maroons, 41, 212
Yellow Horn, Colton, 254
Zubek, Gary, 30